PATHWAYS

SECOND EDITION

Reading, Writing, and Critical Thinking

LAURIE BLASS

MARI VARGO

NATIONAL GEOGRAPHIC
LEARNING

Australia • Brazil • Mexico • Singapore • United Kingdom • United States

NATIONAL GEOGRAPHIC
L E A R N I N G

Pathways
Reading, Writing, and Critical Thinking 2,
Second Edition

Laurie Blass and Mari Vargo

Publisher: Andrew Robinson

Executive Editor: Sean Bermingham

Associate Development Editor: Yvonne Tan

Director of Global Marketing: Ian Martin

Product Marketing Manager: Tracy Bailie

Media Researcher: Leila Hishmeh

Senior IP Analyst: Alexandra Ricciardi

IP Project Manager: Carissa Poweleit

Senior Director of Production:
   Michael Burggren

Senior Production Controller: Tan Jin Hock

Manufacturing Planner: Mary Beth
   Hennebury

Art Director: Brenda Carmichael

Compositor: MPS North America LLC

Cover Photo: Smoke rises from Manam
   Volcano off the coast of Papua New
   Guinea: © WENN Ltd/Alamy

> For product information and technology assistance, contact us at
> **Cengage Learning Customer & Sales Support, cengage.com/contact**
> For permission to use material from this text or product,
> submit all requests online at **cengage.com/permissions**
> Further permissions questions can be emailed to
> **permissionrequest@cengage.com**

Student Book:
ISBN-13: 978-1-337-40777-9

Student Book with Online Workbook:
ISBN-13: 978-1-337-62511-1

National Geographic Learning
20 Channel Center Street
Boston, MA 02210
USA

National Geographic Learning, a Cengage Learning Company, has a mission to bring the world to the classroom and the classroom to life. With our English language programs, students learn about their world by experiencing it. Through our partnerships with National Geographic and TED Talks, they develop the language and skills they need to be successful global citizens and leaders.

Locate your local office at **international.cengage.com/region**

Visit National Geographic Learning online at **NGL.Cengage.com/ELT**
Visit our corporate website at **www.cengage.com**

Printed in China

Print Number: 01 Print Year: 2017

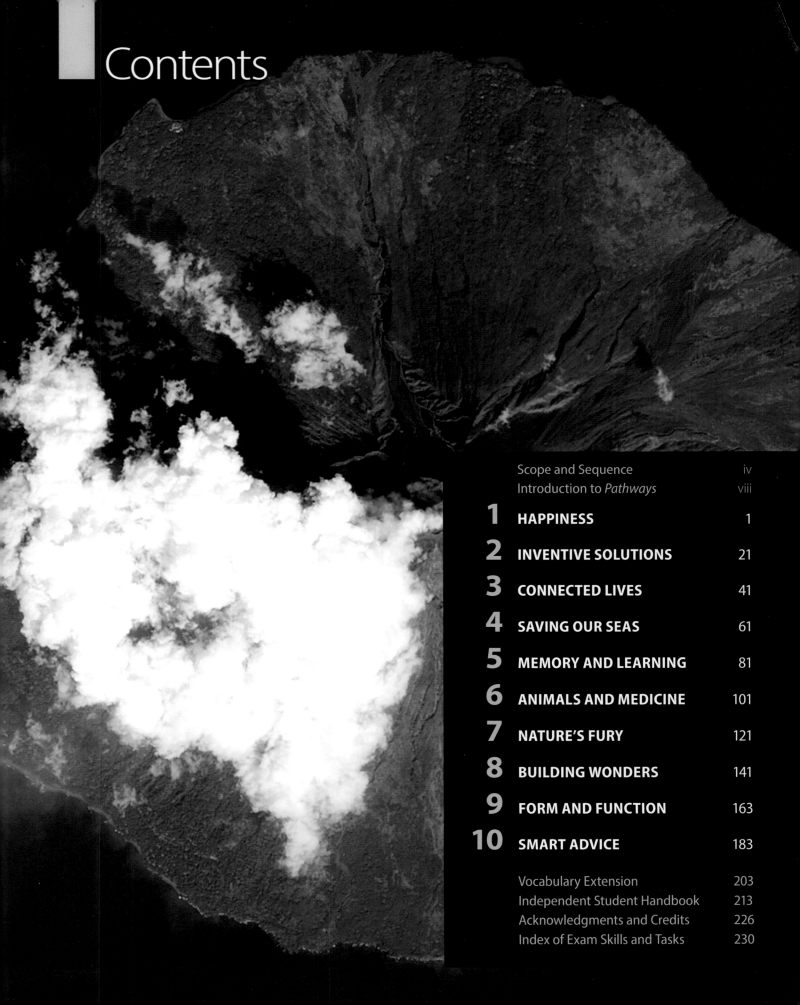

Contents

Scope and Sequence

ACADEMIC SKILLS

Critical Thinking	Writing	Vocabulary Extension
Focus Inferring Meaning from Context Justifying Your Opinion, Synthesizing, Reflecting	**Skill Focus** Writing a Strong Topic Sentence **Language for Writing** Review of the Simple Present Tense **Writing Goal** Writing an opinion paragraph about whether people in your community are happy	**Word Partners** Expressions with *living* **Word Forms** Words as Nouns and Verbs
Focus Analyzing Problems and Solutions Analyzing, Synthesizing, Evaluating	**Skill Focus** Supporting the Main Idea and Giving Details **Language for Writing** Review of the Simple Past Tense **Writing Goal** Writing a problem/solution paragraph about an invention and how it changed people's lives	**Word Partners** adjective + *power* *power* + noun **Word Link** *-able* and *-ible*
Focus Making Inferences Reflecting, Analyzing	**Skill Focus** Writing a Concluding Sentence **Language for Writing** Using the Present Perfect Tense **Writing Goal** Writing a descriptive paragraph about a crowdsourcing project	**Word Partners** adjective + *contribution* **Word Link** *-al*
Focus Evaluating an Argument Synthesizing, Reflecting	**Skill Focus** Explaining a Chart or Graph **Language for Writing** Describing Charts and Graphs **Writing Goal** Writing a paragraph explaining the information presented in a graph	**Word Forms** Changing Nouns into Adjectives **Word Partners** verb + *on*
Focus Applying a Method for Internalization Reflecting, Synthesizing	**Skill Focus** Using an Outline **Language for Writing** Using *By* + Gerund **Writing Goal** Writing a paragraph about how to improve your memory	**Word Forms** Changing Nouns and Adjectives into Verbs **Word Partners** Expressions with *state*

Scope and Sequence

Critical Thinking	Writing	Vocabulary Extension
Focus Understanding Metaphors and Similes Reflecting, Evaluating, Inferring Meaning, Synthesizing	**Skill Focus** Writing an Argumentative Paragraph **Language for Writing** Making Concessions **Writing Goal** Writing a paragraph about whether scientists should use animals for medical research	**Word Link** *en-* **Word Web** Adjectives for Emotion
Focus Evaluating Sources for Credibility Synthesizing	**Skill Focus** Organizing a Process Paragraph **Language for Writing** Describing a Process **Writing Goal** Writing an explanatory paragraph about a natural or biological process	**Word Link** *ex-* **Word Forms** Changing Adjectives into Adverbs
Focus Interpreting Quotes Reflecting, Synthesizing, Evaluating an Argument	**Skill Focus** Writing a Comparison Paragraph **Language for Writing** Using Comparative Adjectives **Writing Goal** Writing a paragraph comparing two different structures	**Word Partners** adjective + *style* **Word Link** *trans-*
Focus Evaluating Evidence Inferring Meaning, Applying, Synthesizing	**Skill Focus** Writing a Summary Paragraph **Language for Writing** Using Synonyms **Writing Goal** Writing a paragraph summarizing a section of the reading passage "Design by Nature"	**Word Partners** adjective + *advantage* **Word Link** *pro-*
Focus Applying an Idea to a New Context Inferring, Synthesizing, Inferring Meaning	**Skill Focus** Giving Details that Support Advice **Language for Writing** Using the Zero Conditional to Give Advice **Writing Goal** Writing a paragraph giving advice about preparing to go to college	**Word Partners** Expressions with *challenge* **Word Partners** Expressions with *quality*

Pathways Reading, Writing, and Critical Thinking, Second Edition uses National Geographic stories, photos, video, and infographics to bring the world to the classroom. Authentic, relevant content and carefully sequenced lessons engage learners while equipping them with the skills needed for academic success. Each level of the second edition features **NEW** and **UPDATED** content.

Academic skills are clearly ▶ labeled at the beginning of each unit.

ACADEMIC SKILLS

READING Identifying pros and cons
WRITING Writing an argumentative paragraph
GRAMMAR Making concessions
CRITICAL THINKING Understanding metaphors and similes

NEW AND UPDATED ▶
Reading passages incorporate a variety of text types, charts, and infographics to inform and inspire learners.

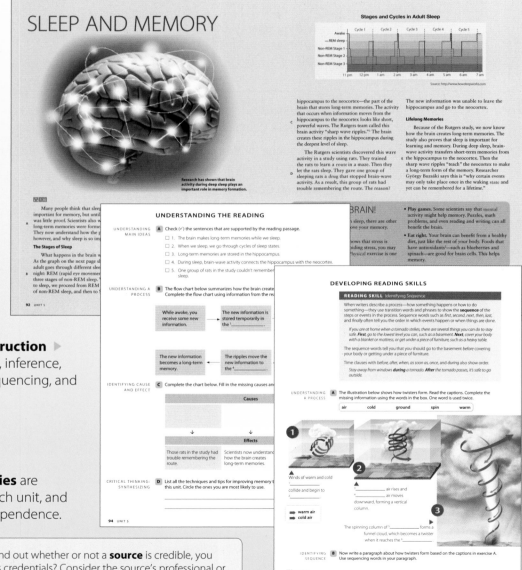

Explicit reading skill instruction ▶
includes main ideas, details, inference, prediction, note-taking, sequencing, and vocabulary development.

▼ **Critical thinking activities** are integrated throughout each unit, and help develop learner independence.

CRITICAL THINKING To find out whether or not a **source** is credible, you **evaluate** it. What are the source's credentials? Consider the source's professional or educational background, experience, and past writing.

Video

Albert Lin rides out to explore a site in Mongolia.

CITIZEN SCIENTISTS

BEFORE VIEWING

A Why do you think people are interested in finding Genghis Khan's tomb? Discuss your ideas with a partner.

BRAINSTORMING

B Read the information about Genghis Khan. Then answer the questions.

LEARNING ABOUT THE TOPIC

Genghis Khan was one of the most feared leaders of all time. Born around 1160, he was originally named "Temujin." At the age of 20, he began building a large army to bring all the people of Mongolia under his rule. As leader of the Mongol Empire, he introduced a new alphabet and a new type of money. He also devised a system of laws and regulations, and allowed freedom of religion—long before that idea spread to other parts of the world. At the same time, however, he launched violent military campaigns against his enemies. After his death, the Mongol Empire grew to become one of the largest of all time. It stretched east to west from the Sea of Japan to Eastern Europe, and north to south from Siberia to Southeast Asia. Today, Genghis Khan is still regarded as one of the most influential people in history.

1. Why is Genghis Khan one of the most feared leaders of all time?

2. List two ways Genghis Khan's empire set a model for modern society.

   a.

   b.

CONNECTED LIVES **49**

◀ **NEW AND UPDATED** *Video* sections use National Geographic video clips to provide a bridge between Readings 1 and 2, and to give learners ideas and language for the unit's writing task.

◀ **NEW** An additional short reading passage provides integrated skills practice.

Reading 1

PREPARING TO READ

BUILDING VOCABULARY

A The words and phrases in blue below are used in the reading passage on pages 145–148. Complete each sentence with the correct word or phrase. Use a dictionary to help you.

| architect | committed to | illustrate | inspiration | sculpture | style | theme |

1. _____ is a form of art that is made by shaping stone, wood, clay, or other materials.

2. If you are _____ something, you give your time and energy to it.

3. If you get _____ from something, it gives you new and creative ideas.

4. A(n) _____ is an important idea or subject found throughout a work of art or literature.

5. A(n) _____ is a person who plans and designs buildings.

6. To _____ an idea means to explain or give examples of it.

7. The _____ of a building refers to its form or design, and is usually characteristic of a particular period or region.

USING VOCABULARY

B Discuss these questions with a partner.

1. Do you know of any famous **architects**? What buildings did they design?
2. What is the architectural **style** of the building you are in right now? Is it modern or traditional?

BRAINSTORMING

C If the style of a building is inspired by nature, what might it look like? Look at the categories listed in the word web below. With a partner, brainstorm some ideas for each category.

The ceiling is painted to look like the sky.

- The sky
- Animals
- Buildings inspired by nature
- Water
- Plants

144 UNIT 6

▲ **Key academic and thematic vocabulary** is practiced, and expanded throughout each unit.

VOCABULARY EXTENSION UNIT 1

WORD PARTNERS Expressions with *living*

Below are definitions for common expressions with the word *living*.

standard of living: the level of wealth someone has
cost of living: the average cost of the basic necessities of life
living the dream: experiencing the achievement of all your career or life goals
make a living: to earn enough money from a job to pay for housing, food, etc.
do (something) for a living: to have a job or career

A Complete each sentence using an expression from the box above.

1. It is hard to _____ as a waiter because wages are often quite low.

2. The well-educated generally enjoy a high _____.

3. The _____ in cities like San Francisco and New York is higher than in rural areas. One of the reasons is that housing is so expensive.

4. She has the job she has always wanted—she is _____!

5. He just finished college but is not sure yet what he wants to _____.

WORD FORMS Words as Nouns and Verbs

Some words can be both nouns and verbs. Some examples are *offer*, *pick*, and *taste*. If a word follows an adjective, it is more likely to be a noun.

NOUN
She is the most hardworking volunteer at the hospital.
VERB
She volunteers at the local hospital every week.

B Read the sentences below. Write N for *noun* or V for *verb* above each underlined word.

1. Many young adults get financial support from their parents when buying their first house.

2. Many homeless shelters need volunteers to help in the kitchen.

3. After three interviews, the company offered me the job.

4. People tend to be happier when they have easy access to good, affordable healthcare.

5. The supermarket rewards customers who shop regularly in the store by giving them a discount.

VOCABULARY EXTENSION **203**

▲ **NEW Vocabulary extension activities** cover word forms, word webs, collocations, affixes, and more, to boost learners' reading and writing fluency.

ix

Writing Skills Practice

Pathways' approach to writing guides students through the writing process and develops learners' confidence in planning, drafting, revising, and editing.

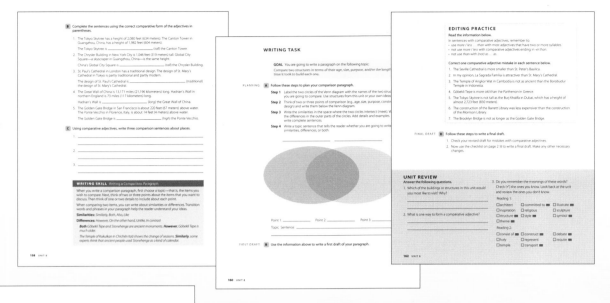

Writing Goals and ***Language for Writing*** sections provide the focus and scaffolding needed for learners to become successful writers.

An **online workbook**, powered by MyELT, includes video clips and automatically graded activities for learners to practice the skills taught in the Student Books.

UPDATED Revising Practice sections incorporate realistic model paragraphs and help learners refine their writing.

NEW Guided online writing practice provides reinforcement and consolidation of language skills, helping learners to become stronger and more confident writers.

HAPPINESS 1

A group of children play inside a jeepney in Cebu City, Philippines.

THINK AND DISCUSS

1 What does it mean to be happy?
2 Think of someone you know who seems happy. Describe that person.

EXPLORE THE THEME

A Look at the information on these pages and answer the questions.

1. Have you been to any of the countries shown here? Why do you think people from these countries are happy?

2. Compare the information about these six countries. Do you see a strong link between GDP per capita and overall happiness? What does this suggest?

B Match the correct form of the words and phrases in blue to their definitions.

_____ (v) to supply or make available

_____ (adj) protected from danger or harm

_____ (n) the level of comfort and amount of money that people have

5 **CANADA**
Rating: 8.0

Population: 35.5 million
Average Life Expectancy:
82.0 years
GDP per capita:
$50,440

3 **MEXICO**
Rating: 8.3

Population: 124.2 million
Average Life Expectancy:
76.7 years
GDP per capita:
$10,450

HAPPY HOT SPOTS

What makes us happy? According to the World Database of Happiness, people are happy if they feel that they have a good quality of life. This may include having a good **standard of living**, feeling safe and **secure**, or living in a society that **provides** basic healthcare for all.

Is it possible to measure happiness? Researchers at the World Database of Happiness think so. The database (2005–2014) brings together scientific reports on happiness from 158 countries around the world. The researchers asked people to rate their enjoyment of life on a scale from 0 to 10. The top six happiest nations are shown here. Oman (18th) is the happiest country in the Middle East. The happiest Asian countries—the Philippines, Thailand, and Singapore—placed 39th, 42nd, and 43rd.

4 ICELAND
Rating: 8.1

Population: 327,400
Average Life Expectancy:
82.9 years
GDP per capita:
$52,470

2 DENMARK
Rating: 8.4

Population: 5.6 million
Average Life Expectancy:
80.7 years
GDP per capita:
$62,430

1 COSTA RICA
Rating: 8.5

Population: 4.8 million
Average Life Expectancy:
79.4 years
GDP per capita:[1]
$10,650

6 SWITZERLAND
Rating: 8.0

Population: 8.2 million
Average Life Expectancy:
83.2 years
GDP per capita:
$85,800

[1] **GDP (Gross Domestic Product) per capita** is the value of goods and services produced by a country, divided by its total population.

Reading 1

PREPARING TO READ

BUILDING
VOCABULARY

A The words and phrases in **blue** below are used in the reading passage on pages 5–6. Complete each sentence with the correct word or phrase. Use a dictionary to help you.

> access   basic necessities   equal   financial   freedom   poverty   socialize

1. When you _____, you spend time with other people for fun.

2. Countries with high levels of _____ should put more social programs in place to help the poor.

3. According to a United Nations report, having _____ to the Internet is a basic human right.

4. If you ask someone for _____ advice, you are concerned about money.

5. People who do the same job should receive _____ pay.

6. _____ of speech is a basic democratic value.

7. In some of the world's poorest countries, obtaining _____ like clean water and shelter is a daily struggle.

USING
VOCABULARY

B Discuss these questions with a partner.

1. Who do you normally **socialize** with?
2. Besides food and shelter, what do you think are the **basic necessities** in life?
3. Is **poverty** a serious problem in your country? If so, what is the government doing to tackle this problem?

BRAINSTORMING

C List six things that you think a person needs in order to be happy. Share your ideas with a partner.

1. _____   3. _____   5. _____

2. _____   4. _____   6. _____

PREDICTING

D Look at the title and the subheads of the reading passage on pages 5–6. What do you think the reading passage is about? Check your answer as you read.

a. how to measure happiness
b. things that make people happy
c. life in the happiest country in the world

IS THERE A RECIPE FOR HAPPINESS?

🎧 1.01

A What makes us happy? Money? Friends? A good job? Are the answers the same for everyone? According to world surveys, Mexico and Singapore are two happy countries—but their people may be happy for different reasons.

SAFETY AND SECURITY

B There are more than 21,000 people per square mile[1] in the small nation of Singapore. People on the island work very long hours and regularly bring work home with them. The country has strict laws against smoking in public, littering,[2] and even jaywalking.[3] But according to the World Database of Happiness, Singapore is one of the happiest countries in Asia. Why?

C One reason for Singapore's happiness is that the government provides the basic necessities, such as housing and healthcare. There is almost no extreme poverty in Singapore. The government "tops up"[4] poorer people's incomes so everyone can have a minimum standard of living. It also offers tax breaks[5] to people who look after their aging parents. The result is a lot of closely connected families with roughly equal standards of living.

D People may not be happy about all the laws, but they are generally happy with the results— they breathe clean air, they don't step in litter, and the streets are safe and orderly. So for Singaporeans, it seems that living in a secure,

[1]A square mile = 2.59 square kilometers.
[2]Littering is leaving trash lying around outside.
[3]Jaywalking occurs when a pedestrian walks across a street at a place where it is not allowed.

[4]If you top something up, you add to it to make it full.
[5]If the government gives someone a tax break, it lowers the amount of tax they have to pay.

clean, and safe place may be more important than having a lot of personal **freedom**. Many societies are trying to find a happy medium between order and freedom. Singapore's ranking on the World Database of Happiness suggests that the country has done a pretty decent job at it.

FRIENDS AND NEIGHBORS

In many ways, Mexico is the opposite of Singapore. There are some parts of Mexico where people do not have a safe or secure life. Many people do not have jobs, enough food, or **access** to education. But, as in Singapore, most people in Mexico feel that they are happy. Why?

One reason is the importance of social interaction. According to psychologists, much of our happiness comes from feeling that we are part of a larger community. Simple acts like smiling at a neighbor or having dinner with friends can greatly increase our overall happiness. People in Mexico **socialize** with family and friends a lot, and this adds to their happiness.

But what about poverty? In Mexico, about half of the population is poor. However, most Mexicans live near people in a similar **financial** situation. If your neighbor doesn't have expensive items—such as a big house or an expensive car—you probably don't feel the need to have those things either. So money, by itself, may not be that important for happiness. What matters more is how much money you have compared to the people around you.

A MIXED RECIPE?

So the question "What makes people happy?" does not seem to have a simple answer. Security, safety, freedom, and socializing with friends and family can all play important roles. As the examples of Singapore and Mexico suggest, there may be no single recipe for happiness. It is up to each of us to find our own.

Festive gatherings and parades help create a strong sense of community in Mexico.

UNDERSTANDING THE READING

A What is the main idea of the reading passage?

UNDERSTANDING THE MAIN IDEA

    a. Happiness means different things to different people.

    b. Personal freedom is the most important thing for happiness.

    c. Everyone needs to feel safe and secure in order to be happy.

B According to the writer, do the following statements (a–e) apply to Mexico, Singapore, or both? Complete the Venn diagram.

UNDERSTANDING DETAILS

    a. Most people here feel that they are happy.

    b. People generally feel safe and secure.

    c. Family connections are important for people's happiness.

    d. Although many people here are poor, most of them are happy.

    e. Most people accept the government's strict rules as part of life.

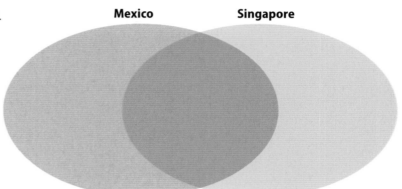

Mexico   Singapore

CRITICAL THINKING   Use the context—the words around a word—to **infer**, or guess, the **meaning** of vocabulary you don't know. The context can also help you decide the word's part of speech (e.g., noun, verb, or adjective). For example:

    The government "tops up" poorer people's incomes so everyone can have a minimum standard of living.

We can guess from this context that *minimum* is probably an adjective used to describe the least or smallest amount required.

C Find and underline the following **bold** words and phrases in the reading passage. Use context to identify their meanings. Then match each word or phrase to its definition.

CRITICAL THINKING: INFERRING MEANING

strict (paragraph B)   **happy medium** (paragraph D)

look after (paragraph C)   **decent** (paragraph D)

    1. _____ (v) to take care of someone or something

    2. _____ (adj) tough; must be obeyed

    3. _____ (adj) good enough; satisfactory

    4. _____ (n) a good choice or condition that avoids any extremes

D Would you prefer to live in Singapore or Mexico? Why? Complete the following sentence and share your ideas with a partner.

CRITICAL THINKING: JUSTIFYING YOUR OPINION

I think I would prefer to live in **Singapore / Mexico** because _____

_____

DEVELOPING READING SKILLS

> **READING SKILL** Identifying the Main Idea
>
> The main idea of a paragraph is the most important idea, or the idea that the paragraph is about. A good paragraph has one main idea and one or more supporting ideas. Read the paragraph below and think about its main idea.
>
> *Researchers have found that the sunny weather in Mexico is one of the reasons that people there are happy. Mexico has many hours of sunlight, so people in Mexico get a lot of vitamin D. Vitamin D is important for overall health and well-being. Also, studies show that when people tan, they make more endorphins—chemicals in our bodies that make us feel happy.*
>
> Which of these statements is the main idea of the paragraph?
>
> a. *People in Mexico are happy because they get a lot of vitamin D.*
>
> b. *Tanning makes us create more endorphins, which make us feel happy.*
>
> c. *Mexico gets a lot of sun, which may make people there happier.*
>
> The last sentence is the main idea. The other two sentences are supporting ideas that explain the main idea.

MATCHING   **A**   Look back at the reading passage on pages 5–6. Match each main idea below to a paragraph (A–H) from the reading passage.

_____ 1. One reason people are generally happy is that the government provides financial support to the poorer members of society.

_____ 2. You don't need to have a lot of money to be happy.

_____ 3. Spending time with family and friends can contribute to happiness.

_____ 4. There are different answers to the question, "What makes people happy?"

_____ 5. Most people are willing to give up certain freedoms to gain more safety and stability.

IDENTIFYING
THE MAIN IDEA   **B**   Read the information about Denmark. Then write the main idea of the paragraph.

It's hard to be happy when you're unhealthy. According to the 2014 World Database of Happiness, Denmark is the second happiest country in the world, and most Danes are fit. They have a lower rate of obesity than many of their European neighbors. Danish cities are designed so it's easy to walk or cycle from one place to another. For instance, many roads in Copenhagen have a special lane just for cyclists. And with a 30-minute walk, you can go from the city of Copenhagen to the ocean, where you can sail or swim, or to the woods, where you can hike. Everyone has easy access to recreation.

Main Idea: _____

_____

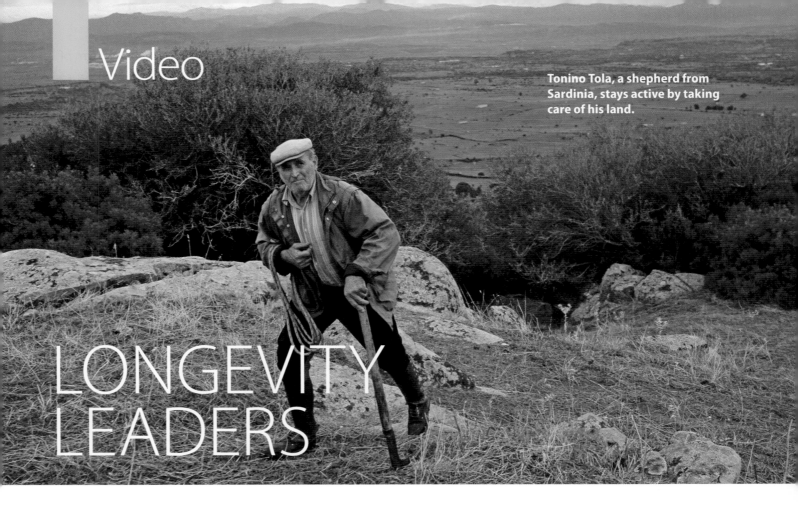

Video

Tonino Tola, a shepherd from Sardinia, stays active by taking care of his land.

LONGEVITY LEADERS

BEFORE VIEWING

A Some people live 100 years or more. What do you think these people do to stay healthy? Discuss your ideas with a partner.

PREDICTING

B Read the information about achieving a long life. Then answer the questions.

LEARNING ABOUT THE TOPIC

In some countries, people are living very long lives. Some are even living beyond 100. What are some of their secrets to longevity? Scientific research shows that eating the right foods plays a big role in determining how long you'll live. A healthy diet includes plenty of fruit, vegetables, and low-fat dairy products. Exercise is also important. A study published in *PLOS Medicine* found that people who exercised at recommended levels gained 3.4 years of life compared to those who were inactive. In addition, research suggests that there is a link between happiness and lifespan—happy people with a positive outlook on life tend to live longer and experience better health than their unhappy peers.

1. What are three things people do that increases their lifespan?

   _____

2. Why do you think there is a connection between happiness and longevity?

   _____

C The words and phrases in **bold** below are used in the video. Match the correct form of each word or phrase to its definition.

> A significant number of Japanese people live very long lives. There are almost 52 **centenarians** per 100,000 people in Japan.
>
> **Processed foods**, such as frozen pizza, aren't good for your health.
>
> Some elderly people prefer to live a **traditional lifestyle**. For example, they eat the same kinds of food their ancestors ate.

1. _____ (n) a way of living that is based on old customs

2. _____ (n) a person who lives to be 100 years old or older

3. _____ (n) food that has been altered from its natural state and that contains added chemicals

WHILE VIEWING

A ▶ Watch the video. According to the video, which of the following is true?

a. The world will struggle to meet the needs of an aging population.
b. Happiness is the most important factor in determining longevity.
c. Both medical science and lifestyle choices can help improve longevity.

B ▶ Watch the video again and answer the questions below.

1. What is one reason the world population is expected to increase in the future?

_____

2. What is one animal that can live a very long time? How long can it live for?

_____

3. What are two characteristics of Okinawa's centenarians that lead to good health?

_____

4. Describe one way younger Okinawans are different from the centenarians.

_____

AFTER VIEWING

A Discuss these questions with a partner.

1. Are there a lot of elderly people in your community? Why do you think this is?
2. In the video, the narrator says, "Some scientists have started to treat aging as a disease instead of a natural part of human life." What do you think this means?

B Compare Okinawa with either Singapore or Mexico. What is one thing people in those places have in common? Complete the following sentence.

People in Okinawa and _____ are generally happy because _____

_____

Reading 2

PREPARING TO READ

A The words in **blue** below are used in the reading passage on pages 12–13. Complete each sentence with the correct form of the word. Use a dictionary to help you.

BUILDING VOCABULARY

mood	community	volunteer	factor
support	long-term	grateful	well-being

1. A person's _____ goals can include saving money for retirement.

2. In some _____ , adult children _____ their elderly parents financially by paying their medical and household bills.

3. Healthy food, exercise, and interpersonal relationships are important for a person's physical and mental _____ .

4. Many people _____ to help those who were affected by the earthquake. The victims were very _____ for the help they received.

5. A person's _____ can change depending on the weather. For example, _____ such as sunlight and higher temperatures can make you feel happier.

B Discuss these questions with a partner.

USING VOCABULARY

1. How would you describe your **community**? What is it like to live there?
2. What are some things that put you in a good **mood**?

C The reading passage on pages 12–13 looks at four basic factors for happiness. Write the factors in the word web below. Then, with a partner, brainstorm some words or phrases that you think might relate to each one.

BRAINSTORMING

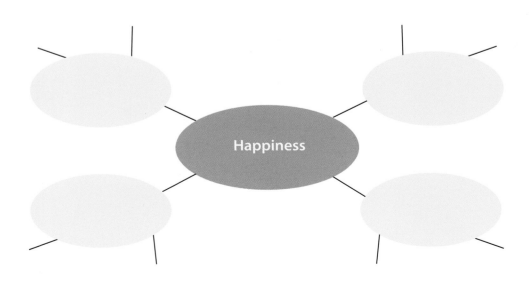

Happiness

FOUR KEYS TO HAPPINESS

A group of Japanese men enjoy a meal outdoors.

Researchers have found that different people need different things to be happy. But there are some basic things that anyone can do to become happier. Here are four areas of your life you can focus on to improve your **long-term** happiness.

1. STAY CONNECTED

Psychiatrist Robert Waldinger directs the Harvard Study of Adult Development, one of the longest-running studies of adult behavior. The study tracked the lives of two groups of men in the United States for over 75 years. One of the main findings from the study is the importance of social connections. "It turns out that people who are more socially connected to family, to friends, to **community**, are happier," says Waldinger. "They're physically healthier, and they live longer than people who are less well-connected." The happiest people meet regularly with friends and family, and **support** each other in difficult times.

2. KEEP ACTIVE

Nic Marks is the founder of the Happy Planet Index, which tracks national **well-being** around the world. One of the most important ways to improve well-being, he believes, is to keep active—healthy people are happier people. "The fastest way out of a bad **mood**," Marks says, is to "step outside, go for a walk, turn the radio on and dance. Being active is great for our positive mood." Being close to nature can also boost happiness. "Our pleasures are really ancient," says psychologist Nancy Etcoff. "We have a response to the natural world that's very profound." Walking a pet in the outdoors, for example, can improve our mood. Pets not only encourage their owners to be healthy, they also provide love and friendship, increasing their owners' self-esteem.

3. BUY LESS

The amount of money you have is a **factor** for happiness—but your salary may be less important than how you use it. Think carefully before buying expensive clothes or a new car, for example. Try to spend money instead on things that will really enrich your life, such as music lessons, or a vacation with family or friends. "We need to think before we buy," urges designer Graham Hill, and "ask ourselves: 'Is that really going to make me happier?'" Too often we buy things we don't really need. The less stuff we have in our lives, Hill argues, the happier we will be.

4. GIVE AWAY

Social science researcher Michael Norton has studied happiness levels around the world. He found that the act of giving money to people has a powerful effect on the giver as well as the receiver. "Almost everywhere we look," says Norton, "we see that giving money away makes you happier than keeping it for yourself." The amount of money isn't so important. "What really matters is that you spent it on somebody else rather than on yourself," he adds. Another way to give away is to donate your time instead of money. People who **volunteer** at homeless shelters, for example, find that it helps take the focus off their own problems and makes them feel **grateful** for what they have. Author David Steindl-Rast believes that being grateful may be the most important foundation for happiness: "It is not happiness that makes us grateful. It's gratefulness that makes us happy."

UNDERSTANDING THE READING

UNDERSTANDING THE MAIN IDEA

A Which sentence best summarizes the reading passage?

a. There are four different types of happy people in the world.
b. There are some small changes everyone can make to increase happiness.
c. Forming social connections is more important for happiness than other factors.

IDENTIFYING MAIN IDEAS

B Read the six scenarios below. Check (✓) the four that follow the advice in the reading passage.

☐ 1. A student installs a budget app on her phone to help control her spending.
☐ 2. A woman offers to take her neighbor's dog for a walk each morning.
☐ 3. A man uses all his savings to pay for an expensive new sports car.
☐ 4. A teenager spends time each Saturday helping at a children's hospital.
☐ 5. A young woman decides to reduce her number of working hours each week.
☐ 6. An elderly man decides to join an art class at a community center.

CRITICAL THINKING: INFERRING MEANING

C Find and underline the **bold** words and phrases below on pages 12–13. Use context to identify their meanings. Then circle the correct answers to complete the definitions.

1. If you have high **self-esteem**, you feel (*confident / unsure*) about yourself.

2. **Salary** is the amount of (*work / money*) that an employee receives.

3. To **enrich** something means to make it (*better / last longer*).

4. If you **take the focus off** something, you give it (*more / less*) attention.

CRITICAL THINKING: REFLECTING

D Choose three factors from the reading passage that you feel are most important for happiness. Write a sentence for each one describing how you can change that area of your life to become happier. Then share your ideas with a partner.

Example: *Keep Active—I can go swimming every week.*

1. _____

_____

2. _____

_____

3. _____

_____

Writing

EXPLORING WRITTEN ENGLISH

A Read the sentences below. Which describe general facts and which describe routines? Circle **F** for fact or **R** for routine. NOTICING

1. There are more than 21,000 people per square mile in the small nation of Singapore. F R
2. I work an average of 50 hours per week. F R
3. The government offers tax breaks to people who look after their aging parents. F R
4. Most people in Mexico live near people in a similar financial situation. F R
5. My friends and I go to the gym three times a week. F R
6. They have lunch together every day. F R
7. Iceland is one of the happiest countries in the world. F R
8. We usually cycle to work. F R
9. She reports to her boss once a month. F R

LANGUAGE FOR WRITING Review of the Simple Present Tense

We use the simple present tense to talk about facts or things that are generally true.
*About 5.6 million people **live** in Singapore.*
*There **are** over seven billion people in the world today.*
*Singapore **doesn't have** a high level of poverty.*

We also use the simple present tense to talk about habits and daily routines—things we do regularly, or things we usually don't do.
*They **walk** to work every day.*
*On most weekends, she **volunteers** at the homeless shelter.*
*I **don't see** my friends on Sundays.*

For simple present tense verbs, we use the base form with *I, you, we,* and *they.* We add -*s* to the base form for third-person singular subjects.

Some verbs have irregular present tense forms:
be: *I am; he/she/it is; you/we/they are*
do: *I/you/we/they do; he/she/it does*
have: *I/you/we/they have; he/she/it has*

To form a negative statement, use *doesn't* or *don't* and the base form of the verb.

B Underline the simple present tense verbs in the sentences in exercise A.

C Complete the sentences using the simple present tense of the verbs in parentheses.

1. According to researchers, happy people _____ (*spend*) a lot of time socializing with family and friends.

2. People in my office _____ (*be*) generally happy because the company _____ (*offer*) a good work-life balance.

3. In Denmark, the government _____ (*provide*) free healthcare and education to its citizens. Everyone _____ (*have*) equal access to basic necessities.

4. When people _____ (*not / feel*) safe in their neighborhood, they generally _____ (*not / be*) very happy.

5. Centenarians in Okinawa and Sardinia _____ (*have*) similar lifestyles— they _____ (*grow*) their own vegetables and _____ (*eat*) natural foods.

D Using the simple present tense, write three sentences about things you do regularly that make you feel happy.

1. _____

_____

2. _____

_____

3. _____

_____

E Using the simple present tense, write three sentences that describe general facts about your country or community.

1. _____

_____

2. _____

_____

3. _____

_____

WRITING SKILL Writing a Strong Topic Sentence

Most paragraphs include a sentence that states the main idea of the paragraph. This sentence is called the topic sentence. It is usually the first sentence in the paragraph, but not always. Topic sentences can also appear within the paragraph or at the end of the paragraph.

A strong topic sentence should introduce the main idea of the paragraph. It should not be too general or too specific. For example, if the paragraph is about how the government helps increase people's happiness, this idea should be included in the topic sentence.

Singaporeans are generally happy. → **weak topic sentence; too general**
One reason Singaporeans are generally happy is that the government provides basic necessities, such as housing. → **strong topic sentence**

As another example, if the paragraph presents the argument that you don't need a lot of money to be happy, this idea should be included in the topic sentence.

About 50 percent of Mexico's citizens live in poverty. → **weak topic sentence; too specific**
Even though many people in Mexico live in poverty, overall reported happiness is still very high. → **strong topic sentence**

F Underline the topic sentence in each paragraph. One of the topic sentences is stronger than the others.

1. In Mexico, family is important. Family members are very close and support one another during difficult times. Grandparents take care of grandchildren so the children's parents can go to work and earn money. When the children grow up, they take care of their parents. This is one of the reasons why people in Mexico are generally happy.

2. Studies have shown that laughter may be an important factor for happiness and that people who laugh a lot are happier. People who laugh more tend to have higher levels of self-esteem. They also tend to be healthier. Laughter is so important for our general well-being that some people go to "laughter therapy," where they laugh with groups of other people.

3. It's important to like your job. In many countries, a lot of people choose their job based on how much it pays or on what other people think about that job. But in Denmark, one of the world's happiest countries, most people take jobs that interest them. That gives them a better chance to feel motivated and happy at work.

G Rewrite the two weak topic sentences from exercise F.

1. _____
   _____

2. _____
   _____

WRITING TASK

GOAL You are going to write a paragraph on the following topic:

Do you think people in your community are generally happy or unhappy? Give three reasons for your answer.

BRAINSTORMING **A** Brainstorm a list of things that make people in your community happy and a list of things that people in your community may be unhappy about.

Things people in my community are happy about	Things people in my community are unhappy about

PLANNING **B** Follow these steps to make notes for your paragraph.

Step 1 Look at your notes above. Do you think people in your community are generally happy or unhappy? Write a topic sentence in the outline below.

Step 2 Choose three things from your notes above that support your topic sentence. Note them in the outline as reasons.

Step 3 For each reason, write one or two details, examples, or facts. Don't worry about grammar or spelling. Don't write complete sentences.

OUTLINE

Topic: Are people in your community generally happy or unhappy?

Topic Sentence: _____

Reason 1: _____

Detail(s): _____

Reason 2: _____

Detail(s): _____

Reason 3: _____

Detail(s): _____

FIRST DRAFT **C** Use the information in your outline to write a first draft of your paragraph.

REVISING PRACTICE

The drafts below are similar to the one you are going to write, but they are on a different topic:

Are you generally happy or unhappy? Describe three things that make you happy or unhappy. Write two or more details about each one, and explain why it makes you feel this way.

What did the writer do in Draft 2 to improve the paragraph? Match the changes (a–d) to the highlighted parts.

a. corrected a verb form
b. added details to explain a reason
c. deleted unrelated information
d. made the topic sentence stronger

Draft 1

I think I'm generally happy. I has a great job. I do work that I feel passionate about, and I like my co-workers. I don't make a lot of money, so sometimes I have to do extra work on the weekends. I want to ask for a raise at work. My family and friends are very supportive. Whenever I have problems, I know that my family and friends will help me. My friends also make me laugh a lot. In addition, I'm healthy.

Draft 2

I think I'm generally happy because I like most things about my life. I have a great job. I do work that I feel passionate about, and I like my co-workers. My family and friends are very supportive. Whenever I have problems, I know that my family and friends will help me. My friends also make me laugh a lot. In addition, I'm healthy. I don't have any illnesses, and I play fun sports such as soccer and basketball.

☐
☐
☐

☐

D Now use the questions below to revise your paragraph.

REVISED DRAFT

☐ Does the paragraph have one main idea?
☐ Does a strong topic sentence introduce the main idea?
☐ Does the paragraph include three reasons that relate to the main idea?
☐ Does the paragraph include one or two details for each reason?
☐ Are all verb forms correct?
☐ Is there any information that doesn't belong?

EDITING PRACTICE

Read the information below.

In sentences using the simple present tense, remember to:

- use the correct verb endings with third-person singular subjects; for example, *he likes*, *she walks*.
- watch out for verbs that have irregular forms in the simple present: *be*, *have*, and *do*.
- use the correct form of *do* and the base form of a verb in negative statements; for example, *don't spend / doesn't spend*.

Correct one mistake with the simple present tense in each sentence below.

1. I enjoy the work that I do because it's very challenging, but I doesn't like my boss.

2. My co-workers are supportive, friendly, and fun, and I enjoying spending time with them after work.

3. It's important to me to spend time with my family members, but it's difficult because they don't lives close to me.

4. Although my house is not big and fancy, my neighborhood are very safe.

5. My friends and I exercises together every day to stay healthy, and that contributes to our happiness.

6. My grandfather is still very active and spend a lot of time outdoors.

7. Most happy people has hobbies like hiking or playing a musical instrument.

FINAL DRAFT **E** Follow these steps to write a final draft.

1. Check your revised draft for mistakes with simple present verb forms.

2. Now use the checklist on page 218 to write a final draft. Make any other necessary changes.

UNIT REVIEW

Answer the following questions.

1. Of the factors for happiness you learned about in this unit, which one do you think is most important?

_____

_____

2. When do you use the simple present tense?

_____

_____

3. Do you remember the meanings of these words? Check (✓) the ones you know. Look back at the unit and review the ones you don't know.

Reading 1:

☐ access AWL   ☐ basic necessities   ☐ equal

☐ financial AWL   ☐ freedom   ☐ poverty

☐ provide   ☐ secure AWL   ☐ socialize

☐ standard of living

Reading 2:

☐ community AWL   ☐ factor AWL   ☐ grateful

☐ long-term   ☐ mood   ☐ support

☐ volunteer AWL   ☐ well-being

INVENTIVE SOLUTIONS 2

Rohim Miniaka (right) learns
how to make a solar lamp in
Tinginaput, India.

THINK AND DISCUSS

1 Do you know of any famous inventors? What did they invent?
2 What inventions do you use every day?

EXPLORE THE THEME

A Look at the information on these pages and answer the questions.

1. Do you agree with the list of the most important inventions? Can you think of other inventions to add?

2. Of these top 10 inventions, how many were developed within the last 200 years? Why do you think this is?

B Match the words in blue to their definitions.

_____ (n) a plan or drawing that shows the look and function of something

_____ (adj) being effective without wasting time or energy

_____ (n) the tools, machines, and other items needed for a particular task

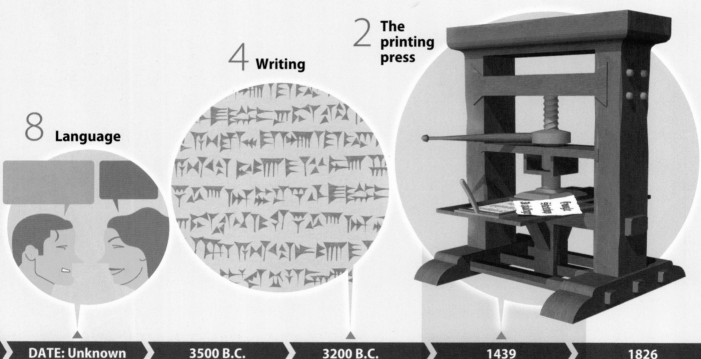

8 **Language**

4 **Writing**

2 **The printing press**

| DATE: Unknown | 3500 B.C. | 3200 B.C. | 1439 | 1826 |

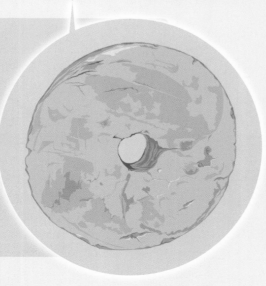

3 **The wheel**

No one knows who invented the wheel, but historians believe that it first appeared in Mesopotamia around 3500 B.C. Today, wheels are used for transportation and in energy-generating **equipment**.

Johannes Gutenberg invented a new type of printing press in 1439. He based his **design** on existing technologies, but his invention had movable type. This made the printing process much faster. Soon, thousands of books were being printed on his presses throughout Europe, and later the world.

6 **The match**

WHAT'S THE WORLD'S GREATEST INVENTION?

The publishing company Raconteur asked over 400 people to name the world's most important inventions. Here are the top 10. Some inventions—like the car—make everyday life easier. Medical inventions—such as antibiotics—save lives. Others—like the smartphone—changed the way we communicate.

And the number one invention? According to survey results, the greatest invention of all time is the World Wide Web, followed by the printing press and the wheel.

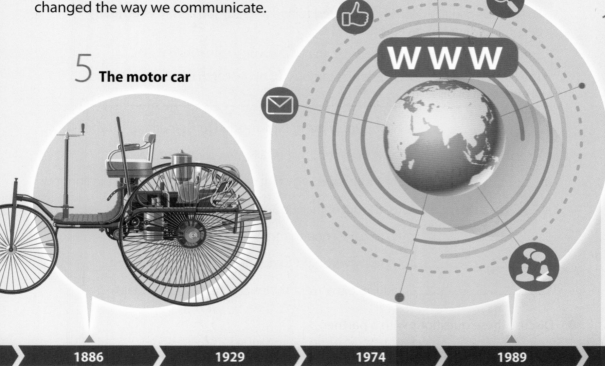

WWW

1 **The World Wide Web**

5 **The motor car**

| 1886 | 1929 | 1974 | 1989 | 1992 |

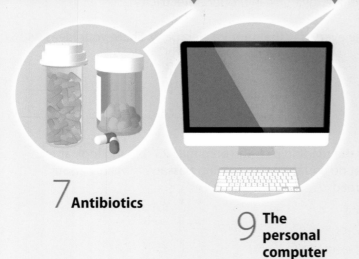

7 **Antibiotics**

9 **The personal computer**

In the 1980s, scientists at the European Organization for Nuclear Research (CERN) needed an **efficient** way to access each other's work. Tim Berners-Lee, a software engineer at CERN, created a system that made it easy to share information. In 1989, he had the idea of creating a similar system for the whole world. This became the World Wide Web—what most people today call "the Internet."

10 **The smartphone**

Reading 1

PREPARING TO READ

BUILDING
VOCABULARY **A** The words in **blue** below are used in the reading passage on pages 25–26. Match the correct form of each word to its definition.

> **Electricity** has many uses—we cook with it, and heat and light our homes with it. It also **powers** our cell phones.
>
> Many people consider Thomas Edison—the inventor of the phonograph—to be one of the greatest **creative** thinkers of all time.
>
> Edison was partially deaf. He **struggled** to find a steady job before **eventually** becoming a famous inventor.
>
> Some inventions are very expensive, so not everyone can **afford** them.
>
> The French chemist Louis Pasteur is famous for his research on the causes and **prevention** of diseases.

1. _____ (v) to supply the energy needed for something to work

2. _____ (adv) in the end, especially after a lot of problems

3. _____ (n) a form of energy that can be used for heating and lighting

4. _____ (n) the act of making sure that something does not happen

5. _____ (v) to have enough money to pay for something

6. _____ (v) to try very hard to do something that is difficult

7. _____ (adj) able to invent things and have original ideas

USING
VOCABULARY **B** Discuss these questions with a partner.

1. Are you a **creative** person? Describe one way in which you are creative.

2. What are some sources of energy that can produce **electricity**?

BRAINSTORMING **C** Make a list of things you use every day that require electricity. Share your ideas with a partner.

1. _____   3. _____   5. _____

2. _____   4. _____   6. _____

PREDICTING **D** Skim the first paragraph of the reading passage on pages 25–26, and look at the pictures and captions. What do you think the reading passage is mainly about? Check your answer as you read.

a. energy shortages in Africa

b. a solution to an energy problem

c. how windmills generate electricity

THE POWER OF CREATIVITY

🎧 1.03

A William Kamkwamba lives in Malawi, Africa, where most people don't have access to **electricity** or running water.[1] They have to cook over open fires and collect water from wells or streams. Poverty is very high; only 2 percent of Malawians can **afford** electricity. In addition, most people have to grow their own food. Life is difficult there, and many people **struggle** to survive.

B In 2001, when William was 14 years old, life in Malawi became even more difficult. There was a severe drought,[2] and most families—including William's— couldn't grow enough food. He explains, "Within five months all Malawians began to starve to death. My family ate one meal per day, at night."

C Because of the drought, William's family couldn't afford to send him to school anymore. However, William wanted to continue his education, so he went to the library near his home one day. He found a science book there called *Using Energy*. It included instructions for building a windmill. Windmills can be very **efficient** sources of electricity, and they can bring water up from underground. William didn't know much English, and he wasn't able to understand most of the book, but it was full of pictures and diagrams.[3] Looking at the pictures, William thought he could build a windmill for his family.

[1]**Running water** is water that is brought into a building through pipes.
[2]A **drought** is a long period of time with no rain.
[3]**Diagrams** are drawings that show how something (e.g., a machine) works.

▲ **William Kamkwamba at a speaking event in 2013**

◀ **William used old bicycle parts and other thrown-away items to build his windmill.**

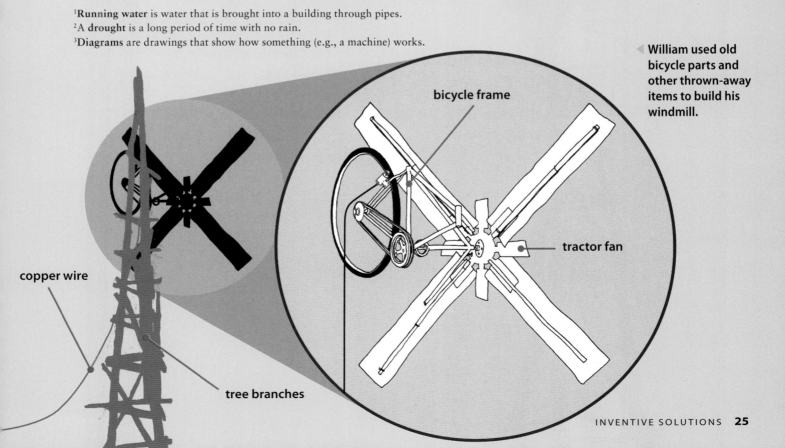

bicycle frame

tractor fan

copper wire

tree branches

Today, William's windmills are up to 12 meters tall.

D When William went home and started building his windmill, a lot of people in his village laughed at him, including his mother. They didn't think he could do it. However, William didn't let that stop him—he was confident. He saw the photo of the windmill in the book. That meant someone else was able to build it, so he knew he could build it, too. William was also **creative**. He didn't have the parts and **equipment** that he saw in the book's diagrams, and he couldn't buy them. So he looked for the parts that he needed in junkyards.[4]

E While building the windmill, William changed and improved his **design** little by little. At first, the windmill **powered** only one lightbulb. Then it powered four lights. **Eventually**, there was enough electricity for four lights and a radio. No one laughed at William after that, and people in his village started to come to his house to get power for their cell phones. Later, William built a second windmill. This one brought water up from underground. After that, he began to teach other people how to build windmills. He also continued to build more of them himself, including one at a primary school.

F Because of his success with the windmills, William was able to go back to school. He also helped to develop a malaria[5] **prevention** program and clean water services in his community. He wrote a book about his life called *The Boy Who Harnessed the Wind: Creating Currents of Electricity and Hope*. In addition, he uses his website to educate people and to give them hope. His main message is this: "To the Africans, and the poor who are struggling with your dreams …, trust yourself and believe. Whatever happens, don't give up."

[4]A **junkyard** is a place where old machines are thrown away.
[5]**Malaria** is a disease spread by mosquitoes.

UNDERSTANDING THE READING

A Choose the best alternative title for the reading passage.

UNDERSTANDING THE MAIN IDEA

   a. Windmills—Africa's Hope for the Future
   b. Advice from a Young Inventor
   c. The Boy Who Brought Electricity—and Hope

B Answer the questions below using information from the reading passage.

UNDERSTANDING DETAILS

   1. Why did life become very difficult for William's family in 2001?

   _____

   2. What did people in William's village think of his idea at first?

   _____

   3. How did William's first windmill help people in his village?

   _____

> **CRITICAL THINKING** To **analyze problems and solutions** in a passage, ask yourself: Does the writer provide enough information to show why the problem is real? Is it clear how the solution matches the problem? If not, what solution(s) would you propose?

C Complete the chart below. Fill in the missing problems and solutions.

CRITICAL THINKING: ANALYZING PROBLEMS AND SOLUTIONS

Problems				
William couldn't afford to go to school.	He couldn't read the book about windmills because he didn't know much English.		The village needed more water.	Other people wanted to build windmills but didn't know how.
↓	↓	↓	↓	↓

Solutions				
	William went to a junkyard.			

D Choose one of the problems mentioned in exercise C. In what other way(s) could William have dealt with it? Discuss with a partner.

CRITICAL THINKING: ANALYZING

DEVELOPING READING SKILLS

READING SKILL Identifying Details

Details tell more about the main idea. They explain, develop, and illustrate the author's main idea by giving reasons and examples. To help locate the details of a paragraph, first identify the main idea. Then turn the main idea statement into a question by using words like *who*, *what*, *when*, *where*, *why*, or *how*.

Look at the paragraph below from the reading passage. What does each colored sentence do?

When William went home and started building his windmill, a lot of people in his village laughed at him, including his mother. They didn't think he could do it. However, William didn't let that stop him—he was confident. He saw the photo of the windmill in the book. That meant someone else was able to build it, so he knew he could build it, too. William was also creative. He didn't have the parts and equipment that he saw in the book's diagrams, and he couldn't buy them. So he looked for the parts that he needed in junkyards.

The main idea of the paragraph is that William was confident and creative in building his windmill. The **red** sentences **give reasons** *why* William was confident. The **blue** sentences **give examples** of *how* William was creative.

IDENTIFYING THE
MAIN IDEA AND
DETAILS

A Read the information about seat belts. Then write the main idea of the paragraph and three details.

Many inventions change lives, but Nils Bohlin's invention has probably helped to save more than a million lives so far. Bohlin invented a new type of seat belt that is in most cars made today. Before Bohlin's invention, seat belts were buckled across the stomach. The buckles often caused injuries during high-speed accidents. Bohlin's seat belt holds the upper and lower body safely in place with one strap across the chest and one across the hips, with a buckle at the side.

Main Idea: _____

_____

Detail 1: _____

Detail 2: _____

Detail 3: _____

IDENTIFYING
DETAILS

B Look back at the reading passage on pages 25–26. Find and underline three details. Then share your answers with a partner.

Video

Workers install solar electric panels on a roof in Camarillo, California.

SOLAR SOLUTIONS

BEFORE VIEWING

A What are some reasons for using solar power? Discuss your ideas with a partner.

B Read the information about solar panels. Then answer the questions.

The energy from the sun's light is enough to fulfill all the world's power needs many times over. There are different ways to use this solar energy. The simplest method is to use solar hot water panels—these can be just boxes of hot water pipes covered with a glass sheet, usually placed on roofs. These turn the sun's visible light into infrared radiation. This heats water in copper pipes that can be used, for example, in a bathroom or kitchen. Solar electric panels, on the other hand, turn sunlight directly into electricity. These panels are made of special materials—such as silicon (made from sand), glass, and metal—that are expensive.

1. What is one advantage of solar power mentioned in the paragraph?

    _____

2. What two types of solar technology are mentioned? Which type do you think is more practical for use in developing countries and why?

    _____

    _____

C Below are some quotes from the video. Match the correct form of each **bold** word or phrase to its definition.

> "The garbage piled everywhere is considered valuable because it's often recycled and reused. Cairo has been **going green** long before it became fashionable."
>
> "The solar heaters allow urban **dwellers** access to a plentiful supply of hot water ...., and they **cut down on** potential energy costs."
>
> "Once they accept that, solar is a **no-brainer** here. It's an easy thing to do."

1. _____ (v) to reduce or decrease

2. _____ (v) to live in an environmentally responsible way

3. _____ (n) something that is easy or obvious

4. _____ (n) a person who lives in a specific place

WHILE VIEWING

A ▶ Watch the video. Check (✓) the goals of Thomas Taha Culhane's project.

☐ 1. to bring affordable hot water to residents of Cairo
☐ 2. to show Egyptians how they can save water
☐ 3. to increase awareness about the importance of recycling

B ▶ Watch the video again and answer the questions below.

1. What are Culhane's solar-powered water heaters made from?

_____

2. Why is Cairo well-suited to Culhane's project?

_____

3. What is one problem with using solar panels in Cairo? What is a simple solution to this problem?

_____

AFTER VIEWING

A Discuss these questions with a partner.

1. Would solar-powered water heaters work well in your country? Why or why not?

2. What does the narrator say at the end of the video? Complete the sentence:

"One man's _____ is another man's _____."

What do you think this saying means?

B List two things William Kamkwamba's windmills and Thomas Taha Culhane's water heaters have in common.

_____

_____

Reading 2

PREPARING TO READ

A The words in **blue** below are used in the reading passage on pages 32–33. Read their definitions and then complete each sentence with the correct form of the word.

A **container** is an object for holding or carrying something.

An **innovation** is a new method, idea, or product.

To **identify** means to be able to name someone or something.

When you **store** something, you keep it for future use.

A **device** is a piece of equipment made or adapted for a particular purpose.

A **benefit** is a good or helpful result or effect.

If something is **valuable**, it is of great use.

To **indicate** means to point out or show something.

1. Research _____ that the global demand for energy is expected to triple by 2050.

2. One _____ of solar power is that it is renewable.

3. There have already been several technological _____ this century, such as the electric car and the tablet computer.

4. The wheel is one of the most _____ inventions of all time. Without it, we would probably have to walk or ride animals to travel long distances.

5. Before refrigerators were invented, people could not easily _____ fresh meat.

6. Blood tests and X-rays can help doctors _____ diseases.

7. Scientists can study the day-to-day movements of an animal by using a tracking _____ .

8. Bottles are useful _____ for water and other liquids.

B Discuss these questions with a partner.

1. What are some recent **innovations** in healthcare?
2. Are there any new **devices** that you really want to get? If so, which ones?

C Skim the first paragraph of the reading passage on pages 32–33, and look at the photos and subheads. How might each item be useful? Discuss your ideas with a partner. Then check your ideas as you read the passage.

BIG IDEAS, LITTLE PACKAGES

🎧 1.04

A Can simple ideas change the world? They just might, one new idea at a time. Creative designers and scientists are working to invent products for communities in developing countries. Some of their innovations might solve even the biggest problems, such as improving access to healthcare and clean water.

INFANT WARMER

B Around 19 million low-birthweight babies are born every year in developing countries. These babies weigh less than 5.5 pounds (2.5 kilograms) when they're born. Low-birthweight babies often have difficulty staying warm because they don't have enough fat on their bodies. Many get too cold and die.

C To solve this problem, American entrepreneur Jane Chen and a team of people invented the Embrace infant warmer. It looks like a small sleeping bag and is specially designed to help keep babies warm. It's filled with wax that easily heats up to 37 degrees Celsius—the normal body temperature.[1] Another benefit of the Embrace infant warmer is that it can work without electricity. It's an easy-to-use, low-cost solution. To date, this simple invention has helped save more than 200,000 babies in Africa, Asia, and Latin America.

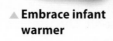

▲ **Embrace infant warmer**

[1] Your **body temperature** is how hot or cold your body is.

WATER CONTAINER

D Clean drinking water is one of the world's most valuable resources. Without it, people get sick and die. But getting clean water can be difficult for many people in developing countries. In poor areas, people often have to walk several miles to get clean water for cooking, cleaning, and drinking. They usually have to carry heavy containers of water on their heads. Most of them make several trips each day to collect water. This is difficult work, especially for women and children.

The Q Drum originated in response to the needs of rural people in South Africa.

HEALTH DETECTOR

F   In many developing countries, doctors work with no electricity or clean water. They have to send medical tests to labs[2] and wait weeks for results. Patients may die while waiting to receive treatment. But a little piece of paper developed by Saudi Arabian scientist Hayat Sindi could change that.

G   Sindi's device is only the size of a postage stamp, but it can help identify health problems. It contains tiny holes that are filled with chemicals. When a person places a single drop of blood on the paper, the chemicals react to the blood and cause the paper to change color. This indicates whether or not the person has an illness. Doctors can then take action immediately, saving time and lives. Since the health detector is made of paper, it's very light and easy to carry. Health workers can easily bring it with them to perform tests in patients' homes. Best of all, this can be done at a very low cost. No electricity, water, or special equipment is needed to use the device. Sindi explains, "It's a tool that allows even the poorest people in the most medically challenged places to get the tests they need."

[2]**Labs** are laboratories—places where scientific research is done.

Hayat Sindi presents her invention at a 2009 conference.

E   A South African engineer, Piet Hendrikse, came up with a solution to the problem of carrying water: the Q Drum. The Q Drum stores 13 gallons (about 50 liters) of water in a rolling container. Made of strong plastic material, it can roll over any kind of ground, no matter how rough. Anyone—even young children—can easily pull the drum with an attached rope. With this innovation, people in developing countries can carry more clean water per journey with less effort.

UNDERSTANDING THE READING

UNDERSTANDING
MAIN IDEAS

A Choose the main purpose of each invention from the pairs of solution statements (a or b).

	Problem	**Solution**
Embrace Infant Warmer	Underweight babies have difficulty staying warm.	a. regulates body temperature of underweight babies b. measures body temperature and indicates when babies are cold
Q Drum	Many people in developing countries don't have easy access to clean water.	a. cleans water and makes it safe for cooking and drinking b. makes it easier for people to transport water
Health Detector	Doctors in remote areas don't have the equipment to process lab results.	a. helps doctors identify diseases quickly and accurately b. tells doctors what the best treatment is for a disease

IDENTIFYING
DETAILS

B Find details in the reading passage to answer each question below.

1. At what weight are babies considered low birthweight?

   _____

2. In developing countries, what is the traditional way of carrying water?

   _____

3. What is Hayat Sindi's health detector made of? What benefit does this have?

   _____

4. List two things the infant warmer, Q Drum, and health detector have in common.

   _____

CRITICAL THINKING:
EVALUATING

C If you gave an award for Best Invention, which of the four listed below would you choose? Consider:

How many people will it help? How much does it cost? Is it easy to make? Are there other inventions that fulfill the same need?

Check (✓) your winning invention. Note your reasons and share your decision with a partner.

☐ Solar-powered water heater   ☐ Q Drum water container

☐ Embrace infant warmer   ☐ Health detector

Reason(s): _____

_____

_____

Writing

EXPLORING WRITTEN ENGLISH

A Below are excerpts from the reading passages. Complete the sentences using the simple past tense of the verbs in parentheses. Then refer back to the reading passages to check your answers.

NOTICING

1. In 2001, when William _____ (*be*) 14 years old, life in Malawi

   _____ (*become*) even more difficult.

2. William _____ (*not / know*) much English, and he

   _____ (*not / be*) able to understand most of the book, but it

   _____ (*be*) full of pictures and diagrams.

3. While building the windmill, William _____ (*change*) and

   _____ (*improve*) his design little by little.

4. American entrepreneur Jane Chen and a team of people _____
   (*invent*) the Embrace infant warmer.

5. A South African engineer, Piet Hendrikse, _____ (*come*) up with a
   solution to the problem of carrying water: the Q Drum.

LANGUAGE FOR WRITING Review of the Simple Past Tense

We use the simple past tense to talk about events that began and ended in the past.

*According to historians, a man named Ts'ai Lun **invented** paper in China around A.D. 105. Before that, people **didn't have** cheap materials to write on. People **wrote** on things such as silk and bamboo, which **were** expensive and difficult to use.*

To form the simple past tense of *be*:

- use *was* or *were* to form affirmative statements.
- use *was not / wasn't* or *were not / weren't* to form negative statements.

To form the simple past tense with other verbs:

- add *-ed* to the end of most verbs to form affirmative statements.
- use *did not / didn't* with the base form of a main verb to form negative statements.

Some verbs have irregular past tense forms in affirmative statements:

go—went	have—had	make—made	take—took
do—did	build—built	find—found	teach—taught

Since there are many different forms for irregular past verbs, it's a good idea to memorize them in context.

*William Kamkwamba **went** to the library and **found** a book called* Using Energy.
*Before people **had** the Q Drum, getting clean water **was** difficult.*
*Before the invention of the printing press, it **took** a very long time to produce a book.*

B Complete the sentences using the simple past tense of the verbs in parentheses.

1. In 2001, there _____ (be) a drought in Malawi.

2. Before William Kamkwamba _____ (build) his windmill, most people in his village _____ (not / believe) he could do it.

3. After his success with the windmills, William _____ (teach) other people how to build them.

4. Before he _____ (invent) the World Wide Web, Tim Berners-Lee _____ (create) a software program that _____ (allow) scientists at CERN to access each other's work.

5. The printing press _____ (make) books more affordable to the general public and _____ (give) many more people access to knowledge.

C Using the simple past tense, write four sentences that describe how people used to do things in the past.

Example: *Before the invention of the printing press, people produced books by hand.*

1. _____

   _____

2. _____

   _____

3. _____

   _____

4. _____

   _____

WRITING SKILL Supporting the Main Idea and Giving Details

As you saw in Unit 1, a strong topic sentence states the main idea of the paragraph. The other sentences in the paragraph relate to and support this main idea.

Supporting idea sentences tell the reader why the topic sentence is true. They often repeat or paraphrase key words from the topic sentence.

When introducing a new supporting idea, use transition words and phrases like *First of all, Secondly, Another, Also, In addition, Furthermore, Finally*, etc. This helps the reader progress from one supporting idea to the next, and shows how the supporting ideas are connected.

Detail sentences give descriptions, reasons, facts, and examples about the supporting ideas to help the reader clearly understand them. In the next paragraph, the **bold** sentences provide details for the writer's three supporting ideas.

The health detector is a perfect medical solution for people in developing countries. First of all, it doesn't need electricity. **It therefore works well in poor countries that have an unreliable power supply.** *Secondly, the device is inexpensive.* **It's made from paper, which is cheap and easy to find almost anywhere in the world.** *Furthermore, this diagnostic tool allows more people to get medical help.* **Health workers can visit up to 200 homes each day, perform tests using the health detector, and take action immediately.**

D Read the topic sentence below. Then write **SI** next to each supporting idea or **D** next to each detail.

Topic Sentence: Solar lanterns are better than kerosene lamps for bringing light to people in developing countries for three main reasons.

_____ 1. For example, they produce 50 times more light than kerosene lamps.

_____ 2. They use solar energy, which is a renewable source of power.

_____ 3. First of all, solar-powered lanterns are more efficient than kerosene lamps.

_____ 4. Finally, solar lanterns are better for our health.

_____ 5. The smoke from kerosene lamps can cause lung damage, but solar-powered lanterns don't use any dangerous chemicals.

_____ 6. Another benefit of solar-powered lanterns is that they are good for the environment.

E Now put the sentences in exercise D (1–6) in order to form a paragraph. Use the transition words and phrases to help you identify the correct order of the sentences.

_____ , _____ , _____ , _____ , _____ , _____

Brick kiln workers in Uttar Pradesh, India, use solar lanterns to brighten their paths.

WRITING TASK

GOAL You are going to write a paragraph on the following topic:

Choose an innovation—either one from this unit or one you personally know about. Describe why it's important and how it changed people's lives.

BRAINSTORMING **A** Brainstorm a list of innovations that you think are important and have improved people's lives. Use ideas from this unit or your own ideas.

_____

_____

PLANNING **B** Follow these steps to make notes for your paragraph.

Step 1 From your brainstorming notes above, choose an innovation to write about.

Step 2 Write a topic sentence for your paragraph in the outline below.

Step 3 Think of two ways this innovation changed people's lives. Note them in the outline as supporting ideas.

Step 4 Give one or two details for each supporting idea. Don't worry about grammar or spelling. Don't write complete sentences.

OUTLINE

Topic: Choose an innovation. How did it change people's lives?

Topic Sentence: _____

_____

Supporting Idea 1: _____

_____

Detail(s): _____

_____

Supporting Idea 2: _____

_____

Detail(s): _____

_____

FIRST DRAFT **C** Use the information in your outline to write a first draft of your paragraph.

REVISING PRACTICE

The drafts below are similar to the one you are going to write. They are on the topic of a particular innovation.

What did the writer do in Draft 2 to improve the paragraph? Match the changes (a–d) to the highlighted parts.

a. added a detail to a supporting idea
b. corrected a verb form
c. added a transition phrase
d. deleted unrelated information

Draft 1

The car is one of the most important inventions in history. It allows people to travel great distances quickly. Before the invention of the car, long-distance travel was slow and difficult. Today, highway traffic jams make travel slow and difficult. Because it was difficult to travel far, most people stayed in their own towns and villages their whole lives. Another benefit of the car is that it improves people's access to opportunities in distant locations. For example, in the past, people have to choose jobs that were near their homes. Now, thanks to cars, people have more choices in terms of where they can work.

Draft 2

The car is one of the most important inventions in history. First of all, it allows people to travel great distances quickly. Before the invention of the car, long-distance travel was slow and difficult. Because it was difficult to travel far, most people stayed in their own towns and villages their whole lives. But now, people can easily travel several hundred miles in a day by car. Another benefit of the car is that it improves people's access to opportunities in distant locations. For example, in the past, people had to choose jobs that were near their homes. Now, thanks to cars, people have more choices in terms of where they can work.

☐
☐
☐
☐

D Now use the questions below to revise your paragraph.

REVISED DRAFT

☐ Does the paragraph have one main idea?
☐ Does a strong topic sentence introduce the main idea?
☐ Does the paragraph include two supporting ideas?
☐ Does the paragraph include one or two details for each supporting idea?
☐ Does the paragraph include transition words or phrases?
☐ Is there any information that doesn't belong?

EDITING PRACTICE

Read the information below.

In sentences using the simple past tense, remember to:
- use the correct verb endings; for most verbs, you add -ed to form the simple past tense, but some verbs have irregular past tense forms.
- use the correct past tense forms of be: was, wasn't, were, and weren't.
- use the base form of the verb with did not / didn't in negative statements.

Correct one mistake with the simple past tense in each sentence below.

1. William Kamkwamba build a windmill using parts he found in junkyards.

2. The people in William Kamkwamba's village wasn't confident about his plan.

3. Before Nils Bohlin's invention, most cars haved seat belts that were buckled across the stomach.

4. The first car didn't went very fast.

5. Orville Wright make the first powered airplane flight in 1903.

6. Alexander Graham Bell, inventor of the telephone, start the Bell Telephone Company in 1877.

7. Ts'ai Lun invented paper in the first century A.D., but it didn't be widely available until many years later.

FINAL DRAFT **E** Follow these steps to write a final draft.

1. Check your revised draft for mistakes with simple past verb forms.

2. Now use the checklist on page 218 to write a final draft. Make any other necessary changes.

UNIT REVIEW

Answer the following questions.

1. Which invention in this unit would you like to know more about? Why?

_____

_____

2. What are two irregular simple past verb forms?

_____

_____

3. Do you remember the meanings of these words? Check (✓) the ones you know. Look back at the unit and review the ones you don't know.

Reading 1:

☐ afford   ☐ creative AWL   ☐ design AWL
☐ efficient   ☐ electricity   ☐ equipment AWL
☐ eventually AWL   ☐ power   ☐ prevention
☐ struggle

Reading 2:

☐ benefit AWL   ☐ container   ☐ device AWL
☐ identify AWL   ☐ indicate AWL   ☐ innovation AWL
☐ store   ☐ valuable

CONNECTED LIVES 3

Participants attend an online gaming
festival in Leipzig, Germany.

READING   Taking notes (Part 1)
WRITING   Writing a concluding sentence
GRAMMAR   Using the present perfect tense
CRITICAL THINKING   Making inferences

THINK AND DISCUSS

1 What do you usually do on the Internet?
2 Do you think our lives have been improved
by the Internet? If so, in what way(s)? If not,
why not?

EXPLORE THE THEME

A Look at the information on these pages and answer the questions.

1. According to Alexa.com, what are the most visited websites in the world? Which are more popular: social media sites or search engines?

2. Which of these websites do you visit regularly? Can you think of other popular websites that aren't on the list?

B Match the correct form of the words and phrases in blue to their definitions.

_____ (n) the act of looking carefully for something

_____ (v) to start or put into operation

_____ (v) to connect to a computer system by typing a particular set of letters or numbers

People in Hong Kong connect with their neighbors and their city while playing Pokémon GO.

THE WORLD'S TOP 10 WEBSITES

How often do you **log in** to Facebook? Is there a website that you check every day? Alexa.com tracks millions of Internet users and compiles lists of the most visited websites. Here are its 2017 rankings of the top 10 websites worldwide.

Unsurprisingly, the world's most popular website is Google. This indicates that the majority of Internet use is driven by the **search** for information. YouTube and Facebook are the next most popular, followed by Baidu (in 4th place). **Launched** in 2000, Baidu is the leading Chinese-language search engine. The Indian version of Google also makes the list (in 8th place).

		Time spent[1]	Pages viewed[2]	Linked sites[3]
1	Google.com	8:34	8.30	2,670,033
2	YouTube.com	9:10	5.30	2,097,022
3	Facebook.com	11:50	4.52	6,442,560
4	Baidu.com	7:56	6.54	96,538
5	Wikipedia.org	4:22	3.30	1,131,376
6	Yahoo.com	4:23	3.80	457,873
7	Reddit.com	15:51	10.38	371,615
8	Google.co.in	8:10	7.05	20,426
9	QQ.com	4:58	4.39	177,323
10	Twitter.com	6:27	3.46	4,494,842

[1] Daily time spent on site (in minutes) per visitor
[2] Daily page views per visitor
[3] Total number of sites that link to this site

Reading 1

PREPARING TO READ

BUILDING VOCABULARY

A The words in **blue** below are used in the reading passage on pages 45–46. Complete each sentence with the correct word. Use a dictionary to help you.

| collaborate | potential | feature | contribution |
| investigate | participant | accurate | |

1. A(n) _____ is a person who takes part in something.

2. When you _____ something, you try to find out what happened or what the truth is.

3. _____ information and statistics are correct to a very detailed level.

4. To _____ means to work together on an activity or project to achieve a common goal.

5. If you make a(n) _____ to something, you help make it successful.

6. Something with _____ has the necessary abilities or qualities to become successful in the future.

7. A(n) _____ of something is an important aspect of it.

USING VOCABULARY

B Discuss these questions with a partner.
1. How often do you **log in** to social media sites? Which is your favorite one?
2. What **contributions** has social media made to society? Can you think of any specific examples?

BRAINSTORMING

C Brainstorm a list of reasons you or people you know have used the Internet to collaborate. Discuss with a partner and note your ideas.

_____

_____

PREDICTING

D Look at the title and the subheads of the reading passage on pages 45–46. Then skim the first paragraph. What do you think the reading passage is mainly about? Check your answer as you read.

a. the different ways archaeologists can collaborate with one another over the Internet
b. how the Internet is changing the field of archaeology
c. how the Internet contributed to a major archaeological discovery

THE POWER OF CROWDS

🎧 1.05

A Every day, people use the Internet to **collaborate** and share information. Today, scientists and archaeologists[1] are using the power of the Internet to **investigate** the past in a new, exciting way. The approach is known as crowdsourcing, and it involves asking the public for help with a project. Crowdsourcing has the **potential** to completely change modern archaeology.

SOLVING A MYSTERY

B Scientists in the United States and Mongolia used the Internet to try to solve an 800-year-old mystery: the location of Genghis Khan's tomb. Genghis Khan was the founder of the Mongol Empire, one of the largest empires in history. When he died in 1227, he was buried in an unmarked grave.

C Experts believe that Genghis Khan's final resting place is somewhere near the Burkhan Khaldun, a sacred[2] Mongolian mountain. It's a difficult place to get to and covers a huge area, so the scientists had to rely on satellite[3] images. However, there were over 85,000 images to study, so they needed a lot of help.

▲ Scientist Albert Lin uses 3-D imaging technology and crowdsourced data to search for a lost tomb.

---

[1] An **archaeologist** is a person who studies human history by digging up items buried underground.
[2] Something that is **sacred** is believed to have a special religious purpose or meaning.
[3] A **satellite** is a device that is sent into space to collect information, to capture images, or to be part of a communications system.

More than 10,000 volunteers or "citizen scientists" joined the **search**. They **logged in** to a website and labeled landmarks[4] on very detailed satellite images of the area. The landmarks could be roads, rivers, modern structures, or ancient structures. **Participants** also labeled anything else that looked unusual.

According to project leader Albert Lin, humans can often do this kind of work better than computers. "What a computer can't do is look for 'weird things,'" he says. Lin's team used the information from the volunteers to decide on the best places to visit and study. The project has identified more than 50 sites that might be related to Genghis Khan's tomb. The exact location is still unknown, but Lin believes that we are getting closer to finding out this great secret.

PROTECTING TREASURES

Crowdsourcing is also being used by National Geographic Explorer and archaeologist Dr. Sarah Parcak. In 2017, Parcak **launched** GlobalXplorer, a citizen science project that aims to find and protect important archaeological sites using satellite images. In particular, it protects sites from looters—people who steal ancient objects and sell them. "If we don't go and find these sites," says Parcak, "looters will." Looting pits are easy to spot in satellite images, so participants can look for signs of looting and illegal construction. The project launched in Peru, which has large numbers of historical sites from many different cultures.

GlobalXplorer is designed like a game. Participants first watch online videos that teach them how to identify certain **features** on satellite images. Then they study and flag[5] satellite images on their own. They look at more than 250,000 square kilometers of land, broken into 100 × 100 meter "tiles." Since the participants don't have professional experience, a certain number of them have to agree on the results before the data is considered useful. Once enough volunteers say that they see the same thing, Parcak and her team will check for themselves before passing the information along to archaeologists on the ground. The "players" receive a score based on how **accurate** they are.

"Most people don't get to make scientific **contributions** or discoveries in their everyday lives," Parcak says. "But we're all born explorers … We want to find out more about other people, and about ourselves and our past." Now, thanks to crowdsourcing projects like GlobalXplorer, anyone with a computer and an Internet connection can be part of a new age of discovery.

[4] A **landmark** is a building or other place (e.g., a large tree or a statue) that is easily noticed and recognized.
[5] When you **flag** something, you mark it for attention.

Archaeologist Sarah Parcak examines a satellite image.

UNDERSTANDING THE READING

A According to the reading passage, the Internet is enabling collaboration through crowdsourcing. How does this work?

UNDERSTANDING THE MAIN IDEA

   a. A small group of people connected to the Internet work together on a project.
   b. A large group of people connected to the Internet contribute toward a shared goal.

B Complete the chart below using information from the reading passage.

IDENTIFYING DETAILS

Lin's Project	Parcak's Project
studies an area in the country of 1 _____	studies sites in the country of 4 _____
aims to find the tomb of 2 _____	aims to protect sites from 5 _____
Participants look at satellite images and label landmarks and other 3 _____ features.	Participants look at satellite images and flag any signs of looting and 6 _____ .

> **CRITICAL THINKING**   You **make inferences** when you make logical guesses about things a writer does not say directly. This is also called "reading between the lines."

C Work with a partner. What can you infer from each statement from the reading passage? Circle the correct inference.

CRITICAL THINKING: MAKING INFERENCES

   1. *More than 10,000 volunteers or "citizen scientists" joined the search.*
      a. A lot of people don't know much about Genghis Khan.
      b. A lot of people are interested in finding Genghis Khan's tomb.

   2. *[GlobalXplorer] protects sites from looters—people who steal ancient objects and sell them.*
      a. Many people don't appreciate the true value of ancient objects.
      b. Ancient objects are worth a lot of money.

   3. *The project launched in Peru, which has large numbers of historical sites from many different cultures.*
      a. Because of its rich history, Peru is an ideal place to start the project.
      b. Peruvians are very proud of their country's rich and diverse history.

D Would you prefer to join Lin's project or Parcak's project? Discuss with a partner and give reasons for your choice.

CRITICAL THINKING: REFLECTING

DEVELOPING READING SKILLS

READING SKILL Taking Notes (Part 1)

Taking notes on a reading passage has two main benefits. First, it helps you understand the information better. It also helps you organize important information for writing assignments and for tests.

It is often helpful to use some kind of graphic organizer when you take notes. Use graphic organizers that best match the type of passage you are reading. Many reading passages are a mixture of text types, so you may want to use more than one graphic organizer:

- **T-chart:** problem-solution, cause-effect, pros-cons, two sides of a topic (see page 47)
- **mind map** (or **concept map** or **word web**): description, classification (see page 11)
- **Venn diagram:** comparison of similarities and differences (see page 7)
- **traditional outline:** any type (see page 38)
- **flow chart** or **timeline:** process or events over time (see below and page 54)

UNDERSTANDING
A PROCESS

A Read the information about how GlobalXplorer works. As you read, underline the different steps in the process.

GlobalXplorer is designed like a game. Participants first watch online videos that teach them how to identify certain features on satellite images. Then they study and flag satellite images on their own. They look at more than 250,000 square kilometers of land, broken into 100 × 100 meter "tiles." Since the participants don't have professional experience, a certain number of them have to agree on the results before the data is considered useful. Once enough volunteers say that they see the same thing, Parcak and her team will check for themselves before passing the information along to archaeologists on the ground. The "players" receive a score based on how accurate they are.

TAKING NOTES

B Complete the flow chart using the information above. Then compare answers with a partner.

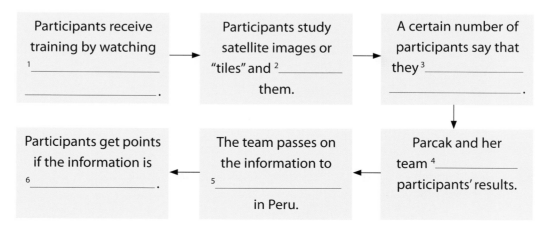

Participants receive training by watching 1_____.

→ Participants study satellite images or "tiles" and 2_____ them.

→ A certain number of participants say that they 3_____.

↓

Participants get points if the information is 6_____.

← The team passes on the information to 5_____ in Peru.

← Parcak and her team 4_____ participants' results.

Video

Albert Lin rides out to explore a site in Mongolia.

CITIZEN SCIENTISTS

BEFORE VIEWING

A Why do you think people are interested in finding Genghis Khan's tomb? Discuss your ideas with a partner.

BRAINSTORMING

B Read the information about Genghis Khan. Then answer the questions.

LEARNING ABOUT THE TOPIC

Genghis Khan was one of the most feared leaders of all time. Born around 1160, he was originally named "Temujin." At the age of 20, he began building a large army to bring all the people of Mongolia under his rule. As leader of the Mongol Empire, he introduced a new alphabet and a new type of money. He also devised a system of laws and regulations, and allowed freedom of religion—long before that idea spread to other parts of the world. At the same time, however, he launched violent military campaigns against his enemies. After his death, the Mongol Empire grew to become one of the largest of all time. It stretched east to west from the Sea of Japan to Eastern Europe, and north to south from Siberia to Southeast Asia. Today, Genghis Khan is still regarded as one of the most influential people in history.

1. Why is Genghis Khan one of the most feared leaders of all time?

   _____

2. List two ways Genghis Khan's empire set a model for modern society.

   a. _____

   b. _____

C Below are some quotes from the video. Match the correct form of each **bold** word or phrase to its definition.

> "Citizen scientists around the world scan the images and **tag** anything that looks unusual."
>
> "These are the most recent tags that have been **uploaded** onto the data pads."
>
> "We're going to scan every single one of the human computation sites that have been picked out on that mountain and try to **figure out** what people saw."

1. _____ (v) to mark or attach a label to

2. _____ (v) to investigate or think something through in order to understand it

3. _____ (v) to transfer data from one computer to a central computer or the Internet

WHILE VIEWING

A ▶ Watch the video. Choose the best alternative title for it.

    a. How Crowdsourcing Led Us to an Ancient Tomb
    b. Journeying on Horseback Across the Burkhan Khaldun
    c. Lessons from a Crowdsourcing Failure

B ▶ Watch the video again and answer the questions below.

1. What is a good indicator that something is man-made?

_____

2. How does the team know that this is not Genghis Khan's tomb?

_____

3. Why is Lin encouraged by the discovery of this tomb?

_____

AFTER VIEWING

A Work with a partner. If you were able to interview Albert Lin, what questions would you ask him?

_____

_____

B Below is an excerpt from the reading passage on page 46:

According to project leader Albert Lin, humans can often do this kind of work better than computers. "What a computer can't do is look for 'weird things,'" he says.

What do you think Lin means by this? Discuss with a partner and include an example from the video to support your answer.

Reading 2

PREPARING TO READ

A The words in **blue** below are used in the reading passage on pages 52–53. Read their definitions and then complete each sentence with the correct word.

BUILDING VOCABULARY

> A **tribe** is a group of people who live in the same place and share a common culture.
>
> **Voting** is the activity of choosing someone or something in an election.
>
> If something exists in the **virtual** world, it exists only on computers or on the Internet.
>
> **Remote** areas are far away from cities and places where most people live.
>
> An **environmentally** responsible person is concerned with the protection of the natural world of land, sea, air, plants, and animals.
>
> When you **advertise** a product, you provide information about it so that more people know about the product.
>
> A **tool** can refer to anything you use for a particular task or purpose.
>
> If something is **global**, it affects all parts of the world.

1. A lot of companies _____ their products on TV and online.

2. Many companies these days are trying to be more _____ friendly. For example, some automobile companies are producing more electric cars.

3. The Internet is a useful _____ for communication.

4. Some online games have _____ cities. These places aren't real; they only exist online.

5. In most democracies, people choose their leaders by _____ for them.

6. There are still some _____ areas in the developing world that don't have Internet access.

7. Most social media sites are _____—people from all over the world can use them.

8. In traditional Fijian society, each _____ has its own chief or leader.

B Discuss these questions with a partner.

USING VOCABULARY

1. What is the most **remote** place you have been to? Did you like it there?
2. Do you generally prefer **virtual** or face-to-face communication? What are the advantages (pros) and disadvantages (cons) of each?

C Skim the reading passage on pages 52–53. Why do you think it is titled "Internet Island"? Note your ideas below. Then check your ideas as you read the passage.

PREDICTING

_____

INTERNET ISLAND

Ben Keene (right) with members of his tribe

THE IDEA

On January 14, 2006, Ben Keene received an email that changed his life. It was from his friend Mark James. The subject line read: "A TRIBE IS WANTED." Keene and James, both 26, had wanted to create an Internet start-up.[1] Here was James's new idea: We will create an online community and call it a tribe. We will make decisions about rules through discussions and online voting. Then we will do something that no one has ever done—our virtual tribe will become a real one. We will travel to a remote island and form a partnership with a local tribe. We will build an environmentally friendly community and share it with the world.

James got this idea from social networking websites. He noticed that people spent a lot of time on these sites, but they spent most of their time posting messages and sharing music. In James's view, these sites could be used for so much more.

THE ISLAND

Keene liked the idea, and he and James named their website Tribewanted.com. Then they began looking for an island for their tribe. Around the same time, Tui Mali—the chief of a tribe in Fiji—wanted to find someone to develop his small island called Vorovoro. Although the main islands of Fiji were becoming very modern, Vorovoro was not. A few people on Vorovoro had cell phones or worked on one of the main islands, but most lived in very small, simple homes with no electricity or running water.

Tui Mali advertised his island on the Internet, and a few weeks later, Keene and James contacted him. They agreed to pay $53,000 for a three-year lease[2] of the island and $26,500 in donations[3] to the community. They also promised jobs for the local tribe members. "We are all excited about Tribewanted," Tui Mali told a local newspaper reporter. "It will provide us with work for the next three years." Tui Mali was happy to have the money, but he also trusted that Keene and James would respect his culture.

THE NEW TRIBE

The Internet tribe attracted people quickly. In a few months, it had 920 members from 25 countries. In September of 2006, Keene and 13 of his tribe members, aged 17 to 59, traveled to the island for the first time. James, meanwhile, stayed at home to manage the website. When Keene's group arrived, the local tribe and Tui Mali were there to greet them.

For several weeks after the newcomers arrived, they worked with the local tribe members. They built buildings, planted crops behind the village, set up clean sources of energy such as solar power, and ate fresh fish from the ocean. As the new and old tribes worked together, they became friends. Eventually, they became one tribe.

Tribewanted brought together groups of people from very different cultures—both on the island and online. Keene and Tui Mali believe the new tribal connections will help Vorovoro develop in a positive way. They hope the island will become more modern without losing its traditional culture.

THE TRIBE KEEPS GROWING

Today, Tribewanted continues to use social networking as a tool to connect in a real environment. Anyone can go to the website to join the online tribe, donate money, or plan a visit. Since Vorovoro, Keene and James have created other tribes in Sierra Leone, Papua New Guinea, Bali, and Italy. They hope to create more communities around the world, bringing people and cultures together in a global Internet tribe.

[1] An **Internet start-up** is a newly created online business.
[2] A **lease** is a contract allowing the use of a building or piece of land.
[3] **Donations** are sums of money or items that someone gives to an organization.

UNDERSTANDING THE READING

UNDERSTANDING MAIN IDEAS

A The statement in **bold** below is an introductory sentence for a brief summary of the reading passage. Complete the summary by choosing three sentences (a–e) that best express the main ideas of the reading passage.

Ben Keene and Mark James created Tribewanted.com, a virtual community that became a real community.

☐ a. They contacted Tui Mali, the leader of a tribe in Fiji who wanted to modernize his island.

☐ b. Members of the website traveled to the island to help develop it, forming new tribal connections with the local community.

☐ c. James did not go to the island; he had to stay at home to manage the website.

☐ d. Each month, one member of Tribewanted was elected co-chief of the island and served alongside Tui Mali.

☐ e. Keene and James have created new tribes in other places around the world and hope to form a global Internet community.

IDENTIFYING DETAILS

B Find details in the reading passage to complete each sentence. The sentences are in random order.

1. James and Keene found a small island for their tribe called _____.

2. In September _____, Keene went to the island with 13 other people.

3. James and Keene paid Tui Mali _____ to lease the island for three years.

4. James and Keene named their website _____.

5. Mark James sent a(n) _____ to his friend Ben Keene about starting a tribe.

6. James and Keene started tribes in other places like _____ in Indonesia.

7. The newcomers worked with the _____ people to develop the island. In the end, both groups became one tribe.

SEQUENCING

C Complete the timeline using the sentences in exercise B (1–7).

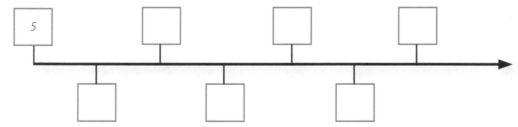

CRITICAL THINKING: MAKING INFERENCES

D Discuss these questions with a partner.

1. What kind of people do you think join Tribewanted?

2. How do you think Tribewanted has changed Tui Mali and his tribe members?

Writing

EXPLORING WRITTEN ENGLISH

A Read the sentences (1–5). Then answer the question below.

NOTICING

1. The project <u>has identified</u> over 50 sites that might be related to Genghis Khan's tomb.
2. Lin and Parcak <u>have used</u> citizen scientists to help them find important sites.
3. Parcak's work <u>has helped</u> to protect sites from looters.
4. Since Vorovoro, Keene and James <u>have created</u> new tribes in other countries.
5. Thousands of people <u>have joined</u> Tribewanted in the past few years.

Which of the following statements is true about the actions described by the underlined verbs?

a. The action started and ended in the past.
b. The action started in the past and continues in the present.

LANGUAGE FOR WRITING Using the Present Perfect Tense

We use the present perfect tense:

- for something that began in the past and continues to the present.
- for something that happened at an unspecified time in the past.
- when the time in the past is not important.

To form the present perfect tense, use *have* or *has* and the past participle of a main verb.

> Tui Mali **has lived** in Fiji all his life.

> We **have advertised** the product on several different social media sites recently.

> I think the Internet **has improved** our lives in many ways.

We often use a phrase with *since* to show when something started in the past.

> She **has posted** over 100 photos on Instagram <u>since last month</u>.

An aerial view of Vorovoro

B Complete the sentences using the present perfect tense of the verbs in parentheses.

1. Facebook _____ (make) it easier for me to keep in touch with my former classmates.

2. Social media sites _____ (change) a lot since they first became popular.

3. I _____ (meet) a lot of great people through social networking sites.

4. Citizen scientists _____ (contribute) to many important research projects in the past few years.

5. GlobalXplorer _____ (form) a partnership with the Sustainable Preservation Initiative (SPI).

6. Since the success of Vorovoro, Tribewanted _____ (expand) into Africa and Europe.

C Write three sentences using the present perfect tense. Write about the impact that the Internet has had on your life, and ways that you have used the Internet.

1. _____

_____

2. _____

_____

3. _____

_____

WRITING SKILL Writing a Concluding Sentence

Formal paragraphs often have concluding sentences. A concluding sentence is the last sentence of a paragraph. It ties the paragraph together.

Concluding sentences can state an opinion (either the author's, or a person mentioned in the paragraph), make a prediction, or ask a question for the reader to think about. They can also restate—or summarize—the main idea of a long or complex paragraph. Here are some examples:

I believe that one of the most important skills we can learn is collaboration.
[states an opinion]

GlobalXplorer will help prevent looting of archaeological sites in Peru.
[makes a prediction]

Which crowdsourcing project would you prefer to join?
[asks a question]

In short, the Internet has transformed the field of archaeology.
[restates the main idea]

D Find and underline these concluding sentences from paragraphs earlier in this unit. What does each sentence do? Write **P** (makes a prediction), **O** (gives an opinion), or **R** (restates the main idea).

_____ 1. *Today, Genghis Khan is still regarded as one of the most influential people in history.* (page 49)

_____ 2. *We will build an environmentally friendly community and share it with the world.* (page 53)

_____ 3. *In James's view, these sites could be used for so much more.* (page 53)

E Write a concluding sentence for each paragraph below.

Everywhere you look these days, people are on their phones, tablets, or computers. Some are talking, some are texting, and some are surfing the Web. It seems like people communicate with each other more on social networks and by text than they do in person. According to Tom Rath and Jim Harter, authors of *Wellbeing: The Five Essential Elements*, people should spend up to six hours a day socializing with friends and family in order to increase happiness. Socializing online probably doesn't have the same effect that socializing in person does.

1. [Write a prediction.] _____

   _____

   _____

In my opinion, reading the news online is better than reading a newspaper or watching the news on TV. One reason for this is that readers can comment on articles that they read online. They can have conversations with other readers, and sometimes even with the writer. Also, online articles provide links to additional information. For example, if an article mentions a name, the name is often linked to another article with more information about that person. Finally, online news articles can be easily updated if something changes during the day. For example, an online news site might post an article about a dangerous storm in the morning. If more information about the storm becomes available later that day, it can be added to the article.

2. [Restate the main idea.] _____

   _____

   _____

WRITING TASK

GOAL You are going to write a paragraph on the following topic:

Describe a crowdsourcing project that you know well. Do some research if necessary. Choose one of the following or your own idea:

EyeWire   Galaxy Zoo   Wild Me   iNaturalist   WildScan

TAKING NOTES **A** Look up the crowdsourcing projects above—or other crowdsourcing projects you know about—online. Choose one project and take notes as you read about it.

_____

_____

_____

PLANNING **B** Follow these steps to make notes for your paragraph.

Step 1 Write a topic sentence in the outline below introducing the crowdsourcing project you chose.

Step 2 Complete the outline with details for each question. Don't worry about grammar or spelling. Don't write complete sentences.

Step 3 Write a concluding sentence for your paragraph.

OUTLINE

Topic: What is one way that people have collaborated on the Internet?

Topic Sentence: _____

_____

What is the purpose of the project? _____

_____

How does it work? _____

_____

What has it accomplished so far? _____

_____

Concluding Sentence: _____

_____

FIRST DRAFT **C** Use the information in your outline to write a first draft of your paragraph.

REVISING PRACTICE

The drafts below are similar to the one you are going to write. They are on the topic of Tribewanted.

What did the writer do in Draft 2 to improve the paragraph? Match the changes (a–d) to the highlighted parts.

a. deleted unrelated information
b. corrected a verb form
c. added a concluding sentence
d. added details to explain an idea

Draft 1

Members of Tribewanted.com has collaborated to create virtual and real-life communities all over the world. The founders of the website are Ben Keene and Mark James. They have been friends for a long time. In 2006, James came up with the idea to launch a website to get members to meet and work together to help a community in need. Keene and James learned about a project to help develop an island in Fiji. By this time, many people had signed up online to join the website. Keene and a few members went to the island and worked with the local people there. Together, they accomplished a lot. Tribewanted has since expanded into other areas like Sierra Leone and Papua New Guinea.

Draft 2

Members of Tribewanted.com have collaborated to create virtual and real-life communities all over the world. The founders of the website are Ben Keene and Mark James. In 2006, James came up with the idea to launch a website to get members to meet and work together to help a community in need. Keene and James learned about a project to help develop an island in Fiji. By this time, many people had signed up online to join the website. Keene and a few members went to the island and worked with the local people there. Together, they accomplished a lot. For example, they planted crops and set up environmentally friendly power sources on the island. Tribewanted has since expanded into other areas like Sierra Leone and Papua New Guinea. The website has successfully brought together people from very different cultures to form a real-world tribe.

D Now use the questions below to revise your paragraph.

REVISED DRAFT

☐ Does a strong topic sentence introduce the main idea?
☐ Does the paragraph include enough details for each supporting idea?
☐ Are all verb forms correct?
☐ Is there any information that doesn't belong?
☐ Does the paragraph have a concluding statement or question?

EDITING PRACTICE

Read the information below.

In sentences using the present perfect tense, remember to:
- use the correct form of *have*.
- use the correct form of the past participle of the main verb. (Be careful with irregular past participles, such as *be—been, do—done, have—had, see—seen,* and *take—taken.*)

Correct one mistake with the present perfect tense in each sentence below.

1. The Internet been in existence for several decades now, but we are still discovering creative ways to use it.

2. Now that it's so easy to share videos, millions of people has posted videos online.

3. Even though I have saw that video a few times, I still find it very funny.

4. Social networks like Facebook and Twitter has changed the way we get our news.

5. The Internet has allow people to share information and collaborate on projects.

6. Sarah Parcak has spend the last several years using satellite images to identify important archaeological sites.

7. Participants in the Galaxy Zoo project have help scientists discover new types of galaxies (star systems) in our universe.

FINAL DRAFT   **E**   Follow these steps to write a final draft.

1. Check your revised draft for mistakes with the present perfect tense.

2. Now use the checklist on page 218 to write a final draft. Make any other necessary changes.

UNIT REVIEW

Answer the following questions.

1. Would you prefer to participate in a crowdsourcing project or join Tribewanted? Why?

_____

_____

2. What are two things a concluding sentence can do?

_____

_____

3. Do you remember the meanings of these words? Check (✓) the ones you know. Look back at the unit and review the ones you don't know.

Reading 1:

☐ accurate AWL   ☐ collaborate   ☐ contribution AWL
☐ feature AWL   ☐ investigate AWL   ☐ launch
☐ log in   ☐ participant AWL   ☐ potential AWL
☐ search

Reading 2:

☐ advertise   ☐ environmentally AWL   ☐ global AWL
☐ remote   ☐ tool   ☐ tribe
☐ virtual AWL   ☐ voting

SAVING OUR SEAS

4

A shipwreck attracts a school of smallmouth grunt fish.

THINK AND DISCUSS

1 Which ocean or sea is nearest your home? When was the last time you saw it?

2 Do you eat seafood? If so, what types do you eat? If not, why not?

A Look at the information on these pages and answer the questions.

1. What does the map show? What do the colors indicate?
2. How is pollution affecting the four places described? What other problems are mentioned?

B Match the words in yellow **to their definitions.**

_____ (adj) concerned with earning money

_____ (v) to continue to live in spite of danger

_____ (n) a group of animals or plants whose members share common characteristics

OCEAN IMPACT

Human activities are affecting all of the world's oceans in some way. These activities include fishing, manufacturing, and offshore oil and gas drilling.

Impact of human activity

Very high | Medium

High | Low

Medium high | Very low

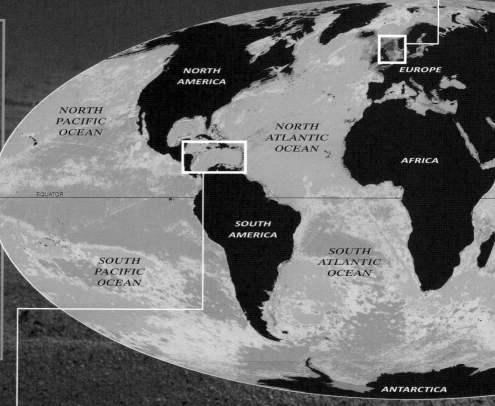

NORTH AMERICA

NORTH PACIFIC OCEAN

EUROPE

NORTH ATLANTIC OCEAN

AFRICA

EQUATOR

SOUTH AMERICA

SOUTH PACIFIC OCEAN

SOUTH ATLANTIC OCEAN

ANTARCTICA

CARIBBEAN SEA

Pollution and overfishing are causing some fish species to disappear. Due to global warming, the temperature of the water is increasing, too. The rising water temperature makes it more difficult for fish to breathe, swim, and find food.

▶ **Garbage washes ashore on the southern edge of Aruba in the Caribbean.**

NORTH SEA

Pollution from shipping and offshore drilling is causing "dead zones"—places without enough oxygen for plants and fish to survive. Overfishing adds to the problem.

◀ Pollution from offshore oil and gas drilling is one cause of the North Sea's dead zones.

EAST CHINA SEA

Several large rivers bring pollution into the sea. It is also a major commercial fishing area and shipping route. Together, these factors cause serious problems for the ocean environment.

◀ Container ships are a common sight on the rivers that flow into the East China Sea.

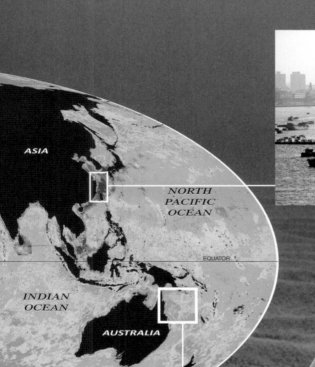

ASIA

NORTH PACIFIC OCEAN

EQUATOR

INDIAN OCEAN

AUSTRALIA

CORAL SEA

The sea absorbs the carbon dioxide produced from human activities. As carbon dioxide in the ocean increases, the water becomes more acidic.[1] Plants, fish, and corals cannot survive in acidic water.

◀ The humphead wrasse is among thousands of fish species living in Australia's Coral Sea.

▲ (Main Photo) Waves of sand cover the ocean floor of Australia's Coral Sea.

[1] If something is **acidic**, it has a pH of less than 7. Very strong acids are able to burn holes in things.

Reading 1

PREPARING TO READ

BUILDING VOCABULARY

A The words in **blue** below are used in the reading passage on pages 65–66. Complete each sentence with the correct word. Use a dictionary to help you.

diverse	estimate	doubled	quantity
reduce	restore	stable	

1. If you _____ something, you make it less.

2. If you _____ something, you make it the way it was before.

3. When you _____ a size or number, you make a guess based on the information available.

4. A(n) _____ environment is made up of things that are very different from one another.

5. Something that is _____ is not likely to change.

6. A(n) _____ is an amount of something that can be counted or measured.

7. If something has _____ in size, it has become twice as much or as many.

USING VOCABULARY

B Discuss these questions with a partner.

1. What do fish need to **survive**? What do humans need to survive?

2. Apart from **species** of fish, what other animal species can we find in the ocean?

3. How can we **reduce** pollution?

PREDICTING

C Skim the reading passage on pages 65–66. Check (✓) the topics that you think the reading passage covers. Then check your answers as you read.

☐ 1. why there are fewer big fish in our oceans

☐ 2. why fish migrate

☐ 3. the growth of the fishing industry

☐ 4. the areas that are most affected by overfishing

☐ 5. the causes and effects of ocean pollution

☐ 6. how to protect and restore ocean life

WHERE HAVE ALL THE FISH GONE?

🎧 1.07

A Throughout history, people have thought of the ocean as a diverse and limitless source of food. Today, however, there are clear signs that the oceans do have a limit. Most of the big fish in our oceans—including many of the fish we love to eat—are now gone. One major factor is overfishing. People are taking so many fish from the sea that species cannot reproduce[1] quickly enough to maintain their populations. How did this problem start? And what is the future for fish?

SOURCE OF THE PROBLEM

B For centuries, local fishermen caught only enough fish to feed their families and their communities. They used traditional gear like spears and hooks that targeted a single fish at a time. However, in the mid-20th century, more people around the world became interested in fish as a source of protein and healthy fats. In response to this, governments gave money and other help to the fishing industry.

As a result, the fishing industry grew. Large commercial fishing companies began catching huge quantities of fish. They made a lot of money selling the

[1]When animals reproduce, they have babies.

C

fish around the world. In addition, they started using new fishing technologies that made fishing easier. These technologies included sonar[2] to locate fish, and dragging large nets along the ocean floor. Modern equipment enabled commercial fishermen to catch many more fish than local fishermen.

RISE OF THE LITTLE FISH

D

In 2010, the Census of Marine Life **estimated** that 90 percent of the big ocean fish populations are gone, mainly due to overfishing. In particular, commercial fishing has greatly **reduced** the number of large fish such as cod, tuna, and salmon. Today, there are plenty of fish in the sea, but they're mostly just the little ones. Small fish, such as sardines and anchovies, have more than **doubled** in number. This is largely because there aren't enough big fish to eat them.

E

This is a problem because, in order to be **stable**, oceans need predators.[3] Predators are necessary to kill the sick and weak fish. Without them, there are too many unhealthy, small fish in the sea. This can cause serious problems for the sea's food chain and the health of our oceans.

A FUTURE FOR FISH?

F

A study published in 2006 in the journal *Science* made a prediction: If we continue to overfish the oceans, most of the fish that we catch now—from tuna to sardines—will disappear by 2050. However, we can prevent this situation if we **restore** the ocean's biodiversity.[4]

G

Scientists say there are a few ways we can do this. First, commercial fishing companies need to catch fewer large fish. This will increase the number of predator fish in the sea. Another way to improve the biodiversity of the oceans is to develop aquaculture—fish farming. Growing fish on farms means that we catch fewer wild fish. This gives wild fish a chance to **survive** and reproduce. In addition, we can make good choices about what we eat. For example, we can stop eating the fish that are most in danger—like bluefin tuna—or only eat fish from fish farms. If we are careful today, we can still look forward to a future with fish.

▽ **Fish farms, such as this one in Turkey, help protect wild seafood populations.**

[2]**Sonar** technology uses sound waves to locate objects on or under the surface of the water.
[3]**Predators** are animals that kill and eat other animals.
[4]**Biodiversity** is the existence of a wide variety of plant and animal species.

UNDERSTANDING THE READING

A Choose the main idea of each section of the reading passage from the pairs of statements (a or b).

UNDERSTANDING MAIN IDEAS

Source of the Problem
a. Traditional gear used by local fishermen is harming the ocean environment.
b. Big companies are using modern technology to catch large numbers of fish.

Rise of the Little Fish
a. It's important for the population of small fish to increase to ensure species diversity.
b. The rising number of small fish in the sea can harm the stability of our oceans.

A Future for Fish?
a. There are several things we can do to protect the ocean populations of big fish.
b. Governments need to take more responsibility for restoring the ocean's biodiversity.

B The flow chart below shows the effects of commercial fishing. Complete the missing information using the words and phrases in the box.

UNDERSTANDING A PROCESS

dropped	increased	too few	too many

Commercial fishing → The number of big fish has 1 _____. → There are 2 _____ predators left.

4 _____ small fish can damage the ocean's ecosystem. ← The number of small fish has 3 _____. ←

C According to the writer, what are three possible solutions to overfishing? Note them in your own words.

IDENTIFYING PROBLEMS AND SOLUTIONS

1. _____

2. _____

3. _____

> **CRITICAL THINKING** When you **evaluate an argument**, ask yourself: What information does the writer use to support their argument? For example, does the writer provide any facts or statistics? Is the information convincing?

D Work with a partner. Discuss the following questions about the reading passage.

CRITICAL THINKING: EVALUATING AN ARGUMENT

1. What statistics does the writer use to show that overfishing is a real problem?

2. How convincing is this argument? What other kinds of statistics or supporting information could the writer have provided?

DEVELOPING READING SKILLS

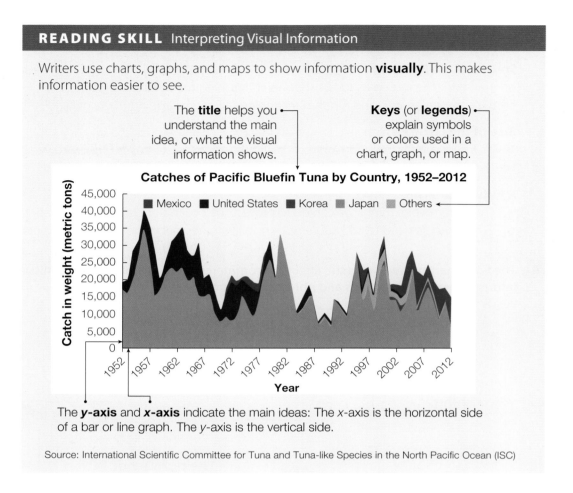

READING SKILL Interpreting Visual Information

Writers use charts, graphs, and maps to show information **visually**. This makes information easier to see.

The **title** helps you understand the main idea, or what the visual information shows.

Keys (or **legends**) explain symbols or colors used in a chart, graph, or map.

Catches of Pacific Bluefin Tuna by Country, 1952–2012

■ Mexico ■ United States ■ Korea ■ Japan ■ Others

(y-axis: Catch in weight (metric tons), 0 to 45,000)
(x-axis: Year, 1952 to 2012)

The **y-axis** and **x-axis** indicate the main ideas: The x-axis is the horizontal side of a bar or line graph. The y-axis is the vertical side.

Source: International Scientific Committee for Tuna and Tuna-like Species in the North Pacific Ocean (ISC)

INTERPRETING
GRAPHS

A Look at the graph above and answer the following questions.

1. What does the graph show? What do the colors represent?

   _____

2. According to the graph, which countries were the only ones to fish for Pacific bluefin tuna before the 1970s?

   _____

3. Approximately how many metric tons of Pacific bluefin tuna were caught in 2012?

   _____

4. When was the lowest catch of Pacific bluefin tuna recorded? When was the highest?

   _____

INTERPRETING
MAPS

B Look at the map on pages 62–63 again and answer the following questions.

1. Which areas are most affected by human activities? _____

2. Which areas are least affected by human activities? _____

Video

SAVING BLUEFIN TUNA

▲ A school of caged
bluefin tuna

BEFORE VIEWING

LEARNING ABOUT
THE TOPIC

A Read the information about the bluefin tuna. Then answer the questions.

The bluefin tuna is one of the biggest and fastest fish in the world. There are three species: Atlantic, Pacific, and Southern. This blue- and silver-colored fish can grow to about 6.5 feet (2 meters) in length and 550 pounds (250 kilograms) in weight. It grows to this size by eating enormous quantities of smaller fish, crustaceans, squid, and eels. Its powerful fins help it swim up to 43 miles (70 kilometers) per hour. However, the bluefin is also known for its meat, which is often eaten raw, as sushi or sashimi. Due to the high demand for this fish, it's now an endangered species. In 2014, scientists reported that the Pacific bluefin tuna population was down to only 4 percent of what it was before commercial fishing began.

1. List two special characteristics of the bluefin tuna.

2. What is driving the high demand for the bluefin tuna?

3. What do you think can be done to help increase bluefin tuna populations?

B The words in **bold** below are used in the video. Match the correct form of each word to its definition.

> Fish **breed** by laying eggs or by giving birth to live fish.
>
> Some animals exist only in **captivity**, in places like zoos and wildlife parks.
>
> Most fish **hatchlings** are left on their own to survive immediately after leaving the egg.

1. _____ (n) a baby animal that has just come out from an egg

2. _____ (n) the state of being kept somewhere and not being free

3. _____ (v) to produce young animals

WHILE VIEWING

A ▶ Watch the video. How is Shukei Masuma helping the bluefin tuna population grow?

a. by breeding bluefins in tanks and pools until they can be returned to the sea

b. by removing adult bluefins from the wild and sending them to protected areas

c. by tracking bluefins in the wild to study their breeding behavior

B ▶ Watch the video again. Circle the correct words to complete the summary.

Shukei Masuma is trying to save the bluefin tuna from extinction by raising some in captivity. Bluefin tuna breed by [1] **laying eggs / giving birth to live fish**. Masuma faced difficulties in finding a stable water [2] **temperature / pressure** and the right [3] **tank size / food** for the baby fish. But after years of hard work, he succeeded. He shows ocean scientist Sylvia Earle the [4] **fins / eyes** of a fish as they begin to form.

AFTER VIEWING

A The narrator says that the Atlantic bluefin tuna population is now only one-fifth of its population in the 1970s. How does this compare with Pacific bluefin? Using the graph below, discuss these questions with a partner.

1. How does the Pacific bluefin population in 2012 compare with that in the early 1970s? Is this similar or different to the Atlantic bluefin?

2. How does the population in 2012 compare with that in the early 1960s?

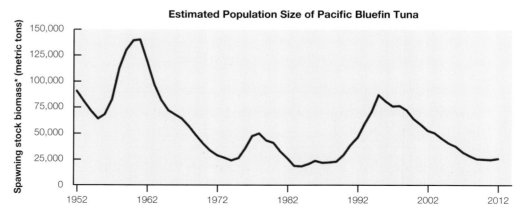

Estimated Population Size of Pacific Bluefin Tuna

*Population of adult fish capable of breeding

Source: ISC

Reading 2

PREPARING TO READ

A The words and phrases in **blue** below are used in the reading passage on pages 72–73. Read their definitions and then complete each sentence with the correct form of the word or phrase.

BUILDING VOCABULARY

If something is **declining**, it is becoming less.

If something is **definitely** true, it is for sure and without doubt.

An **individual** is a single person.

Something that is **essential** is extremely important or absolutely necessary.

If you make an **informed** decision, you understand the facts of the situation.

To **rely on** something means to need or depend on it.

To make an **impact** on something means to have an effect or influence on it.

If a problem is described as **severe**, it is very bad or serious.

1. If pollution is a global problem, what can we as _____ do about it?

2. Overfishing has led to _____ populations of predator fish. This is _____ having a negative effect on the ocean's ecosystem.

3. Protection of big fish species is _____ for the health of the oceans. If predator fish die out, the ocean's ecosystem will be unbalanced.

4. You can make _____ choices about seafood by researching which fish are endangered and which aren't.

5. Our love of sushi has led to _____ overfishing of bluefin tuna.

6. The use of modern equipment in commercial fishing has had a large _____ on the ocean's ecosystem.

7. Larger fish _____ smaller fish as a source of food.

B Discuss these questions with a partner.

USING VOCABULARY

1. What are three things you think are **essential** for the health of the planet?
2. How do you stay **informed** about environmental issues?
3. What are some negative **impacts** of global warming?

C Note some ideas about things you can do to help keep the oceans healthy. Share your ideas with a partner.

BRAINSTORMING

_____

_____

AN INTERVIEW WITH BARTON SEAVER

A Barton Seaver is a chef and conservationist[1] who wants our help to save the oceans. He believes that our eating choices have a direct **impact** on the ocean's health. In this interview, Seaver discusses how **individuals** can make a big difference by making **informed** choices.

Should people stop eating seafood?

B There are certain species that have been overfished and that people should **definitely** avoid for environmental reasons. But I don't think we need to stop eating seafood altogether. I believe that we can save the oceans while continuing to enjoy seafood. For example, some types of seafood, such as Alaskan salmon, come from well-managed fisheries. And others, such as farmed mussels and oysters, actually help to restore **declining** wild populations and clean up polluted waters.

Barton Seaver

What kind of seafood should people eat? What should they not eat?

C My general advice is to eat fish and shellfish that are lower on the food chain and that can be harvested[2] with little impact on the environment. Some examples include farmed mussels, clams and oysters, anchovies, sardines, and herring. People should not eat the bigger fish of the sea, like tuna, orange roughy, shark, sturgeon, and swordfish. Otherwise, we will face **severe** shortages of these species and upset the balance of life in the oceans.

| LEVEL 4 | **TOP PREDATORS** Animals that eat carnivores |

Why did you choose to dedicate[3] your life to the ocean?

D I believe that the next great advance in human knowledge will come not from making new discoveries, but rather, from learning how we relate to our natural world. Humans are an **essential** part of nature, yet most humans do not have a very strong relationship with the world around them. I have dedicated myself to helping people understand our place on this planet through the foods that we eat.

Why do you believe people should care about the health of the oceans?

E The health of the oceans is directly linked to the health of people. The ocean provides most of the air that we breathe. It has a big effect on the weather that we **rely on** for crops and food production. It also provides a necessary and vital[4] diet for billions of people on the planet. So I don't usually say that I am trying to save the oceans. I prefer to say that I am trying to save the vital things that we rely on the ocean for.

ATLANTIC BLUEFIN TUNA

ORANGE ROUGHY

---

[1]A **conservationist** is someone who works to protect the environment.
[2]When you **harvest** food, you gather it from the fields or the sea.
[3]When you **dedicate** yourself to something, you give it a lot of time and effort.
[4]Something that is **vital** is very important.

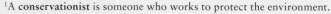

ATLANTIC SALMON

WHAT WE EAT MAKES A DIFFERENCE

F

When we eat predator fish, we increase our impact on the ocean. This is because predators sit at the top of the sea's food chain. They eat smaller fish and help to keep populations of other species from growing too large. At the bottom of the food chain are plants. They make their own food and produce all the oxygen in the ocean, just as plants on land do. Below is an illustration of an ocean food chain. The species can be classified into different levels.

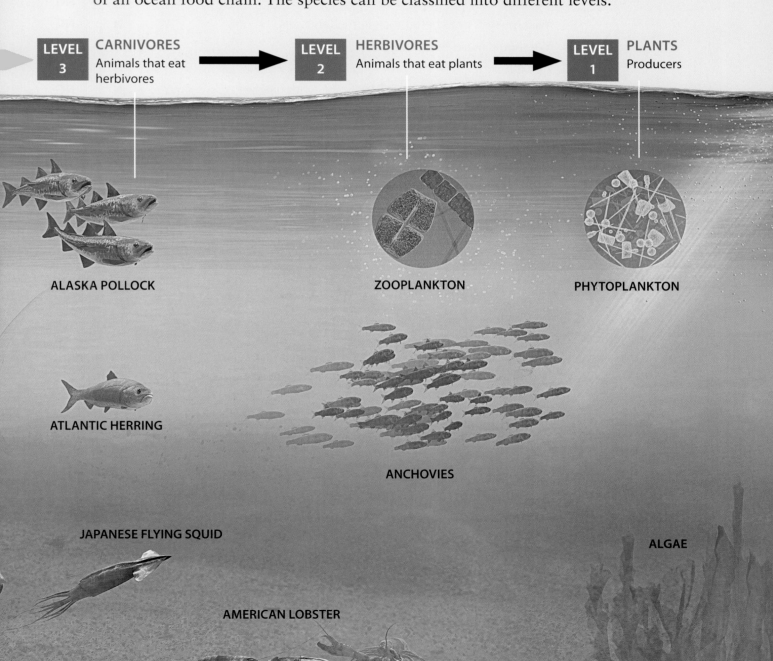

LEVEL 3 CARNIVORES Animals that eat herbivores →

LEVEL 2 HERBIVORES Animals that eat plants →

LEVEL 1 PLANTS Producers

ALASKA POLLOCK

ZOOPLANKTON

PHYTOPLANKTON

ATLANTIC HERRING

ANCHOVIES

JAPANESE FLYING SQUID

ALGAE

AMERICAN LOBSTER

UNDERSTANDING THE READING

A What is Barton Seaver's main message in his interview?

a. People should stop eating seafood so the ocean's ecosystem can be restored.

b. We need to protect the ocean because it provides most of the food that we eat.

c. Individuals can have a positive impact on the ocean by making good food choices.

B Based on his responses, would Barton Seaver agree with the following statements? Circle **Y** (Yes), **N** (No), or **NG** (Not Given) if there isn't enough information in the reading passage.

1. It's OK to eat seafood from well-managed fisheries.	**Y**	**N**	**NG**
2. Fish farms are bad for the ocean.	**Y**	**N**	**NG**
3. Wild mussels taste better than farmed mussels.	**Y**	**N**	**NG**
4. We should avoid eating big fish.	**Y**	**N**	**NG**
5. Fish is a better source of protein than meat.	**Y**	**N**	**NG**
6. Most humans have a strong relationship with nature.	**Y**	**N**	**NG**
7. Healthy oceans will make people healthier.	**Y**	**N**	**NG**

C Look at the illustration on pages 72–73 and answer the questions below.

1. What is one example of a top predator fish? _____

2. What kind of animals do top predators eat? _____

3. What is a herbivore? _____

4. What is one example of a herbivorous fish? _____

5. What is one species of fish that eats herbivores? _____

6. Why are plants called producers? _____

D Look at the information on pages 72–73 again. Which species of fish in the illustration would Barton Seaver say are OK and not OK to eat? List two examples of each in the chart below.

Fish that are OK to eat	Fish we should avoid
1.	1.
2.	2.

E Based on what you have learned in this unit, do you plan to change any of your eating choices? Why or why not? Discuss with a partner.

Writing

EXPLORING WRITTEN ENGLISH

A Read the sentences below. What do they describe? Write **UT** for an upward trend (something that increased), **DT** for a downward trend (something that decreased), or **NC** for no change.

NOTICING

_____ 1. As the graph shows, the big ocean fish populations have fallen by 90 percent since the middle of the 20th century.

_____ 2. The data show that small fish, such as sardines and anchovies, have more than doubled in number.

_____ 3. We can see from the chart that the number of commercial fishing companies remained stable between 2016 and 2017.

_____ 4. This chart shows that the price of bluefin tuna rose sharply between 2008 and 2013.

_____ 5. According to the graph, the quantity of fish caught dropped slightly between 1970 and 1972.

LANGUAGE FOR WRITING Describing Charts and Graphs

We use these phrases to introduce a description of a chart or graph (followed by a comma):

According to the graph, …   As the chart shows, …   As we can see from the chart, …

These are common verbs used to describe charts and graphs (usually in simple past tense):

↑ _rose to/by, increased to/by, grew, doubled (= ×2), tripled (= ×3), quadrupled (= ×4), peaked, reached a high point of_

↓ _declined, decreased, dipped, dropped, fell, reached a low point of_

→ _remained stable/steady, stayed (about) the same_

Prepositions are often used to describe information in charts and graphs.

• Use _to_ with most verbs to talk about a number or amount that something reached.
• Use _by_ with most verbs to talk about how much something changed.
• Use these words to talk about time:
   over—a period of time
   between—a period from one year to another
   _by_—at a certain time
   _in_—during a number of years

As the graph shows, _sales_ **rose to** _$50 million_ **by** _2010._
According to the graph, _seafood sales_ **fell by** _20 percent_ **over** _two years._
As the chart shows, _sales of orange roughy_ **doubled in** _five years._

B Look at the graph below. Then complete the sentences using the words or phrases in the box. Two options are extra.

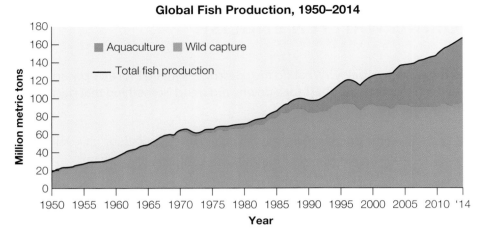

Global Fish Production, 1950–2014

Source: Food and Agriculture Organization of the United Nations (FAO)

| decreased | doubled | increased | remained stable | tripled |

1. According to the graph, production from fish farming _____ by about 20 million metric tons between 1995 and 2005.

2. Total fish production roughly _____ between 1985 and 2014.

3. The amount of fish caught in the wild _____ between 1995 and 2014.

C Look at the graph on page 70. Write three sentences about the graph.

1. _____

2. _____

3. _____

WRITING SKILL Explaining a Chart or Graph

We usually begin a description of a chart or graph by explaining its main idea or purpose.

The chart shows that eating top predators has a severe impact on the ocean's ecosystem.

According to the graph, the quantity of small fish in the oceans has increased steadily.

We then provide details—specific data that support the main idea.

Eating one pound of a top predator, such as orange roughy, is like eating 10 pounds of a smaller fish, such as herring.

In the last 100 years, the number of small fish—such as herrings, anchovies, and sardines—has more than doubled.

D Look at the graph below. Check (✓) the sentences that correctly describe the graph.

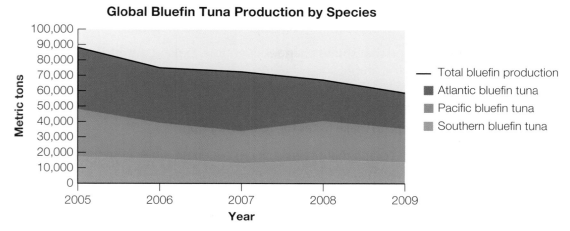

Global Bluefin Tuna Production by Species

— Total bluefin production
■ Atlantic bluefin tuna
■ Pacific bluefin tuna
■ Southern bluefin tuna

Source: FAO

☐ 1. However, production of Southern bluefin tuna remained more or less stable.

☐ 2. The graph shows global production for each species of bluefin tuna in metric tons per year.

☐ 3. In 2005, total bluefin production was almost 70,000 metric tons; by 2009, that number had fallen to about 60,000.

☐ 4. According to the graph, total production of bluefin tuna increased steadily between 2005 and 2009.

☐ 5. As for production level by species, both Atlantic and Pacific bluefin tuna showed some variation between 2005 and 2009.

E Correct the sentences above that contain errors.

F Now put the five sentences in order to write a paragraph. Use the transition words and phrases and the graph descriptions to help you identify the correct order of the sentences.

_____

_____

_____

_____

_____

_____

_____

_____

_____

WRITING TASK

> **GOAL** You are going to write a paragraph on the following topic:
>
> Choose a graph that shows changes over time. Explain the information presented in the graph.

PLANNING **A** Follow these steps to make notes for your paragraph.

Step 1 Choose a graph that shows changes over time, either from this book or from another source.

Step 2 Decide what the main idea of the graph is. Write a topic sentence that introduces the main idea in the outline below.

Step 3 Give three details that support the main idea of the graph. Don't worry about grammar or spelling. Don't write complete sentences.

Step 4 Complete the outline by noting the most recent piece of data in the graph.

OUTLINE

Topic: Describing a Graph

What is the main idea of the graph? _____

_____

What is one detail that supports the main idea of the graph? _____

_____

What is another detail that supports the main idea of the graph? _____

_____

What is another detail that supports the main idea of the graph? _____

_____

What is the most recent piece of data in the graph? _____

_____

FIRST DRAFT **B** Use the information in your outline to write a first draft of your paragraph.

REVISING PRACTICE

The drafts below are similar to the one you are going to write. They describe this graph.

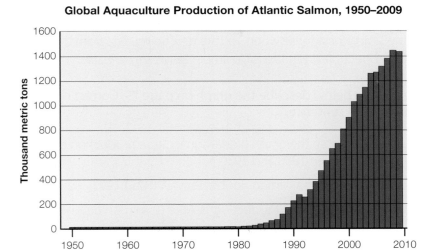

Global Aquaculture Production of Atlantic Salmon, 1950–2009

What did the writer do in Draft 2 to improve the paragraph? Match the changes (a–d) to the highlighted parts.

a. corrected a preposition
b. added recent data to conclude
c. corrected a detail about the graph
d. made the graph's main idea clearer

Draft 1

According to the graph, farming of Atlantic salmon began in the 1950s. Between 1980 and 1985, production of Atlantic salmon rose slightly. Around 1985, production began to increase more significantly. It rose from about 40 metric tons in 1985 to over 200,000 in just five years. Production fell slightly between 1991 and 1992, but then it rose again between 1993. It continued to rise to the year 2000 and beyond.

Draft 2

According to the graph, farming of Atlantic salmon started to become popular in the 1980s, and after a slow start, it grew quickly. Between 1980 and 1985, production of Atlantic salmon rose slightly. Around 1985, production began to increase more significantly. It rose from about 40,000 metric tons in 1985 to over 200,000 in just five years. Production fell slightly between 1991 and 1992, but then it rose again in 1993. It continued to rise to the year 2000 and beyond. By 2009, global aquaculture production of Atlantic salmon reached almost 1.5 million metric tons.

C Now use the questions below to revise your paragraph.

REVISED DRAFT

☐ Does the topic sentence introduce the main idea of the graph?
☐ Does the paragraph include at least three details that support the main idea?
☐ Is there any information that is incorrect?
☐ Does the concluding sentence give the most recent piece of data in the graph?

EDITING PRACTICE

Read the information below.

In sentences describing a chart or graph, remember to:
* use a comma after a phrase that introduces a description of the chart or graph.
* use the simple past tense when you are describing data from the past.
* use the correct prepositions; for example, *between*, *by*, *in*, *to*.

The sentences below describe the graph on page 79. Correct one grammatical mistake in each sentence.

1. As we can see from the graph global aquaculture production of Atlantic salmon was stable between 1950 and 1980.

2. Production of Atlantic salmon doubled by 1990 and 1995.

3. Between 1991 and 1992, production of Atlantic salmon decline slightly.

4. Between 1999 and 2001, production of Atlantic salmon grow by about 200,000 metric tons.

5. Production of Atlantic salmon decreased slightly to 2009.

FINAL DRAFT **D** Follow these steps to write a final draft.

1. Check your revised draft for language mistakes in describing charts and graphs.

2. Now use the checklist on page 218 to write a final draft. Make any other necessary changes.

UNIT REVIEW

Answer the following questions.

1. Which idea in this unit do you think is the most effective way to restore the ocean's biodiversity?

_____

_____

2. When describing a chart or graph, what is one word or phrase that indicates the following:

An upward trend? _____

A downward trend? _____

No change? _____

3. Do you remember the meanings of these words? Check (✓) the ones you know. Look back at the unit and review the ones you don't know.

Reading 1:

☐ commercial ☐ diverse AWL ☐ doubled
☐ estimate AWL ☐ quantity ☐ reduce
☐ restore AWL ☐ species ☐ stable AWL
☐ survive AWL

Reading 2:

☐ declining AWL ☐ definitely AWL ☐ essential
☐ impact AWL ☐ individual AWL ☐ informed
☐ rely on AWL ☐ severe

MEMORY AND LEARNING

5

Artist Stephen Wiltshire sketches the New York City skyline from memory.

THINK AND DISCUSS

1 What is your earliest memory?
2 Why do you think some people have better memories than others?

EXPLORE THE THEME

A Look at the photo for 30 seconds and answer the questions.

1. How many items can you remember? Close your book and make a list.

2. Compare lists with a partner. Who remembered more items correctly? Were some items easier to remember than others?

B What does the graph on the next page show about how memory changes with age?

C Match the correct form of the words in blue to their definitions.

_____ (n) a special way of doing something

_____ (adv) slowly and in small stages or amounts

_____ (adj) having parts that connect or go together in complicated ways

HOW WE REMEMBER

The brain is the most **complex** organ in the human body. It has about 100 billion nerve cells, or neurons. We make memories when connections are made between the brain's neurons. The more connections there are, the easier it is to recall information.

Memories about childhood and things that happened long ago are called long-term memories. Telephone numbers and the names of people we just met are stored in our brains as short-term memories.

There are certain **techniques** we can use to improve memory. However, as the graph shows, our ability to remember—or recall—things **gradually** worsens over time. This is because, as we age, connections between neurons weaken or are lost.

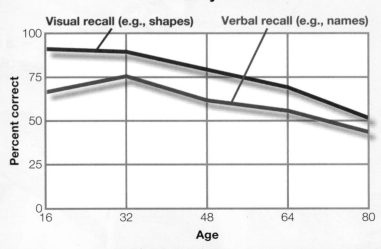

Adult Ability to Recall

Visual recall (e.g., shapes) Verbal recall (e.g., names)

Percent correct / Age

Reading 1

PREPARING TO READ

BUILDING
VOCABULARY

A The words in **blue** below are used in the reading passage on pages 85–86. Complete each sentence with the correct word. Use a dictionary to help you.

> familiar   visualize   memorize   external   text   achievement   internal

1. If something looks _____ to you, you recognize it or know it well.

2. A(n) _____ is a book or other written or printed work.

3. Things that exist inside a particular person, object, or place are _____.

4. Things that exist outside a particular person, object, or place are _____.

5. When you _____ something, you form a picture of it in your mind.

6. To _____ means to learn something so that you will remember it exactly.

7. A(n) _____ is something that is done successfully, especially after a lot of effort.

USING
VOCABULARY

B Discuss these questions with a partner.

1. What places are you **familiar** with? Describe a place that you know well.
2. What **external** conditions make it difficult for you to study?

CLASSIFYING

C Do you ever make lists to remember things? Do you ever try to memorize things? Complete the chart below. Then compare your answers with a partner.

Things I make lists for	Things I try to memorize

PREDICTING

D Scan the reading passage on pages 85–86 quickly. List two other nouns or verbs that appear two or more times.

_____*memory*_____   _____   _____

Now look at the words you wrote. What do you think the reading passage is about? Share your ideas with a partner. Then check your ideas as you read the passage.

In the BBC series *Sherlock*, detective Sherlock Holmes—played by Benedict Cumberbatch—uses the loci method to recall information.

THE ART OF MEMORY

🎧 1.09

A We all try to remember certain things in our daily lives: telephone numbers, email addresses, facts that we learn in class, and important tasks. We use memory **techniques** like repetition—the idea that the more we repeat a piece of information, the better we can recall it. But did you know that memory training goes all the way back to the days of ancient Greece?

B People began to value memory as a skill about 2,500 years ago. That's when the Greek poet Simonides of Ceos came up with a powerful technique known as the loci[1] method. Simonides realized that it's easier to remember places and locations than it is to remember lists of names. According to the loci method, if you think of a very **familiar** place and **visualize** certain things in that place, then you can keep those things in your memory for a long time.

C Simonides called this imagined place a "memory palace." Your memory palace can be any place that you know well, such as your home or your school. Here's how to use the loci method to remember a list of tasks: Let's say your memory palace is based on your house. Visualize yourself walking through it. Imagine yourself doing each task in a different room. Later, when you want to recall your list of tasks, visualize yourself walking through your house again. You will remember your list of tasks as you see yourself doing each one.

[1] **Loci** is the plural form of the Latin noun *locus*, meaning "place."

In the 15th century, an Italian man named Peter of Ravenna used the loci method to **memorize** books and poems. He memorized religious **texts**, 200 speeches, all of the laws of that time, and 1,000 poems. By using the loci method, he was able to "read" books stored in his memory palaces. "When I [travel] I can truly say I carry everything I own with me," he wrote.

When Simonides and Peter of Ravenna were alive, most people did not have books or pens to write notes with. They had to remember what they learned. In her book titled *The Book of Memory*, Mary Carruthers writes about these memory techniques of the past. She explains that ancient people considered memory to be a great virtue.[2] A person with a good memory was special because they could help preserve the society's cultural heritage.[3]

After Simonides developed the loci method, other people continued to study the art of memory. Memorization gained a **complex** set of rules and instructions. Students of memory learned what to remember and techniques for how to remember it. In fact, memory training is still an important activity in many parts of the world today. In some cultures, memorizing religious texts is considered a great **achievement**. Other cultures value people who can tell myths and folktales from the past, as there is often no written record of these things.

Over the past millennium,[4] though, many things have changed. We've **gradually** replaced our **internal** memory with **external** memory. We've invented devices so we don't have to store information in our brains. We now have photographs to record our experiences, calendars to keep track of our schedules, and the Internet and computers to store our ideas. As a result, we've gone from remembering many things to remembering very little. Nowadays, when we want to know something, we just look it up. But how does this affect us and our society? Did we lose an important skill?

▼ Competitors memorize names and faces at the World Memory Championships, London.

[2] A **virtue** is a very good personal quality.
[3] **Heritage** is something that is handed down from the past (e.g., a society's traditions, achievements, and beliefs).
[4] A **millennium** is a period of one thousand years.

UNDERSTANDING THE READING

A Choose the best alternative title for the reading passage.

UNDERSTANDING
THE MAIN IDEA

  a. Modern Memory Techniques
  b. Memorization Throughout History
  c. Internal and External Memory

B Answer the questions below using information from the reading passage.

UNDERSTANDING
DETAILS

  1. What is the loci method? Explain it in your own words.

  _____

  2. What benefit did the loci method have for Peter of Ravenna?

  _____

  3. According to Mary Carruthers, why was memory so important in the past?

  _____

  4. What is one example of the important role of memory in certain cultures today?

  _____

C Read the list of memory techniques and devices below. If the item relates to internal memory, circle **I**. If it relates to external memory, circle **E**.

CLASSIFYING

  1. repetition   I   E
  2. books   I   E
  3. photographs   I   E
  4. loci method   I   E
  5. tablet computers   I   E

> **CRITICAL THINKING** **Applying information**, such as a method or procedure, can help you internalize it more easily. For example, using the loci method yourself will help you understand the concept and remember how it works.

D Imagine you have these problems. How might you solve them by using the loci method? Share your ideas with a partner.

CRITICAL THINKING:
APPLYING A METHOD

  1. You are learning a foreign language. You are having trouble remembering new words.
  2. You are taking a history class. It's hard for you to remember when important events happened and the names of the people involved.

E The author writes:

CRITICAL THINKING:
REFLECTING

We've gradually replaced our internal memory with external memory. … We've gone from remembering many things to remembering very little.

Do you think we have lost an important skill? Why or why not? Discuss with a partner and give examples from your own lives.

DEVELOPING READING SKILLS

> **READING SKILL** Identifying Cause and Effect
>
> A **cause** is something that makes another event happen. The resulting event is the **effect**. Recognizing causes and effects can help you better understand a reading passage. Look at the sentence below. Does the underlined portion show a cause or an effect?
>
> *If you think of a very familiar place and visualize certain things in that place, then you can keep those things in your memory for a long time.*
>
> The underlined portion shows the effect. Visualizing things within a familiar place is the cause. Keeping memories for a long time is the effect.
>
> You can sometimes identify cause-and-effect relationships by finding certain connecting or signal words. These include *because, so, if … then, therefore, as a result,* and *by* verb + *-ing.*
>
> *We don't have to remember phone numbers now **because** we can store them in our cell phones.*
>
> *I enter my email password three times a day, **so** I remember it easily.*

IDENTIFYING CAUSE AND EFFECT

A Read the information about memorization techniques. How many cause-effect relationships can you find? Circle the causes and underline their effects.

Techniques for remembering things like lists, numbers, and facts are called mnemonic devices. People often use mnemonics—like poems or pictures—because it's easier to remember rhymes or images than plain facts and lists.

Acronyms are one type of mnemonic. For example, it may be hard to remember the colors of the rainbow in the order that they appear. Someone therefore made an acronym for this: ROY G BIV. The letters in the acronym are the first letters in the names for the colors: red, orange, yellow, green, blue, indigo, and violet. The name Roy G. Biv is meaningless, but it's short, so it's easier to remember than the list.

English spelling rules can also be difficult to learn, so some students use rhymes to help them remember the rules. By learning "*i* before *e* except after *c* (where you hear *ee*)," students of English can remember the spelling of words like *niece* and *receipt*.

IDENTIFYING CAUSE AND EFFECT

B Look back at the reading passage on pages 85–86. Circle three causes and underline their effects.

Video

HOUSE OF CARDS

▲ Nelson Dellis is a four-time USA Memory Champion.

BEFORE VIEWING

A Read the information about the USA Memory Championship. Then answer the questions.

LEARNING ABOUT THE TOPIC

The USA Memory Championship is an annual competition in which participants compete in memorization tasks. In one event, participants have to memorize the order of a shuffled[1] deck of cards. First, they are given five minutes to memorize the order of the cards. Then they are given five minutes to arrange a second deck of cards in the same order. The participant who recalls all the cards correctly in the shortest time period wins.

[1]If a deck of cards is **shuffled**, the cards are mixed up in a random order.

1. What do you think the record time for the card event is? Note your answer. Then check the answer on the bottom of page 100. Does this surprise you?

_____

2. How might a person use the loci method to memorize the order of a deck of cards?

_____

B The words and phrases in **bold** below are used in the video. Match each word or phrase to its definition.

VOCABULARY IN CONTEXT

People often **code** information by using mnemonic devices, like poems or pictures.

Information is easier to recall if it has an **associated** rhyme or image.

Most people have a **mental map** of their home or neighborhood.

1. _____ (n) a picture in a person's mind of an area

2. _____ (adj) connected with something else

3. _____ (v) to give a name, number, or symbol to something

WHILE VIEWING

UNDERSTANDING MAIN IDEAS

A ▶ Watch the video. How does Nelson Dellis memorize the cards? Order the steps (a–e). Two sentences are extra.

Step 1: _____   Step 2: _____   Step 3: _____

a. He groups three cards at a time to create brief stories.
b. He connects each card to someone familiar, with an associated action and object.
c. He groups the whole deck of cards into four piles.
d. He counts the number of cards in each pile.
e. He places the images around a familiar mental map in his mind.

UNDERSTANDING DETAILS

B ▶ Watch the video again. Complete the labels in Dellis's memory palace below. Then draw a line connecting each label (2–4) to the correct image. See the example provided.

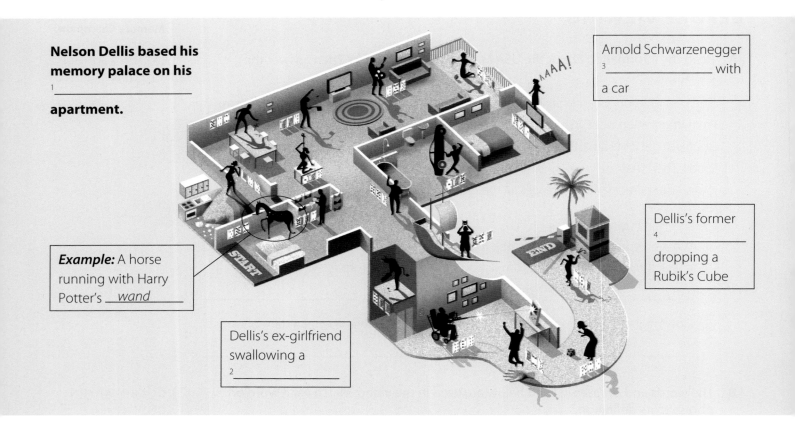

Nelson Dellis based his memory palace on his 1 _____ **apartment.**

Example: A horse running with Harry Potter's _wand_____

Dellis's ex-girlfriend swallowing a 2 _____

Arnold Schwarzenegger 3 _____ with a car

Dellis's former 4 _____ dropping a Rubik's Cube

AFTER VIEWING

REACTING TO THE VIDEO

A Many images in Dellis's memory palace are very strange or unusual. Why do you think this is? Discuss with a partner.

CRITICAL THINKING: APPLYING A METHOD

B Imagine you are at a party and you have to memorize the names of 20 people. What method or system would you use? Share your ideas with a partner.

Reading 2

PREPARING TO READ

BUILDING VOCABULARY

A The words in **blue** below are used in the reading passage on pages 92–93. Read their definitions and then complete each sentence with the correct form of the word.

A **mental** activity uses and exercises the mind.

A **physical** activity uses and exercises the body.

If you have **proof**, you have evidence that shows something is true.

A **route** is a way or path taken to get from one place to another.

A **drug** is a chemical intended to affect the structure or function of the body.

If you are experiencing **stress**, you are worried about problems in your life.

To **transfer** something means to move it from one place to another.

A person's **state** refers to the condition they are in at a certain time.

1. Scientists can give a rat a _____ to make it go to sleep or stay awake.

2. Doing a _____ activity such as a crossword puzzle can improve memory.

3. Because of a recent study, we now have _____ that sleep is important for memory.

4. A person in a _____ of confusion isn't sure what is happening.

5. If a student is under too much _____, they may perform badly.

6. Research shows that regular _____ activity—such as cycling or dancing—has significant benefits for memory.

7. Storing phone numbers in cell phones is an example of _____ information from internal to external memory.

8. People with a good sense of direction are good at remembering _____.

USING VOCABULARY

B Discuss these questions with a partner.

1. What kinds of **physical** activities do you enjoy doing? Why?
2. Which **routes** do you find easy to remember? Which routes are harder to memorize? Why do you think this is?

PREDICTING

C Underline the key words in the title and the subheads of the reading passage on pages 92–93. Use the underlined words to help you complete the sentence below. Then check your answer as you read the passage.

I think the reading passage is about _____

_____

SLEEP AND MEMORY

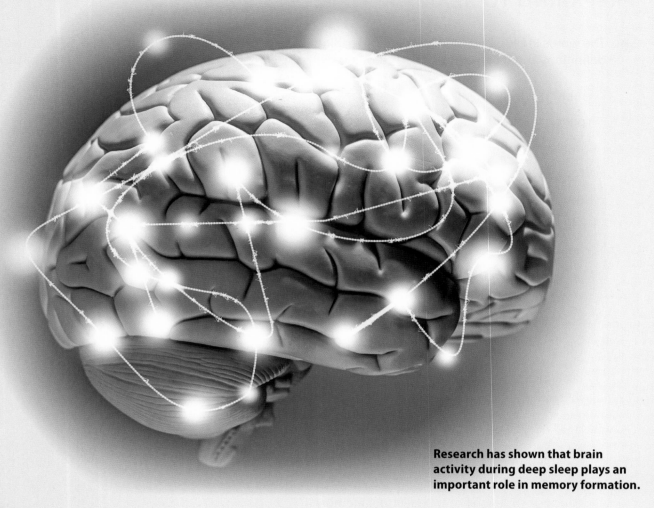

Research has shown that brain activity during deep sleep plays an important role in memory formation.

🎧 1.10

A Many people think that sleep must be important for memory, but until recently there was little proof. Scientists also weren't sure how long-term memories were formed in the brain. They now understand how the process happens, however, and why sleep is so important.

The Stages of Sleep

B What happens in the brain when we sleep? As the graph on the next page shows, the average adult goes through different sleep stages each night: REM (rapid eye movement) sleep, and three stages of non-REM sleep. When we first go to sleep, we proceed from REM sleep to Stage 1 of non-REM sleep, and then to Stages 2 and 3.

Non-REM Stage 3 is the deepest level of sleep. After that, we go back through the stages (Stage 3 → Stage 2 → Stage 1) and have a period of REM sleep before entering non-REM sleep again. We repeat this cycle four or five times each night. With each new cycle, the time spent in deep Stage 3 sleep decreases and the time spent in REM sleep increases.

Memory and the Brain

In 2009, a research team at Rutgers University discovered new information about the role of sleep in creating memories. The team found a type of brain activity that happens during sleep. The activity transfers new information from the

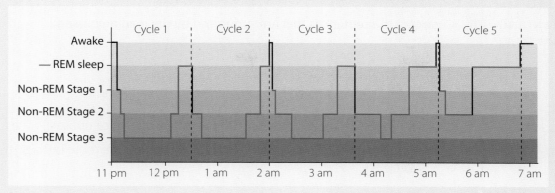

Stages and Cycles in Adult Sleep

Source: http://www.howsleepworks.com

hippocampus to the neocortex—the part of the brain that stores long-term memories. The activity that occurs when information moves from the hippocampus to the neocortex looks like short, powerful waves. The Rutgers team called this brain activity "sharp wave ripples."[1] The brain creates these ripples in the hippocampus during the deepest level of sleep.

The Rutgers scientists discovered this wave activity in a study using rats. They trained the rats to learn a **route** in a maze. Then they let the rats sleep. They gave one group of sleeping rats a **drug** that stopped brain-wave activity. As a result, this group of rats had trouble remembering the route. The reason?

The new information was unable to leave the hippocampus and go to the neocortex.

Lifelong Memories

Because of the Rutgers study, we now know how the brain creates long-term memories. The study also proves that sleep is important for learning and memory. During deep sleep, brain-wave activity transfers short-term memories from the hippocampus to the neocortex. Then the sharp wave ripples "teach" the neocortex to make a long-term form of the memory. Researcher György Buzsáki says this is "why certain events may only take place once in the waking **state** and yet can be remembered for a lifetime."

TRAIN YOUR BRAIN!

Apart from getting enough sleep, there are other things you can do to improve your memory. Here are some tips:

- **Avoid stress.** Research shows that stress is bad for the brain. By avoiding stress, you may improve your memory. **Physical** exercise is one way to reduce stress.

- **Play games.** Some scientists say that **mental** activity might help memory. Puzzles, math problems, and even reading and writing can all benefit the brain.

- **Eat right.** Your brain can benefit from a healthy diet, just like the rest of your body. Foods that have antioxidants[2]—such as blueberries and spinach—are good for brain cells. This helps memory.

[1]A **ripple** is a slight movement of a surface (e.g., water).
[2]An **antioxidant** is a substance in food and other products that can prevent harmful chemical reactions from taking place in your body.

UNDERSTANDING THE READING

UNDERSTANDING
MAIN IDEAS

A Check (✓) the sentences that are supported by the reading passage.

☐ 1. The brain makes long-term memories while we sleep.

☐ 2. When we sleep, we go through cycles of sleep states.

☐ 3. Long-term memories are stored in the hippocampus.

☐ 4. During sleep, brain-wave activity connects the hippocampus with the neocortex.

☐ 5. One group of rats in the study couldn't remember the route because they got less sleep.

UNDERSTANDING A
PROCESS

B The flow chart below summarizes how the brain creates long-term memories. Complete the flow chart using information from the reading passage.

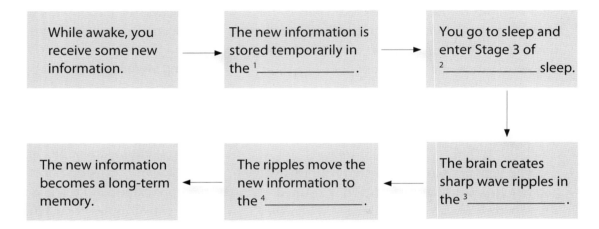

While awake, you receive some new information. → The new information is stored temporarily in the ¹_____. → You go to sleep and enter Stage 3 of ²_____ sleep.

The new information becomes a long-term memory. ← The ripples move the new information to the ⁴_____. ← The brain creates sharp wave ripples in the ³_____.

IDENTIFYING CAUSE
AND EFFECT

C Complete the chart below. Fill in the missing causes and effects.

Causes		
		You eat a lot of blueberries and spinach, which are high in antioxidants.
↓	↓	↓

Effects		
Those rats in the study had trouble remembering the route.	Scientists now understand how the brain creates long-term memories.	

CRITICAL THINKING:
SYNTHESIZING

D List all the techniques and tips for improving memory that you have learned about in this unit. Circle the ones you are most likely to use.

_____

_____

Writing

EXPLORING WRITTEN ENGLISH

A Read the sentences below. Above each underlined portion, write **C** if it shows the cause or **E** if it shows the effect.

NOTICING

1. <u>By using the loci method</u>, Peter of Ravenna was able to "read" books stored in his memory palaces.

2. <u>You can memorize the colors of the rainbow in the order that they appear</u> by using the acronym ROY G BIV.

3. By learning "*i* before *e* except after *c* (where you hear *ee*)," <u>students of English can remember the spelling of words like *niece* and *receipt*</u>.

4. <u>Nelson Dellis set a record in the card event of the USA Memory Championship</u> by creating a coding system for his cards.

5. <u>By taking part in regular physical activity</u>, you can increase self-esteem and reduce stress.

6. By avoiding stress, <u>you may improve your memory</u>.

LANGUAGE FOR WRITING Using *By* + Gerund

There are many ways to show cause-and-effect relationships in your writing. One way to do this is with a *by* + gerund phrase. A gerund is a verb form that ends in *-ing*.

In a *by* + gerund phrase, you describe an activity that is the cause of something. The rest of the sentence expresses the result or effect. So, *by* + gerund expresses how to reach a result.

> **By exercising** *regularly, you can improve your memory.*
>   cause   effect

By + gerund phrases can appear at the beginning or at the end of a sentence. Use a comma when they appear at the beginning of a sentence.

> *You can improve your memory* **by getting** *enough sleep.*
> **By getting** *enough sleep, you can improve your memory.*

> *You can keep your brain healthy* **by eating** *foods that are high in antioxidants.*
> **By eating** *foods that are high in antioxidants, you can keep your brain healthy.*

B Combine the sentence parts using *by* + gerund.

Example: eat right / you can increase your brain power

   By eating right, you can increase your brain power.

1. get a good night's sleep / you help your brain form long-term memories

   _____

   _____

2. you can memorize the order of a deck of cards / use the loci method

   _____

   _____

3. the scientists stopped the rats' brain waves / give them a drug

   _____

   _____

4. make a shopping list / you can remember what items you need to buy

   _____

   _____

C Write three sentences using the *by* + gerund form. Describe ways you relieve stress and ways you can improve your diet.

1. _____

2. _____

3. _____

WRITING SKILL Using an Outline

Using an outline helps you to organize and develop your ideas before you write. A good outline is like a map: It gives you something to follow while you write.

To write an outline for a paragraph, first think about the topic and list a few supporting ideas. Then write a topic sentence that introduces your supporting ideas. The topic sentence should clearly state the main idea of the paragraph. Finally, write down details that explain each supporting idea. The details might be examples, a list of reasons, or steps in a process. Apart from the topic sentence, don't write complete sentences in an outline.

By following an outline, you improve the flow of your writing. It also helps you make sure that you don't miss any important points or include any unrelated information.

D Look at the outline below and read the paragraph that follows. Match the sentences in the paragraph (a–j) to the parts of the outline. Three sentences are extra.

OUTLINE

Topic: How to Memorize a Route

Topic Sentence: _____

Supporting Idea 1: memorize as steps _____

        Details: write names, directions _____

           read and repeat _____

Supporting Idea 2: create mental picture _____

        Details: study a map _____

           imagine following route _____

a. When you have to memorize a route, you should use a technique that works well for you. **b.** Many people use driving apps nowadays, so they don't need to memorize a route. **c.** One technique is to memorize directions as a set of steps. **d.** To do this, write the street names and directions in the correct order on a piece of paper. For example, Step 1 might be: "Drive three miles down Main Street." Step 2 might be: "Turn right on Oak Street." **e.** Read what you have written several times. After a while, you won't have to look at the paper anymore. **f.** You can also memorize a route by creating a mental picture of it. **g.** That is, you can form an image of the streets and the places on the streets in your mind. **h.** To do this, study the route as it appears on a map. **i.** Then close your eyes and imagine yourself following the route. Turn your body to the right and to the left as you make the turns and pass the buildings. By visualizing the route, you will learn it faster. **j.** There are other ways to learn routes; use the method that works best for you.

E Look again at the three sentences that didn't match the outline. Match each sentence to a description.

_____ provides an explanation of a key concept

_____ provides a concluding statement

_____ is not relevant to the main idea of the paragraph

F Look back at sentences a–j in exercise D. Find and underline three cause-effect relationships.

WRITING TASK

GOAL You are going to write a paragraph on the following topic:

What can a person do to improve their memory?

BRAINSTORMING **A** Look back at your list for exercise D on page 94. Work with a partner. Can you think of any other ways a person could improve their memory? Add ideas to your list.

_____

_____

PLANNING **B** Follow these steps to complete an outline for your paragraph.

Step 1 From your notes above and on page 94, choose your best two or three techniques and note them as your supporting ideas in the outline below.

Step 2 Write a topic sentence that introduces your supporting ideas.

Step 3 Now write two details or examples for each supporting idea. Don't worry about grammar or spelling. Don't write complete sentences.

OUTLINE

Topic: How to Improve Your Memory

Topic Sentence: _____

_____

Supporting Idea 1: _____

Details: _____

_____

Supporting Idea 2: _____

Details: _____

_____

Supporting Idea 3: _____

Details: _____

_____

FIRST DRAFT **C** Use the information in your outline to write a first draft of your paragraph.

REVISING PRACTICE

The drafts below are similar to the one you are going to write. They are on the topic of how people can keep lasting memories.

What did the writer do in Draft 2 to improve the paragraph? Match the changes (a–d) to the highlighted parts. Some can be used more than once.

a. added a detail to a supporting idea
c. corrected a verb form

b. made the topic sentence stronger
d. deleted unrelated information

Draft 1

You can record the important events in life so that they will become lasting memories. One way is to keep a written journal. This is a written record of events, activities, and thoughts. You can also include photos in your journal. Another way to create lasting memories is to keep a video journal. With a video journal, you can record activities and events as they are happening. You can also make recordings afterwards of yourself talking about the events or activities. My phone has a video recorder, but sometimes it doesn't work very well. By use these methods, you can create lasting memories that you will enjoy for many years.

Draft 2

There are two main ways to record the important events in life so that they will become lasting memories. One way is to keep a written journal. This is a written record of events, activities, and thoughts. You can write it by hand in a notebook, or type it on a computer. You can also include photos in your journal. Label each one by date, place, and the names of the people in the photos so that you'll be able to remember them later. Another way to create lasting memories is to keep a video journal. With a video journal, you can record activities and events as they are happening. You can also make recordings afterwards of yourself talking about the events or activities. By using these methods, you can create lasting memories that you will enjoy for many years.

D Now use the questions below to revise your paragraph.

REVISED DRAFT

- ☐ Does a strong topic sentence introduce the main idea?
- ☐ Are there two or three different supporting ideas?
- ☐ Are there at least two details or examples for each supporting idea?
- ☐ Are all verb forms correct?
- ☐ Is there any information that doesn't belong?
- ☐ Is there a concluding sentence?

EDITING PRACTICE

Read the information below.

In cause-and-effect sentences using a *by* + gerund phrase, remember to:
- use the *-ing* form of the verb.
- use a comma when the *by* + gerund phrase appears at the beginning of a sentence.

Correct one *by* + gerund mistake in each sentence below.

1. You can't remember all of the information in a lecture just by listen to it.

2. By taking notes while you listen you can remember information better.

3. By write a summary of your notes after a lecture, you will remember the information more easily.

4. By taking notes and make lists, you transfer information from internal to external memory.

5. One study shows that by getting a good night's sleep people remember a skill (such as playing the piano) 30 percent better.

6. You can improve your memory by eating a healthy diet and exercise regularly.

FINAL DRAFT **E** **Follow these steps to write a final draft.**

1. Check your revised draft for mistakes with the *by* + gerund form.

2. Now use the checklist on page 218 to write a final draft. Make any other necessary changes.

UNIT REVIEW

Answer the following questions.

1. In your opinion, which memorization technique mentioned in this unit is most effective?

   _____

   _____

2. Why do writers use the *by* + gerund phrase in sentences?

   _____

   _____

3. Do you remember the meanings of these words? Check (✓) the ones you know. Look back at the unit and review the ones you don't know.

Reading 1:

☐ achievement **AWL**	☐ complex **AWL**	☐ external **AWL**
☐ familiar	☐ gradually	☐ internal **AWL**
☐ memorize	☐ technique **AWL**	☐ text **AWL**
☐ visualize **AWL**		

Reading 2:

☐ drug	☐ mental **AWL**	☐ physical **AWL**
☐ proof	☐ route **AWL**	☐ state
☐ stress **AWL**	☐ transfer **AWL**	

Answer to **Before Viewing** A-1, page 89: 16.96 seconds (set in 2016 by Alex Mullen)

ANIMALS AND MEDICINE 6

Nudibranchs—colorful sea slugs—have toxins that are used for cancer treatment.

ACADEMIC SKILLS

READING	Identifying pros and cons
WRITING	Writing an argumentative paragraph
GRAMMAR	Making concessions
CRITICAL THINKING	Understanding metaphors and similes

THINK AND DISCUSS

1 Have you ever been bitten or stung by an animal? If so, by what?

2 Which animals are often used in medical research? Why do scientists use them?

A Look at the information on these pages and answer the questions.

1. Why are animals used in medical research? Give two reasons.

2. All the animals shown here can improve our health. Which species do you think makes the greatest contribution to human health? How?

B Match the correct form of the words and phrases in blue to their definitions.

_____ (n) understanding of or information about a subject

_____ (n) something that shows potential or a capacity for future success

_____ (n) an unintended, unpleasant effect of a drug

ANIMALS IN MEDICAL RESEARCH

Research involving animals can lead to many medical breakthroughs. For example, scientists often test a new drug on monkeys or rats before giving it to human patients. This way, they can see how effective the drug is or if there are any side effects.

But animals can be sources of medicines, too. Scientists are constantly looking in nature for new possibilities in drug development. Here are a few animals that have helped to advance our medical knowledge.

SPECIES: Atlantic cod
MEDICAL USE: Cod liver oil is used as a source of vitamins A and D.

SPECIES: Gila monster
MEDICAL USE: A hormone in its saliva can treat diabetes.

SPECIES: Jameson's mamba
MEDICAL USE: Its venom[1] has been used to develop a drug that treats heart disease.

[1] **Venom** is a toxic liquid produced by animals such as snakes, spiders, and scorpions. It can be deadly to other animals.

Reading 1

PREPARING TO READ

BUILDING
VOCABULARY
A The words in **blue** below are used in the reading passage on pages 105–106. Complete each sentence with the correct form of the word. Use a dictionary to help you.

> cure   disease   target   specific   concerned   endangered   resource

1. A(n) _____ is a person or object that you aim at and try to hit.

2. If you are _____ about something, you are worried about it.

3. A(n) _____ is an illness caused by infection or poor health.

4. Medicines help doctors _____ illnesses.

5. When you talk about something _____, you talk about one particular topic.

6. If you have _____, you have materials, money, and other things you need in order to do something.

7. A(n) _____ animal is one that may not exist in the future or is at risk of becoming extinct.

USING
VOCABULARY
B Discuss these questions with a partner.

1. What are some examples of **endangered** species?
2. What are some **side effects** of common medications?
3. What are some **diseases** that doctors can't **cure**?

BRAINSTORMING
C Scientists often look for medicines and cures in nature. What are some problems or challenges that these scientists might face? Discuss with a partner and note your ideas.

_____

_____

PREDICTING
D Skim the reading passage on pages 105–106. Which sentence do you think is the best description of Zoltan Takacs? Check your answer as you read the passage.

a. He studies endangered snakes to prevent them from becoming extinct.
b. He collects snake venom because it can be used to create important medicines.
c. He develops antivenoms for the treatment of snake bites.

Zoltan Takacs with a banded sea krait, a highly venomous sea snake

THE SNAKE CHASER

🎧 2.01

A As a boy, Zoltan Takacs caught snakes and kept them in his room. Now he pursues them in the world's most remote jungles, deserts, and oceans.

B Takacs collects snake venom so that he can study it. He is searching for venom components—called "toxins"—that can be used as medicine to cure various diseases. Usually, he travels alone with only a backpack, a camera bag, and equipment for collecting venom. He often flies small planes to reach remote places, and has traveled to more than 160 countries. His trips are often dangerous: He has faced pirates,[1] wars, and angry elephants. He has also survived six venomous snake bites. Takacs's adventures are like action movies, but he is driven by his desire to make new scientific discoveries. "Animal venoms," he explains, "are the source of over a dozen lifesaving medications. They have been used to develop drugs that treat high blood pressure, heart attacks, diabetes, and other diseases."

[1]**Pirates** are people who attack ships to rob them.

Many drugs produce certain side effects. These side effects happen because the drugs affect more than one target in the body. For example, cancer drugs sometimes can't tell the difference between cancer cells and healthy cells—so the drugs kill both. This causes side effects like severe headaches, hair loss, nausea,[2] and vomiting. Toxins are a good model for medications because they can hit a single target. But finding the right toxin to fight a specific disease can take years of work. That's why Takacs and his colleagues have developed a new technology called "Designer Toxins." This allows the creation of "toxin libraries."

Designer toxin libraries—which could eventually hold the venom toxins of every animal on Earth—help researchers identify which toxin might cure a specific disease. With this new technology, testing can happen much more quickly and efficiently. A researcher can test many different toxins at once to see if any of them have an effect on a specific disease. Takacs believes the technology will help researchers develop new toxin-based drugs. But he is also concerned that a lot of possible toxin-based drugs are being lost.

So far, scientists have studied only a couple thousand toxins. But according to Takacs, some 20 million more exist in nature. Some of these venom toxins come from endangered species. So if a venomous animal becomes extinct, it's possible that a new drug is lost, too. The venom of an endangered snake could potentially lead to a medicine that saves human lives.

Once a species becomes extinct, there's no way to bring it back. Takacs says, "For me, losing biodiversity means losing beauty and a wealth of knowledge and resources, including possibilities for treating diseases." Losing species, he explains, is "like peeling[3] out pages from a book we've never read, then burning them."

[2]**Nausea** is a feeling of sickness in the stomach. People who suffer from nausea often feel they are going to vomit.
[3]When you **peel** something, you remove layers from it one at a time.

A king cobra prepares to strike.

WHY DOESN'T SNAKE VENOM AFFECT THE SNAKE?

A snake's venom aims only at a specific target in the body. However, if contact with the target is blocked, the toxin has no effect. When researchers inject[4] a cobra with its own venom, nothing happens. This is because cobras have a molecule[5] that "disguises"—or hides—the target and stops the toxin from making contact.

[4]When you **inject** something such as medicine, you put it into a person or an animal using a needle.
[5]A **molecule** is two or more atoms held together by chemical bonds.

UNDERSTANDING THE READING

A Match each section from the reading passage (1–3) to a suitable heading.

_____ 1. Paragraph C
_____ 2. Paragraph D
_____ 3. Paragraphs E–F

a. Why Are We Losing Potential Drugs?
b. Why Do Toxins Make Good Medications?
c. How Does the Technology Work?

UNDERSTANDING MAIN IDEAS

B Answer the questions below using information from the reading passage.

UNDERSTANDING DETAILS

1. Why does Zoltan Takacs study snakes?

   _____

2. Why are toxins a good model for medications?

   _____

3. What reason does Takacs give for protecting endangered species?

   _____

4. Why are cobras not affected by their own venom?

   _____

> **CRITICAL THINKING** **Metaphors and similes** are types of figurative language.
> They allow a writer to compare one thing to another. For example:
>
> _The alligator's teeth are white daggers._ (metaphor)
>
> _Sam swims like a fish._ (simile)
>
> As you read, think about how the two things being compared are similar.

C What is the writer's or speaker's meaning in each sentence? Circle a or b.

CRITICAL THINKING: UNDERSTANDING METAPHORS AND SIMILES

1. _Takacs's adventures are like action movies._
   a. Takacs's life is similar to the life of a famous movie actor.
   b. Takacs's job sometimes seems like the events in a movie.

2. _Designer toxin libraries—which could eventually hold the venom toxins of every animal on Earth—help researchers identify which toxin might cure a specific disease._
   a. In a toxin library, toxins are arranged in order on shelves, like books in a library.
   b. In a toxin library, a lot of information is stored in a way that is easy to search.

3. _"[Biodiversity loss is] like peeling out pages from a book we've never read, then burning them."_
   a. Biodiversity loss is a problem because we lose species before we understand them.
   b. Biodiversity loss often results from burning large areas of forest.

D Would you like to have a job like Zoltan Takacs's? Why or why not? Discuss with a partner.

CRITICAL THINKING: REFLECTING

DEVELOPING READING SKILLS

READING SKILL Identifying Pros and Cons

Pros are advantages (positive effects) of something, and **cons** are disadvantages (negative effects). Writers often provide both pros and cons of an issue in order to make a more balanced argument. Identifying the pros and cons of an issue will help you evaluate the strength of a writer's arguments. It will also help you form your own opinion.

Look at the facts below about the reading passage on pages 105–106. Is each fact a pro or a con for studying snake venom?

a. *His job can be very dangerous.*
b. *A snake's venom might be used as medicine to cure a serious disease.*
c. *Snake venom is a good model for medications.*

The first fact is a con (a disadvantage of studying snake venom). The other two are pros.

IDENTIFYING PROS
AND CONS

A Read the information about the study of viruses. Then write notes in the chart.

Scientists called virologists study viruses[1] to discover how they work and how to stop people from getting infected. In the past few years, some virologists have begun studying extinct viruses—ones that died out long ago. They discovered that all humans have pieces of very old viruses in their bodies. The virologists were able to rebuild some of the viruses and bring them back to life.

Some people argue that rebuilding viruses is not worth the risk. If a person is infected with an extinct virus, it's unlikely that there would be a cure for it. Also, our immune systems[2] probably wouldn't have the ability to fight an extinct virus. However, virologists argue that extinct viruses can teach us more about how viruses cause disease. They also believe that by studying extinct viruses, we can learn a lot about how our species developed in the past. In addition, scientists can develop vaccines[3] in case these extinct viruses reappear one day and begin infecting people again.

[1] A **virus** is a tiny organism that can cause disease.
[2] Your **immune system** consists of all the organs and processes in your body that protect you from illness and infection.
[3] A **vaccine** is a substance given to people, usually by injection, to prevent them from getting a particular disease.

Pros of Studying Extinct Viruses			
Cons of Studying Extinct Viruses			

CRITICAL THINKING:
EVALUATING

B Now look at your list of pros and cons. Do you think virologists should continue studying extinct viruses? Share your opinion with a partner and give reasons for it.

Video

THE FROG LICKER

Scientist Valerie Clark with a golden Mantella frog

BEFORE VIEWING

A Look at the photo above. Why do you think this person is licking the frog? Discuss your ideas with a partner.

PREDICTING

B Read the information about poisonous animals. Then answer the questions.

LEARNING ABOUT THE TOPIC

Poisonous animals use their toxins in different ways. Animals such as snakes use toxins to attack their prey. They inject their venom into other creatures by biting them. Poisonous frogs, on the other hand, release toxins through their skin. This protects them from predators. One well-known species is the poison dart frog. Found in the rain forests of Colombia, it is coated in poison. A single frog—just two inches (five centimeters) long— has enough poison on its skin to kill 10 adult humans. However, not all animal toxins are deadly. Centipedes, for example, produce a venom that is painful to humans but doesn't normally kill.

1. What are two ways that animals deliver their toxins?

   _____

2. How might the toxins from poison dart frogs be useful to traditional hunters in Colombia?

   _____

3. Which animal is more dangerous: a poison dart frog or a centipede? Why?

   _____

C The words and phrases in **bold** below are used in the video. Match the correct form of each word or phrase to its definition.

> Mackerel and herring are good **sources** of fish oil.
>
> Many plants and animals typically found in **primary forests** cannot survive in forests that have been replanted.
>
> The "toxin libraries" developed by Zoltan Takacs help researchers identify new **leads** for drug development.

1. _____ (n) a piece of information that allows a discovery to be made

2. _____ (n) a place, person, or thing from which something comes

3. _____ (n) an area of old land with many trees, where there has been little or no human activity

WHILE VIEWING

A ▶ Watch the video. Check (✓) the types of information Valerie Clark hopes to learn from Mantella poison frogs.

☐ 1. how they reproduce

☐ 2. their location

☐ 3. what kinds of insects they eat

B ▶ Watch the video again and answer the questions below.

1. Aside from licking the frog, what is another way to test the toxins in a frog's skin?

_____

2. Why is it safe for Clark to lick the Mantella poison frog?

_____

3. Name one way we can save the Mantella poison frogs of Madagascar.

_____

AFTER VIEWING

A In the video, the narrator says:

*"Poison frogs aren't born poisonous. Instead, they are proof of the old saying: **'You are what you eat.'"***

What do you think the expression in **bold** means?

_____

_____

B How are Zoltan Takacs's and Valerie Clark's jobs similar? How are they different? Discuss with a partner.

Reading 2

PREPARING TO READ

A The words in blue below are used in the reading passage on pages 112–113. Read their definitions and then complete each sentence with the correct form of the word.

BUILDING VOCABULARY

> An **experiment** is a scientific test to discover if something works or is true.
>
> A **laboratory** is a room or building where people do scientific research.
>
> A **procedure** is a way of doing something, especially the correct or usual way.
>
> An **emotional** person has strong feelings of joy, sadness, anger, etc.
>
> An **invasive** medical treatment examines the inside of a person's or animal's body.
>
> An **advance** in a particular subject is any development or improvement in it.
>
> A **mission** is an aim that is very important to a person or organization.
>
> When you **conduct** an activity or task, you organize it and carry it out.

1. The _____ of cancer researchers is to find better ways to prevent and treat cancer.

2. It's important that scientists follow certain safety _____ when working with animal toxins.

3. Nutritionists sometimes _____ surveys to find out things like how often people exercise or what kinds of food they eat.

4. Scientists carry out _____ in _____ to test the effectiveness of new drugs.

5. Researchers involved in animal testing are trying to use techniques that are less _____.

6. Thanks to _____ in medical science, many illnesses can now be cured.

7. Animal testing is a(n) _____ issue for animal rights activists. They strongly believe it is wrong to use animals for medical research.

B Discuss these questions with a partner.

USING VOCABULARY

1. What kinds of scientific **experiments** have you **conducted** in school?
2. What are some important **advances** that have been made in medicine?

C How have chimpanzees and other apes been used in medical research? With a partner, brainstorm some ideas and note them below.

BRAINSTORMING

_____

_____

A HAVEN FOR CHIMPS

Retired lab chimps hang out in an enclosure at Chimp Haven, Louisiana.

A It's early morning at Chimp Haven, a sanctuary[1] for retired research chimpanzees. The air fills with hoots and cries. The chimps are excited. It's snack time. Veterinarian Raven Jackson is bringing them juice and frozen bananas.

B The younger chimps run around and play on the grass. The older chimps are less active; some suffer from illnesses like heart disease. However, both the old and the young chimps have one thing in common: They will never have to be subjects[2] in medical experiments again.

FROM LAB TO PLAYGROUND

C For nearly a hundred years, laboratories have used chimpanzees to test drugs and medical procedures. This is because of their genetic[3] similarity to humans. Lab chimps used to have a hard life. They often lived by themselves in small cement cages. Some never went outdoors. And many of them were given HIV and hepatitis[4] viruses in order to test vaccines.

D What has changed? A U.S. law protecting chimpanzees as an endangered species used to apply only to wild chimps. But in 2015, the law changed to protect all chimps. As a result, the National Institutes of Health (NIH) is retiring its research chimpanzees. To help with the change, specially designed places like Chimp Haven are opening their doors to these great apes.

E At the sanctuaries, chimps can socialize with each other—it's the first time some of them have ever seen another chimpanzee. At Chimp Haven, they live in play yards with climbing platforms, ropes, and swings. There are also two large forested areas surrounded by a moat[5] and fences. After years of captivity, research chimpanzees now have the chance to learn how to be wild.

[1]A **sanctuary** is a place where someone or something is protected.
[2]The **subject** of an experiment is the person or animal that is being tested.
[3]Anything **genetic** has to do with genes and DNA.
[4]**Hepatitis** is a serious disease of the liver.
[5]A **moat** is a long hole dug around a place and filled with water.
[6]**Ebola** is a deadly disease marked by fever and internal bleeding.
[7]If you **bring** something **to a halt**, you cause it to stop immediately.

SPLIT OPINIONS

F Conservationists have been working for years to rescue research chimpanzees. They're happy that the NIH is finally ending this practice. It means people will stop capturing chimpanzees in the wild and selling them for research. If they are no longer being used in labs, chimps may someday no longer be endangered.

G Studies have also shown that chimpanzees have intelligent, emotional natures, similar to those of humans. Animal rights activists are therefore against using chimps in medical research, especially in invasive experiments.

H On the other hand, some scientists argue that animal testing is important for making advances in human health. Chimps have been used to study infectious diseases and reproduction, among other things. After the NIH announced that it was stopping its chimp program, Frankie Trull—president of the Foundation for Biomedical Research—expressed concern about the decision. "Given NIH's primary mission to protect public health, it seems surprising," she said in a 2015 *Nature* article.

I In addition, some scientists experiment on chimpanzees to find cures for diseases that affect chimps—not just humans. Disease ecologist Peter Walsh has been working on an Ebola[6] vaccine for wild chimps. He worries that the NIH decision will bring his research to a halt[7] and hurt the health of the species. The United States is the world's leading nation for chimpanzee conservation research. Besides the United States, Walsh argues, "there really is no other place to do conservation-related trials."

J The debate over using chimpanzees in medical research continues. Under the new law, some scientists may be allowed to conduct experiments on chimps if the goal is the preservation of the species itself. "It doesn't mean the NIH is eliminating chimpanzee research altogether," stresses Jen Feuerstein, the director of Save the Chimps, a sanctuary in Florida. However, it's likely that the focus will shift to more non-invasive forms of research instead.

UNDERSTANDING THE READING

A Which sentence best summarizes the reading passage?

a. Because scientific experiments on chimpanzees have been so valuable to medicine, the NIH continues to use chimps for research.

b. In order to give chimpanzees a better life, researchers are now conducting less invasive experiments on them.

c. The NIH has recently stopped its chimp program, but there is still a debate over the use of chimpanzees in medical experiments.

B Read the sentences. Circle **T** for true, **F** for false, or **NG** for not given.

1. Researchers still conduct experiments on the chimps at Chimp Haven.　　**T　F　NG**

2. Scientists only recently began using chimps in medical experiments.　　**T　F　NG**

3. In the past, chimps were intentionally given malaria and cancer.　　**T　F　NG**

4. Chimps in labs were often not able to socialize with each other.　　**T　F　NG**

5. Chimps may live as long as 50 or 60 years in captivity.　　**T　F　NG**

6. Some scientists are trying to cure diseases that affect chimps.　　**T　F　NG**

C Read the sentences below. What does the underlined pronoun in each sentence refer to? Circle the correct answer.

1. *Both the old and the young chimps have one thing in common: They will never have to be subjects in medical experiments again.*

   a. old chimps　　　　b. young chimps　　　　c. old and young chimps

2. *For nearly a hundred years, laboratories have used chimpanzees to test drugs and medical procedures. This is because of their genetic similarity to humans.*

   a. laboratories　　　　b. chimpanzees　　　　c. drugs and procedures

D Complete the chart below using information from the reading passage.

Pros of Experimenting on Chimps	Cons of Experimenting on Chimps

E Now look at your list of pros and cons. Do you think scientists should continue using chimps in medical research? Discuss with a partner.

Writing

EXPLORING WRITTEN ENGLISH

A Read the two parts of each sentence. Then answer the question below.

NOTICING

1. (a) Even though products that haven't been animal-tested are more expensive,

   (b) buying them saves animals' lives.

2. (a) Although it's important to test the safety of eye makeup products,

   (b) testing them on rabbits' eyes can blind the animals.

3. (a) The drug Botox is very popular

   (b) even though it's made from a poisonous substance called botulinum toxin.

4. (a) Even though studying extinct viruses can be dangerous,

   (b) it is a good way to learn more about human evolution.

Which side of each issue does the writer think is more important: (a) or (b)? Circle your answer. Underline the words that help show this.

LANGUAGE FOR WRITING Making Concessions

Making a concession is saying that one idea is true, but another idea is stronger or more important. We use *although* and *even though* to make concessions.

The clause starting with *although* or *even though* is the concession clause. It contains the less important idea. The rest of the sentence is the main clause. The concession clause can come before or after the main clause. If the concession clause comes first, separate the two with a comma.

> **Although** botulinum toxin can be deadly, it can also treat muscle disorders.
>   concession clause   main clause

In the sentence above, the writer concedes that botulinum toxin is dangerous. However, the writer believes that its ability to treat muscle disorders is more important. In other words, scientists should continue to work with the toxin.

If the concession clause comes second, a comma is usually not needed.

> Botulinum toxin can be deadly **even though** it can also treat muscle disorders.
>   main clause   concession clause

Here, the writer concedes that botulinum toxin can treat muscle disorders. However, the writer believes that the fact that it is dangerous is more important, so scientists should stop working with the toxin.

B Use concessions to connect the ideas below.

Example: more important: *Zoltan Takacs still hunts snakes for a living.*
less important: *Zoltan Takacs has been bitten by several venomous snakes.*

<u>*Even though Zoltan Takacs has been bitten by several venomous snakes, he still hunts*</u>
<u>*them for a living.*</u>

1. more important: *Arsenic is still used to treat certain diseases.*
   less important: *A small amount of arsenic can be deadly.*

   Although _____

   _____

2. more important: *The poison dart frog is highly toxic.*
   less important: *The poison dart frog is just two inches long.*

   _____

   even though _____

3. more important: *Invasive research on chimpanzees has been largely banned.*
   less important: *Chimpanzee experimentation can lead to advances in human health.*

   Even though _____

   _____

C Using *although* or *even though*, write two sentences that make concessions. Use ideas from this unit, ideas from previous units, or your own ideas.

1. _____

   _____

2. _____

   _____

WRITING SKILL Writing an Argumentative Paragraph

In an argumentative paragraph, you try to convince the reader that your point of view is valid or true. First, you state the issue. Then you state your argument, and give reasons why you think it is valid.

For example, in a writing assignment you may be asked to agree or disagree with a particular viewpoint. There are certain phrases you can use to respond to this type of question:

I (generally) agree (with the idea) that …   I support the viewpoint that …
There are a number of strong arguments to support the idea that …

I disagree (with the idea) that …   I do not share the view that …
There are some important reasons to disagree with the idea that …

Making concessions can also help strengthen your argument. Concessions show that you have thought about both sides of the issue, but you believe that your argument is stronger. They make your paragraph more convincing.

D Read the paragraph about zoos. Underline the three sentences that make a concession.

Many people enjoy going to the zoo with family and friends. However, there are a number of strong arguments to support the idea that it is wrong to keep animals in zoos. First, although zoos allow people to see animals they might not otherwise be able to see, living in zoos negatively affects animals' routines and habits. For example, unlike lions that live in the wild, zoo lions aren't able to hunt for food in their natural habitats. Not being able to hunt can make lions more aggressive. This in turn makes them more dangerous to zoo employees and visitors. In addition, although keeping animals in zoos does help protect endangered animals, it does not increase their populations in the wild. Animals born in zoos usually stay in zoos their whole lives; they are not reintroduced into their natural habitats. Finally, even though zoos—like those in the United States—are supposed to at least meet the minimum requirements spelled out in documents like the Animal Welfare Act, standards aren't always enforced. For example, zebras at a zoo in Washington, D.C., died because they weren't given enough food.

E Complete the outline below using information from the paragraph in exercise D.

OUTLINE

Issue: Keeping Animals in Zoos

Main Argument: _____

Supporting Idea 1: _____

Concession: _____

Details: _____

_____

Supporting Idea 2: _____

Concession: _____

Details: _____

_____

Supporting Idea 3: _____

Concession: _____

Details: _____

_____

WRITING TASK

GOAL You are going to write a paragraph on the following topic:

Scientists should be allowed to use animals for medical research. Do you agree or disagree?

BRAINSTORMING **A** Work with a partner. Brainstorm a list of pros and cons of using animals for medical research.

Pros	Cons

PLANNING **B** Follow these steps to plan your argumentative paragraph.

Step 1 Decide whether you think scientists should be allowed to use animals for medical research. Write a sentence that states your main argument in the outline below.

Step 2 From your brainstorming notes above, choose two supporting ideas for your main argument and write them in the outline.

Step 3 Now write a concession and details for each supporting idea. Don't worry about grammar or spelling. Don't write complete sentences.

OUTLINE

Issue: The Use of Animals for Medical Research

Main Argument: _____

_____

Supporting Idea 1: _____

Concession: _____

Details: _____

_____

Supporting Idea 2: _____

Concession: _____

Details: _____

_____

FIRST DRAFT **C** Use the information in your outline to write a first draft of your paragraph.

REVISING PRACTICE

The drafts below are similar to the one you are going to write, but they are on a different topic:

Scientists should be allowed to use toxins in beauty products. Do you agree or disagree?

What did the writer do in Draft 2 to improve the paragraph? Match the changes (a–d) to the highlighted parts.

a. added a concession
b. added a detail sentence
c. added a concluding sentence
d. stated the main argument

Draft 1

Many beauty products these days contain toxins. Botox, for example, is made from botulinum toxin, which is produced by a form of bacteria. The toxin reduces the appearance of wrinkles on your face. Studying toxins can be very dangerous. Scientists should not risk their lives, and possibly ours, in order to help people look more beautiful. Furthermore, even though scientists created a safe cosmetic product with botulinum toxin, we can't be sure that other toxins will be safe. Perhaps the next toxin that researchers work with will cause an outbreak of disease.

Draft 2

Many beauty products these days contain toxins. Botox, for example, is made from botulinum toxin, which is produced by a form of bacteria. The toxin reduces the appearance of wrinkles on your face. However, I do not share the view that scientists should be allowed to use toxins in beauty products. Even though the study of toxins can lead to the creation of useful medications, it can also be very dangerous. Scientists should not risk their lives, and possibly ours, in order to help people look more beautiful. Furthermore, even though scientists created a safe cosmetic product with botulinum toxin, we can't be sure that other toxins will be safe. Perhaps the next toxin that researchers work with will cause an outbreak of disease. Or perhaps a toxin-based product will cause medical problems after several years of use. Many people want to be more beautiful, but using toxins in beauty products is not worth the risk.

D   Now use the questions below to revise your paragraph.

REVISED DRAFT

- ☐ Does the paragraph present the issue?
- ☐ Does the paragraph state the main argument?
- ☐ Does the paragraph include at least two supporting ideas?
- ☐ Does the paragraph include one or two details for each supporting idea?
- ☐ Does the paragraph include concessions?
- ☐ Is there a concluding sentence?

EDITING PRACTICE

Read the information below.

In sentences that make concessions, remember to:
- put the less important idea after *although* or *even though*.
- use a comma after the concession clause when it appears at the beginning of a sentence.
- include a subject and a verb in both clauses.

Correct one mistake with making concessions in each sentence below.

1. Even though she's afraid of snakes she wants to study snake venoms.

2. Although the golden poison dart frog is very small, it very deadly.

3. Even though the NIH is retiring its research chimpanzees, will continue to use other animals for medical research.

4. Although there are potentially millions of toxins in the wild scientists have studied only a couple thousand.

5. Even though black widow spider bites can be deadly to small children, are not usually strong enough to kill an adult human.

FINAL DRAFT **E** Follow these steps to write a final draft.

1. Check your revised draft for mistakes with making concessions.

2. Now use the checklist on page 218 to write a final draft. Make any other necessary changes.

UNIT REVIEW

Answer the following questions.

1. What is one surprising thing you learned in this unit?

_____

_____

2. What are two words or phrases you can use to introduce a concession?

_____

_____

3. Do you remember the meanings of these words? Check (✓) the ones you know. Look back at the unit and review the ones you don't know.

Reading 1:

☐ concerned   ☐ cure   ☐ disease

☐ endangered   ☐ knowledge   ☐ possibility

☐ resource AWL   ☐ side effect   ☐ specific AWL

☐ target AWL

Reading 2:

☐ advance   ☐ conduct AWL   ☐ emotional

☐ experiment   ☐ invasive   ☐ laboratory

☐ mission   ☐ procedure AWL

NATURE'S FURY

Lightning strikes over the town of Barr, France.

ACADEMIC SKILLS

READING	Identifying sequence
WRITING	Organizing a process paragraph
GRAMMAR	Describing a process
CRITICAL THINKING	Evaluating sources

THINK AND DISCUSS

1 What types of extreme natural events can you think of?
2 Which of these natural events are the most dangerous? Why?

A **Look at the information on these pages and answer the questions.**

  1. Which events have natural causes? Which event is normally caused by human activity?

  2. Which event can cause another to start? Which event can create its own weather system?

B **Match the correct form of the words in blue to their definitions.**

  _____ (v) to happen
  _____ (v) to hit something suddenly
  _____ (adj) very strong or powerful

Lightning, tornadoes, and wildfires all cause destruction. **Lightning strikes** somewhere on Earth about 100 times every second. It's extremely hot—it can heat the air around it to temperatures five times hotter than the surface of the sun. In most cases, lightning is caused by electrical activity in clouds.

Tornadoes, also called twisters, are born from thunderstorms. They **occur** when warm, moist (wet) air meets cold, dry air. Moving at up to 250 mph (400 kph), tornadoes are the fastest winds on Earth. They can form at any time of the day, but they happen most often in the late afternoon, when large thunderstorms are common.

Wildfires move at speeds of up to 14 mph (23 kph). Four out of five wildfires are caused by human activity. A natural event such as lightning can also start a wildfire. A large, **violent** wildfire can create its own weather system: Air around the fire gets warmer, the warm air rises, and this process sometimes creates winds.

EXTREME NATURE

A tornado develops from a thunderstorm over farmland in Colorado.

A firefighter tackles a wildfire near San Andreas, California.

Reading 1

PREPARING TO READ

BUILDING
VOCABULARY

A The words and phrases in **blue** below are used in the reading passage on pages 125–126. Complete each sentence with the correct form of the word or phrase. Use a dictionary to help you.

| climate | collide | condition | data | extend | on record | coast |

1. _____ are facts and statistics that you can analyze.

2. If things _____, they crash into each other.

3. _____ refers to the general weather pattern in a particular place.

4. The _____ is an area of land that is next to the sea.

5. A(n) _____ is the state that something is in.

6. If something is _____, it is officially measured and noted.

7. If something _____ from one place to another, it covers that area or distance.

USING
VOCABULARY

B Discuss these questions with a partner.
1. What is the **climate** like in your country?
2. What extreme natural events **occur** in your region?
3. Can you think of a recent example of a **violent** natural event? What caused it?

BRAINSTORMING

C What are some possible effects of a tornado? Make a list and share your ideas with a partner.

_____

_____

PREDICTING

D Skim the first paragraph of the reading passage on pages 125–126. Note the dates and the names of places you find.

_____

_____

Now look at the information you wrote. What do you think the reading passage is mainly about? Check your answer as you read.
a. where tornadoes strike around the world
b. a deadly tornado season in the United States
c. violent tornadoes that are expected in the future

WHEN TORNADOES STRIKE

2.03

A On April 25–28, 2011, a huge number of tornadoes hit the southern United States, striking areas like Mississippi, Alabama, Tennessee, and Georgia. In fact, more violent tornadoes struck the United States in April 2011 than in any other month on record. On April 27—its worst day—there were more than 120 separate twisters. They moved through six states and killed at least 316 people on that day alone.

THE "PERFECT STORM"

B Most tornadoes in the United States occur in a region called Tornado Alley, between the Rocky Mountains and the Gulf of Mexico. Warm, wet air from the Gulf of Mexico collides with the cold, dry mountain air, creating ideal conditions for a storm. Sometimes, "perfect storm" conditions lead to extremely violent tornadoes.

C The "perfect storm" conditions that occurred in April 2011 gave birth to a monster twister in Tuscaloosa, Alabama. Tornadoes usually touch the ground for only a few miles before they die. The Tuscaloosa tornado, however, stayed on the ground for an unusually long time. It traveled approximately 300 miles (482 kilometers) across a region extending from Alabama to Georgia, with winds of over 260 mph (418 kph). "There were no limitations," said tornado expert and storm chaser Tim Samaras.[1] "It went absolutely crazy. It had nothing but hundreds of miles to grow and develop."

[1]Sadly, Tim Samaras was killed by a tornado in May 2013.

CONFLICTING THEORIES

D   What caused the outbreak of violent tornadoes in 2011? Experts aren't sure. Some think warmer-than-normal water temperatures in the Gulf of Mexico—a result of global warming—were the cause. Russell Schneider, director of the U.S. Storm Prediction Center, thinks the outbreak occurred largely because of a weather pattern called "La Niña." La Niña occurs when cold water in the Pacific Ocean rises to the surface off the coast of South America. This can also affect the climate in the United States and create more thunderstorms and tornadoes.

E   Pablo Saide, a scientist at the University of Iowa, has another theory. He believes that fires in Central America may be part of the cause. These fires are set every year to clear land for farming. Smoke drifting[2] into the United States raises air temperature, which can lead to cloud formation and irregular wind patterns—common risk factors for tornadoes. "We're not saying that the outbreak happened because of the smoke," says Saide. "We're saying that, given the conditions already in place, the smoke intensified the tornadoes."

F   Scientists around the world continue to gather data about tornadoes. One day, their research will help us to better understand the conditions that cause violent tornadoes to form. Eventually, we may be able to predict how strong they will be and where they will hit, and take preventive measures to minimize loss of life.

▽ **Tornadoes may occur wherever warm, moist air collides with cool, dry air.**

[2]When something **drifts** somewhere, it is carried there by the movement of wind or water.

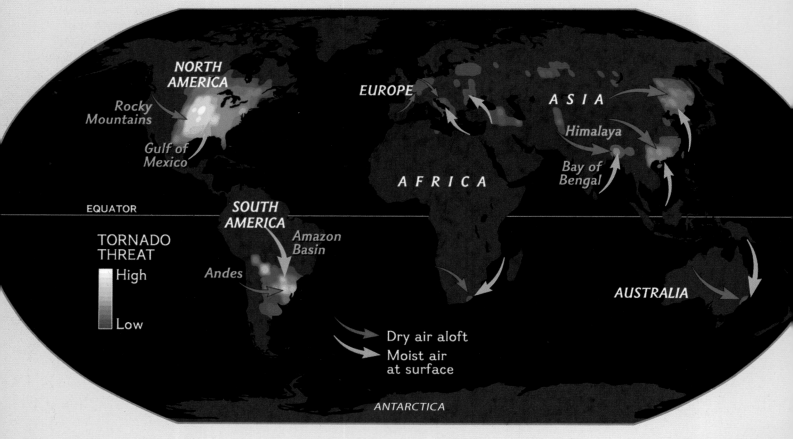

UNDERSTANDING THE READING

A Match each section from the reading passage (1–4) to its purpose.

UNDERSTANDING
MAIN IDEAS

_____ 1. Paragraph A   a. to highlight an area where tornadoes usually occur
_____ 2. Paragraph B   b. to give possible reasons for the violent tornadoes
_____ 3. Paragraph C   c. to explain what was unusual about the Tuscaloosa tornado
_____ 4. Paragraphs D–E   d. to provide some facts about the April 2011 tornado season

B What may have caused the violent tornadoes in April 2011? Fill in the missing information in the flow chart below.

UNDERSTANDING
CAUSE AND EFFECT

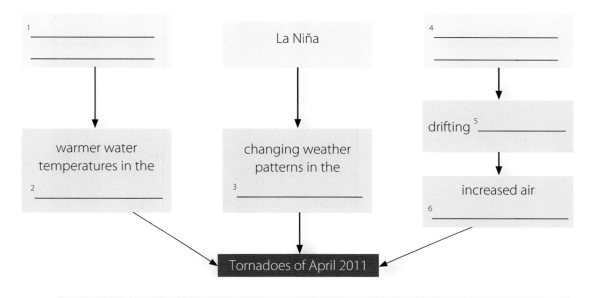

> **CRITICAL THINKING**   To find out whether or not a **source** is credible, you **evaluate** it. What are the source's credentials? Consider the source's professional or educational background, experience, and past writing.

C Read the following excerpts from the reading passage. Then discuss the questions with a partner.

CRITICAL THINKING:
EVALUATING
SOURCES

"There were no limitations," said tornado expert and storm chaser Tim Samaras. "It went absolutely crazy. It had nothing but hundreds of miles to grow and develop."

Russell Schneider, director of the U.S. Storm Prediction Center, thinks the outbreak occurred largely because of a weather pattern called "La Niña."

Pablo Saide, a scientist at the University of Iowa, has another theory. He believes that fires in Central America may be part of the cause.

1. How does the writer describe Samaras, Schneider, and Saide? For which source(s) do you have more specific information?

2. Do you find each of these sources credible? Why or why not?

D Look at the map on page 126. Apart from North America, where else do tornadoes strike? Discuss with a partner.

INTERPRETING
MAPS

DEVELOPING READING SKILLS

READING SKILL Identifying Sequence

When writers describe a process—how something happens or how to do something—they use transition words and phrases to show the **sequence** of the steps or events in the process. Sequence words such as *first, second, next, then, last,* and *finally* often tell you the order in which events happen or when things are done.

*If you are at home when a tornado strikes, there are several things you can do to stay safe. **First**, go to the lowest level you can, such as a basement. **Next**, cover your body with a blanket or mattress, or get under a piece of furniture, such as a heavy table.*

The sequence words tell you that you should go to the basement *before* covering your body or getting under a piece of furniture.

Time clauses with *before, after, when, as soon as, once,* and *during* also show order.

*Stay away from windows **during** a tornado. **After** the tornado passes, it's safe to go outside.*

UNDERSTANDING
A PROCESS

A The illustration below shows how twisters form. Read the captions. Complete the missing information using the words in the box. One word is used twice.

| air | cold | ground | spin | warm |

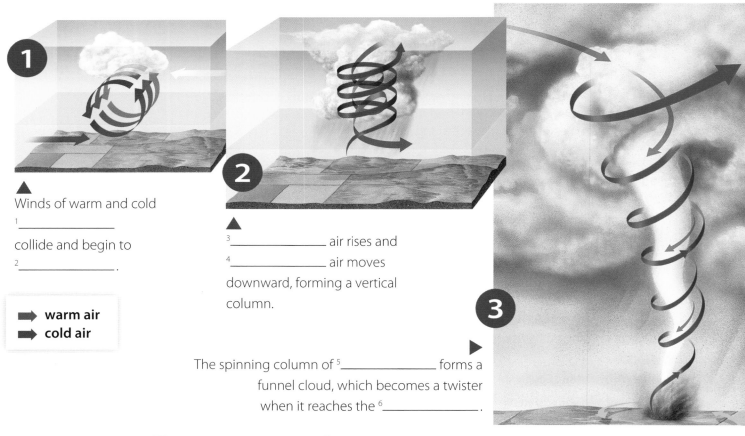

1

▲ Winds of warm and cold
¹_____
collide and begin to
²_____ .

➡ **warm air**
➡ **cold air**

2

▲ ³_____ air rises and
⁴_____ air moves
downward, forming a vertical
column.

3

► The spinning column of ⁵_____ forms a
funnel cloud, which becomes a twister
when it reaches the ⁶_____ .

IDENTIFYING
SEQUENCE

B Now write a paragraph about how twisters form based on the captions in exercise A. Use sequencing words in your paragraph.

Video

LIGHTNING

A lightning storm lights up the sky over a desert.

BEFORE VIEWING

A Read the sentences and guess if they are correct. Circle **T** for true or **F** for false. You will learn the answers while watching the video.

PREDICTING

1. Lightning is electricity.   **T**   **F**
2. Lightning occurs about 1,000 times a second worldwide.   **T**   **F**
3. Lightning strikes are more common in Europe than in South America.   **T**   **F**
4. On average, more people in the United States are killed by lightning than by tornadoes.   **T**   **F**

B Read the information about lightning. Then answer the questions.

LEARNING ABOUT THE TOPIC

Lightning is extremely hot. A bolt of lightning can raise air temperature by as much as 50,000 degrees Fahrenheit (27,700 degrees Celsius); that's five times hotter than the surface of the sun. When lightning strikes sand, it can melt it, creating a tube-shaped rock called a fulgurite. Lightning can even kill people. The average American has about a 1 in 5,000 chance of being struck by lightning during their lifetime. In the United States, most lightning happens during the summer months. The Fourth of July is historically one of the deadliest times of year for lightning in the country.

1. What can happen to sand when lightning hits it?

_____

2. Why do you think the Fourth of July is such a dangerous time for lightning strikes?

_____

C The words in **bold** below are used in the video. Match the correct form of each word to its definition.

> When tiny **particles** of ice collide within thunderclouds, the contact creates an electrical **charge**.
>
> A fully charged car battery should measure at 12.6 **volts** or above.
>
> Lightning strikes can cause forest fires; when drought conditions exist in the forest, fires often **expand** quickly.

1. _____ (v) to get bigger

2. _____ (n) a unit used to measure the force of an electric current

3. _____ (n) a very small piece of matter

4. _____ (n) the type of electricity that something contains (existing in a positive or negative form)

WHILE VIEWING

A ▶ Watch the video. Check (✓) the topics that are discussed.

☐ 1. where in the world lightning frequently occurs

☐ 2. how lightning is formed

☐ 3. warning signs of lightning and thunderstorms

☐ 4. what to do if you are caught in a thunderstorm

☐ 5. how to protect your home from lightning

B ▶ Watch the video again. Circle the correct words.

1. Regions that have the most lightning strikes include Central Africa, the Himalayas, and **Europe / South America**.

2. In a storm cloud, lighter particles become **positively / negatively** charged, while heavier particles become **positively / negatively** charged.

3. The sound of thunder is caused by the **expanding air / electrical charges** around the lightning.

4. During a lightning storm, you can stay safe by **getting in a car / standing under a tree**.

AFTER VIEWING

A Check your answers to exercise A of **Before Viewing**. Were your predictions correct? Did any information from the video surprise you?

B Look back at the map on page 126. Discuss these questions with a partner.

1. Where in the world do both tornadoes and frequent lightning occur?

2. Based on what you have learned in this unit, where are the safest regions in the world to live?

Reading 2

PREPARING TO READ

A The words and phrases in **blue** below are used in the reading passage on pages 132–133. Read their definitions and then complete each sentence with the correct form of the word or phrase.

BUILDING VOCABULARY

> If something is **appropriate**, it is suitable for a particular situation.
>
> To **block** something means to make its movement difficult or impossible.
>
> If something is **frequent**, it happens often.
>
> **Fuel** is a material (such as coal, wood, oil, or gas) that is burned to produce heat or power.
>
> If you do something **on purpose**, you do it intentionally.
>
> **Particularly** means more than usual or more than other things.
>
> If something is described as **significant**, it is large enough to be noticeable.
>
> Something that **threatens** a person or thing is likely to cause harm.

1. _____ lightning storms are dangerous. Many storms in a short period of time can cause fires that _____ people's lives.

2. Fires that occur in places where a lot of people live are _____ dangerous.

3. Many fires are the result of accidents. However, firefighters sometimes set small, controlled fires _____ to prevent larger fires later on.

4. Different types of fire extinguishers are designed to fight different types of fire. To successfully put out a fire, you must use the _____ extinguisher.

5. Corridors and stairwells should be kept clear of any objects that might _____ people's exit during a fire.

6. In 2016, a series of wildfires burned across the state of California, consuming all the _____ in their path—such as trees, grass, and homes—and causing _____ damage.

B Discuss these questions with a partner.

USING VOCABULARY

1. Do fires occur **frequently** in your community? Why or why not?
2. If there is a fire in a crowded building, what is the **appropriate** thing to do?

C Look at the illustration on pages 132–133. What do you think the reading passage is mainly about? Check your answer as you read.

PREDICTING

a. the main causes or sources of wildfires
b. how to prevent wildfires from spreading
c. the effect of wildfires on the environment

WILDFIRES!

🎧 2.04

A Wildfires occur all around the world, but they are most **frequent** in areas that have wet seasons followed by long, hot, dry seasons. These conditions exist in parts of Australia, South Africa, southern Europe, and the western regions of the United States. These places therefore experience **particularly** dangerous fires.

B A wildfire can move quickly and destroy large areas of land in just a few minutes. There are three conditions that need to be present in order for a fire to burn: **fuel**, oxygen, and a heat source. Fuel can be anything in the path of the fire that can burn—trees, grass, and even homes. Air supplies the oxygen. Heat sources include lightning, hot winds—like the Santa Ana winds in California— and even heat from the sun. However, most wildfires are caused by people, not nature, especially from cigarettes and campfires.

C When trying to put out a fire, firefighters must consider three main factors: the shape of the land, the weather, and the type of fuel in the path of the fire. For example, fire often moves faster uphill. Southern sides of mountains are sunnier and drier, so they are more likely to burn than the northern sides. Also, strong winds can suddenly change the direction of a fire. This could put firefighters directly in the fire's path and **threaten** their safety. Sudden changes in wind direction also make it hard to predict the spread of a fire. Lastly, dry grass and dead trees tend to burn faster than trees with lots of moisture.

D From past experience, we know that it is difficult to prevent wildfires, but it is possible to stop them from becoming too big. One strategy is to cut down trees. Another is to start fires **on purpose** to clear land. Both of these strategies limit the amount of fuel available for fires by removing plants and trees. In addition, people who live in areas where wildfires frequently occur can build fire-resistant[1] homes, says fire researcher Jack Cohen. Cohen has studied wildfires for more than two decades and is an expert on how houses catch fire. "In California there were **significant** cases of communities that did not burn," he says, "because they were fire-resistant."

E Most experts agree that no single action will solve the wildfire problem entirely. The best method is to consider all these strategies and use each of them when and where they are the most **appropriate**.

[1]If something is **fire-resistant**, it does not catch fire easily.

FIGHTING FIRE

- To control a wildfire, firefighters on the ground first look for something in the area that can **block** the fire, such as a river or a road. Then they dig a deep trench[2] along it. This is a "fire line"—a line that fire cannot cross. **❶**

- While firefighters on the ground create a fire line, planes and helicopters drop water or chemical fire retardant[3] on the fire. **❷** Pilots communicate with firefighters on the ground so they know which areas to hit.

- After the fire line is created, firefighters cut down any dead trees in the area between the fire line and the fire. **❸** This helps keep flames from climbing higher into the treetops.

- At the same time, other firefighters on the ground begin backburning[4] in the area between the fire line and the fire. **❹**

[2]A **trench** is a long, narrow hole that is dug in the ground.
[3]**Fire retardant** is a type of chemical that slows the burning of fire.
[4]**Backburning** involves removing fuel (such as plants and trees) in a fire's path by burning it in a controlled way.

UNDERSTANDING THE READING

UNDERSTANDING
MAIN IDEAS

A Match each paragraph from the reading passage to its purpose.

_____ 1. Paragraph A   a. to describe the necessary conditions for a fire
_____ 2. Paragraph B   b. to explain how to protect ourselves from wildfires
_____ 3. Paragraph C   c. to highlight areas where wildfires are most common
_____ 4. Paragraph D   d. to describe what firefighters should look out for in a fire

UNDERSTANDING
DETAILS

B What are the main factors that firefighters consider when they are trying to put out a fire? What are examples of each one? Complete the chart using information from the reading passage.

Factor	Shape of the land		
Examples			dry grass, dead trees

UNDERSTANDING
A PROCESS

C How do firefighters control a wildfire? Read the sentences. Circle **T** for true or **F** for false.

1. Firefighters dig a trench to create a fire line.   **T   F**

2. Planes and helicopters drop fire retardant on the fire line.   **T   F**

3. Firefighters cut down dead trees in the area to control the fire.   **T   F**

4. Firefighters backburn the area behind the fire line, far away from the   **T   F**
   oncoming fire.

CRITICAL THINKING:
EVALUATING SOURCES

D Discuss these questions with a partner.

1. Who is Jack Cohen? How does the writer describe him?

2. What idea does Cohen's quote support?

3. On a scale from 1 to 3, how credible a source do you think Cohen is? (1 = not credible; 3 = very credible) Share your rating with a partner and discuss your reasons.

4. What other information about Cohen could the writer have provided?

CRITICAL THINKING:
EVALUATING SOURCES

E If you were writing this passage, who would you include as an additional source? Circle your answer and note your reasons. Then share your decision with a partner.

a. a wildland firefighter who has just completed basic training
b. an experienced pilot of a firefighting plane
c. a scientist who has studied fire ecology for 30 years
d. an owner of a fire-resistant home

Reason(s): _____

_____

Writing

EXPLORING WRITTEN ENGLISH

A The sentences below describe the rainwater cycle. Read each sentence and underline the verb(s).

NOTICING

1. The sun raises the temperature of water in rivers, lakes, and oceans.

2. When the water heats up, some of it turns into vapor or steam.

3. The vapor rises into the air.

4. As the vapor rises, it gets cold and turns into tiny water droplets that form clouds in the sky.

5. The clouds get heavy, and water falls back to Earth in the form of rain.

6. The cycle continues.

What tense are the underlined verbs? _____

LANGUAGE FOR WRITING Describing a Process

Writers usually use the simple present tense to describe a natural or biological process—that is, to explain how something happens. For example:

*Warm air **moves** upward.*

*When vapor in the air **gets** cold enough, it **changes** back into tiny water droplets.*

*These water droplets **combine** with dust particles in the air and **form** visible clouds.*

*Within a thundercloud, tiny particles of ice **bump** into each other as they **move** around in the air.*

*All of these collisions **create** an electrical charge.*

*After a while, the whole cloud **fills** up with electrical charges.*

Remember to make subjects and verbs agree when you use the simple present tense.

B The following sentences describe how snow is formed. Complete the sentences using the correct form of the verbs in parentheses.

1. When the temperature in the clouds _____ (*be*) very low, the vapor in the air _____ (*freeze*) and _____ (*turn*) into tiny ice crystals.

2. When the tiny ice crystals _____ (*collide*), they _____ (*stick*) together in clouds and _____ (*form*) snowflakes.

3. Each snowflake _____ (*start*) out very small and then _____ (*grow*) bigger.

4. When the snowflakes _____ (become) too heavy, they
   _____ (fall) to the ground.

5. After snow _____ (fall) to the ground, it either _____
   (melt) or _____ (stay) frozen, depending on the land surface
   temperature.

C In your own words, write three sentences in the simple present tense about how
tornadoes, lightning, and/or wildfires form.

1. _____

   _____

2. _____

   _____

3. _____

   _____

WRITING SKILL Organizing a Process Paragraph

When you write a process paragraph, you explain steps or events in **chronological order**—the first event appears first, then the next event, and so on.

To plan a process paragraph, first list each step or event in the correct order. When you write your paragraph, use sequence words and phrases to help the reader follow the order.

First, Initially, To begin with → These sequence words and phrases are used to indicate the beginning of a process.

Second, Third, Then, Next, After, After that → These sequence words and phrases show the following steps.

While, At the same time, During → These sequence words and phrases show actions or steps that happen at the same time.

Finally, Last, Eventually → These sequence words are used to indicate the final step.

Note: *When, As soon as,* and *Once* describe an event that happens just before another event.

First, *the water evaporates and turns into vapor that rises into the air.*
After that, *the water vapor turns back into a liquid.*

Once *the snowflakes become too heavy, they start to fall from the clouds.*
As soon as *the land surface temperature rises, the snow on the ground begins to melt.*

A process paragraph should be more than a list of steps. It is also important to include details that help the reader understand the steps or events.

D The sentences below describe the stages of a wildfire. Read the sentences and underline the sequence words or phrases. Then number the sentences (1–5) to put the stages in the correct order.

_____ Next, as the flames get bigger and spread farther, the fire reaches its hottest stage. At this point, the fire is fully developed.

_____ First, an ember[1] lands close to a fuel source, such as dry grass or leaves. As the ember reacts with oxygen, it increases in heat and strength.

_____ Finally, the fire is reduced to embers and ash. It often takes weeks to fully extinguish all the embers from a large fire.

_____ The combination of heat, oxygen, and fuel increases the likelihood of the fire growing to the second stage. This is when the fire begins to spread to the surrounding areas.

_____ Once all the fuel has been consumed, the fire begins to die out. However, any introduction of new fuel sources or an increase in oxygen can cause the fire to flare up again.

[1]An **ember** is a small piece of burning coal or wood.

E Now write the sentences from exercise D in the correct order to form a paragraph. Replace the underlined sequence words or phrases with others from the Writing Skill box.

When a wildfire starts, it goes through several different stages of growth. _____

_____

_____

_____

_____

_____

_____

_____

_____

_____

_____

_____

_____

WRITING TASK

GOAL You are going to write a paragraph on the following topic:

Explain a natural process that you know well. Choose one of the following or use your own idea:

- a volcanic eruption
- photosynthesis
- an earthquake
- a hurricane

TAKING NOTES **A** List a few natural or biological processes that you are familiar with. Do some research and take notes if necessary. Then try explaining the processes to a partner.

_____

_____

PLANNING **B** Follow these steps to plan your process paragraph.

Step 1 Choose a topic from your notes above and write it down in the outline below.

Step 2 List up to eight steps or events for your process in order in the outline. Don't worry about grammar or spelling. Don't write complete sentences.

Step 3 Write a topic sentence that introduces your process.

Step 4 Now write any details that will help the reader to better understand your steps or events.

OUTLINE

Topic: _____

Topic Sentence: _____

_____

Steps or Events   Details

1. _____   _____

2. _____   _____

3. _____   _____

4. _____   _____

5. _____   _____

6. _____   _____

7. _____   _____

8. _____   _____

FIRST DRAFT **C** Use the information in your outline to write a first draft of your paragraph.

REVISING PRACTICE

The drafts below are similar to the one you are going to write, but they are on a different topic:

Explain how a caterpillar turns into a monarch butterfly.

What did the writer do in Draft 2 to improve the paragraph? Match the changes (a–d) to the highlighted parts. Some can be used more than once.

a. added a detail to a step
b. added a sequence word or phrase
c. corrected a verb form
d. added a concluding sentence

Draft 1

The monarch butterfly has a life cycle that is different from that of most other insects. First, a monarch butterfly lay its eggs on a milkweed plant. After about four days, the eggs hatch into baby caterpillars. The caterpillars eat the milkweed in order to grow. When they are fully grown, they start the pupa stage. Each caterpillar attaches itself to a stem or a leaf and hangs upside down. It forms a chrysalis—a protective shell—around its body. Once it is in this chrysalis, its body begins to change. This transformation is called a metamorphosis. An adult butterfly flies out of the chrysalis and looks for a mate.

Draft 2

The monarch butterfly has a life cycle that is different from that of most other insects. First, a monarch butterfly lays its eggs on a milkweed plant. ☐
After about four days, the eggs hatch into baby caterpillars. As soon as they ☐
are born, the caterpillars eat the milkweed in order to grow. When they are fully grown, they start the pupa stage. Each caterpillar attaches itself to a stem or a leaf and hangs upside down. It forms a chrysalis—a protective shell—around its body. Once it is in this chrysalis, its body begins to change. It grows wings, legs, and other butterfly parts. This transformation is called a ☐
metamorphosis. After the metamorphosis, an adult butterfly flies out of the ☐
chrysalis and looks for a mate. This starts the cycle all over again. ☐

▲ **A monarch butterfly emerges from its chrysalis.**

D Now use the questions below to revise your paragraph.

☐ Does the topic sentence introduce the main idea?
☐ Are the steps in the correct order?
☐ Are there sequence words and phrases to show order?
☐ Are there detail sentences for some of the steps?
☐ Is there a concluding sentence?

REVISED DRAFT

EDITING PRACTICE

Read the information below.

In sentences that explain how something happens, remember to:

- use the simple present tense.
- use verbs that agree with subjects in the simple present tense.

Correct one mistake with the simple present tense in each sentence below.

1. Tornadoes occur when warm, wet air collide with cold, dry air.

2. The rapid expansion of the air surrounding the path of a lightning bolt has caused the sound of thunder.

3. When lightning hits a tree, the moisture inside the tree turns into gas and cause the tree to expand and blow up.

4. A wildfire needed three conditions: fuel, oxygen, and a heat source.

5. Water take three forms: solid (ice), liquid, and gas (vapor).

6. When tiny ice crystals in a cloud collides, they form snowflakes.

FINAL DRAFT **E** Follow these steps to write a final draft.

1. Check your revised draft for mistakes with simple present verb forms.

2. Now use the checklist on page 218 to write a final draft. Make any other necessary changes.

UNIT REVIEW

Answer the following questions.

1. Which of the natural events in this unit would you like to know more about? Why?

_____

_____

2. What are three examples of sequence words or phrases that show order in a list of steps?

_____

_____

3. Do you remember the meanings of these words? Check (✓) the ones you know. Look back at the unit and review the ones you don't know.

Reading 1:
- ☐ climate
- ☐ coast
- ☐ collide
- ☐ condition
- ☐ data AWL
- ☐ extend
- ☐ occur AWL
- ☐ on record
- ☐ strike
- ☐ violent

Reading 2:
- ☐ appropriate AWL
- ☐ block
- ☐ frequent
- ☐ fuel
- ☐ on purpose
- ☐ particularly
- ☐ significant AWL
- ☐ threaten

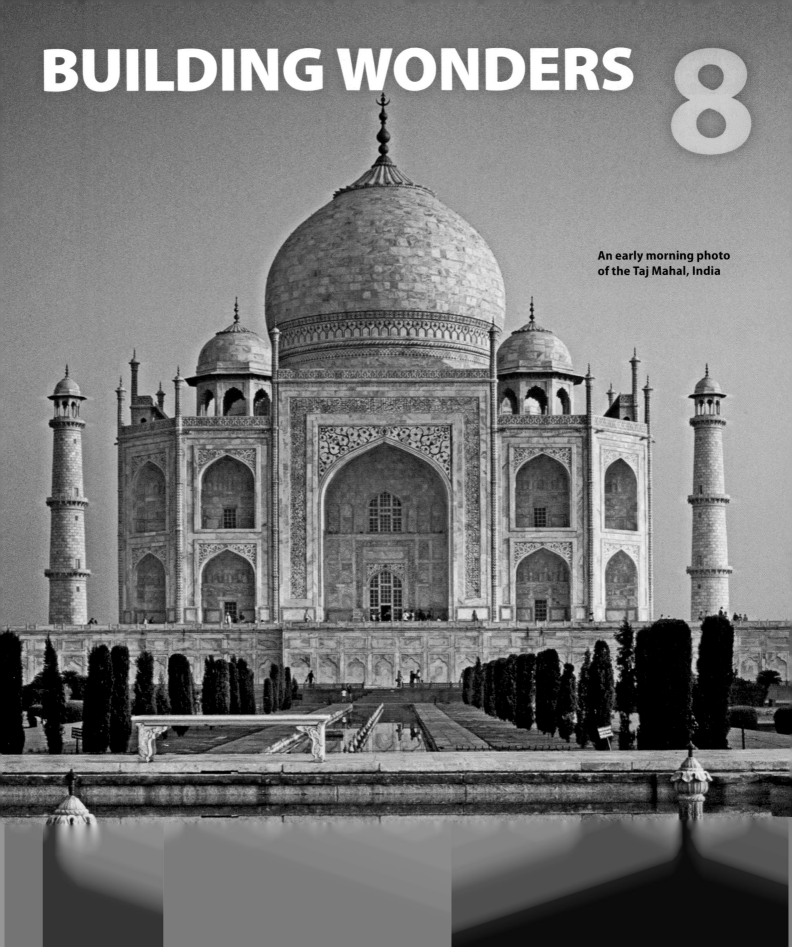

BUILDING WONDERS

8

An early morning photo of the Taj Mahal, India

A Look at the information on these pages and answer the questions.

1. Why do humans build monuments and other large buildings? List as many reasons as you can.

2. Which of the monuments mentioned below would you most like to visit? Give reasons for your choice.

B Match the correct form of the words in blue to their definitions.

_____ (adj) having or showing belief in a god or a group of gods

_____ (n) a shape, design, or object that represents something else

_____ (n) something that has been built

GREAT MONUMENTS

Throughout history, humans have felt a need to build huge structures. Buildings or structures of historical interest are known as monuments. UNESCO (the United Nations Educational, Scientific, and Cultural Organization) protects many important monuments as World Heritage Sites.

There are many reasons for building monuments. Some are tombs for great people. For example, ancient Egyptians built pyramids to protect their kings after death. Centuries later, the ruler Shah Jahan built the Taj Mahal in India as a symbol of love for his dead wife.

Some monuments remind us of great leaders from the past, such as Mount Rushmore's giant carvings of American presidents. Other monuments have religious purposes, such as Göbekli Tepe, one of the oldest man-made structures on Earth. The purpose of some monuments—such as the ancient stone circle of Stonehenge in England—is still a mystery.

The Sankore Mosque in Timbuktu, Mali, is a UNESCO World Heritage Site.

Reading 1

PREPARING TO READ

BUILDING
VOCABULARY

A The words and phrases in **blue** below are used in the reading passage on pages 145–148. Complete each sentence with the correct word or phrase. Use a dictionary to help you.

> architect   committed to   illustrate   inspiration   sculpture   style   theme

1. _____ is a form of art that is made by shaping stone, wood, clay, or other materials.

2. If you are _____ something, you give your time and energy to it.

3. If you get _____ from something, it gives you new and creative ideas.

4. A(n) _____ is an important idea or subject found throughout a work of art or literature.

5. A(n) _____ is a person who plans and designs buildings.

6. To _____ an idea means to explain or give examples of it.

7. The _____ of a building refers to its form or design, and is usually characteristic of a particular period or region.

USING
VOCABULARY

B Discuss these questions with a partner.

1. Do you know of any famous **architects**? What buildings did they design?
2. What is the architectural **style** of the building you are in right now? Is it modern or traditional?

BRAINSTORMING

C If the style of a building is inspired by nature, what might it look like? Look at the categories listed in the word web below. With a partner, brainstorm some ideas for each category.

The ceiling is painted to look like the sky.

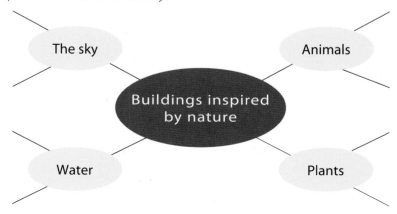

UNFINISHED MASTERPIECE

🎧 2.05

A It's a **structure** that isn't finished, yet two million people visit it every year. Antoni Gaudí began building his church, La Sagrada Família, in 1883—and work continues to this day.

B The **architect** Antoni Gaudí was born in 1852 near the town of Reus, in the Catalonian region of Spain. As a child, he was interested in the natural wonders of the Catalonian countryside. When he grew up, he went to Barcelona to study architecture. Gaudí designed many structures in Barcelona during his career, but he was most **committed to** La Sagrada Família. In fact, after 1910, he stopped working on nearly all other projects to focus on it.

INSPIRED BY NATURE

C Gaudí experimented with many **styles** early in his career, but eventually developed his own ideas about architecture. The natural world was the main **inspiration** for Gaudí's designs. "Nothing is art if it does not come from nature," he believed. Gaudí understood that the natural world is full of curved forms, not straight lines. With this idea in mind, he based his structures on a simple idea: If nature is the work of God, then the best way to honor God is to design buildings based on nature.

D The architect's love of nature combined with his **religious** beliefs guided the design of La Sagrada Família. Gaudí designed the inside of La Sagrada Família to feel like a forest. Inside the church, pillars rise up like trees. This **theme** continues outside. The outside of the church is decorated with **sculptures** of wildlife. For example, a turtle—a **symbol** of the sea—and a tortoise—a symbol of the land—are carved[1] into the base of two columns. Carvings of other animals, such as reptiles and birds, appear throughout the structure.

[1]If something is **carved** from wood or stone, it is cut into a shape or pattern.

Barcelona's Natural Wonder

■ Finished section (as of 2010)
■ Unfinished section

Work on La Sagrada Família is moving slowly. It is scheduled for completion in 2026.

Barcelona
★ Madrid
SPAIN

Forms in nature influenced Gaudí's architectural style. There are many examples of his nature-inspired designs throughout the church.

Natural Windows

Gaudí's windows are similar to shapes found in nature, such as in this algae, a tiny sea animal.

Pyrite crystal ▲

Vine Lines

Gaudí often used vine shapes to decorate the walls of the church.

▼ Passion fruit vine

Tower Tops

Some of the decorations on La Sagrada Família are modeled on Gaudí's study of crystals, grains, and grasses.

Tree Structures

Gaudí made a "forest" inside the church by creating columns that look like trees. He even carved shapes that look like places where branches were removed.

Spiral Stairways

The spiral is a common shape in nature. It exists in plants and animals. Gaudí used spirals in many parts of the church.

Garden snail ▼

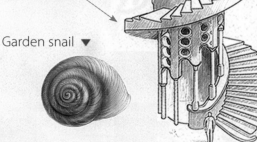

AN END IN SIGHT

E   Gaudí died in 1926. Before his death, he made three-dimensional[2] models of his plans for the building, hoping that others could complete his masterpiece.[3] Many of these models were lost during the Spanish Civil War (1936–1939), but some survived. These models have helped Gaudí's successors.[4] For example, Mark Burry, an architect from New Zealand, has worked on La Sagrada Família for almost 40 years. He uses computer technology and the surviving models to bring Gaudí's plans to life.

[2]A **three-dimensional** object can be measured in three directions: length, width, and depth.

[3]A **masterpiece** is an extremely good work of art.

[4]A **successor** is someone who takes a job or position previously held by someone else.

F   Gaudí's work **illustrates** a timeless truth. As the architectural historian Joan Bassegoda wrote: "The lesson of Gaudí is ... to look at nature for inspiration ... [N]ature does not go out of fashion." In fact, you might say Gaudí's architectural style was ahead of its time. The architect's nature-inspired designs can be seen as an early example of the modern science of biomimetics—a science that uses designs in nature to solve modern problems.

G   Work on La Sagrada Família is expected to be finished in 2026, a hundred years after Gaudí's death. Gaudí was once asked why La Sagrada Família was taking so long to complete. "My client is not in a hurry," he said.

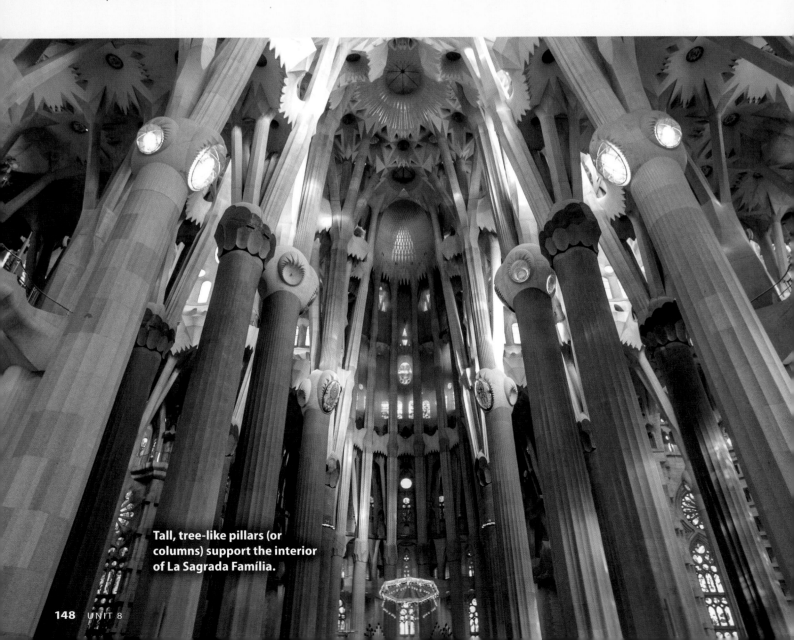

Tall, tree-like pillars (or columns) support the interior of La Sagrada Família.

UNDERSTANDING THE READING

A Match each paragraph from the reading passage to its purpose.

UNDERSTANDING MAIN IDEAS

_____ 1. Paragraph B   a. to explain Gaudí's ideas about architecture

_____ 2. Paragraph C   b. to show a link between Gaudí's work and biomimetics

_____ 3. Paragraph D   c. to provide some biographical information about Gaudí

_____ 4. Paragraph E   d. to describe what inspired the design of La Sagrada Família

_____ 5. Paragraph F   e. to explain how other architects have continued Gaudí's work

B How is the design of La Sagrada Família inspired by nature? Complete the chart using examples from pages 145–147.

UNDERSTANDING DETAILS

Object in La Sagrada Família	Shape or Object in Nature
pillars	trees
sculptures and carvings	
wall decorations	

> **CRITICAL THINKING** Writers often use **quotations** (quotes) from relevant, authoritative sources to add credibility to their claims. When you read a quote, ask yourself: What does this quote mean? How does it relate to the main idea?

C Discuss these questions with a partner.

CRITICAL THINKING: INTERPRETING QUOTES

1. "Nothing is art if it does not come from nature." How does this quote relate to Gaudí's ideas about architecture?
2. According to Joan Bassegoda, "Nature does not go out of fashion." What do you think this means?
3. Gaudí once said, "My client is not in a hurry." Who do you think he was referring to?

D What do you think about Gaudí's design for La Sagrada Família? Complete the following sentence and share your ideas with a partner.

CRITICAL THINKING: REFLECTING

I **like** / **don't like** the design of La Sagrada Família because _____

_____

DEVELOPING READING SKILLS

READING SKILL Identifying Relevant Information

Scanning a passage helps you find relevant information quickly. When you scan, you only look for particular things. For example, to get information about times, dates, and distances, look for **numbers**. To get information about people and places, look for **capitalized words**. Read the words around the numbers or capitalized words to understand the context.

For example, to answer the question "When did Gaudí start work on La Sagrada Família?", first scan the text to find a year. Then read the words before and after the year for information about "starting work."

Antoni Gaudí began building his church, La Sagrada Família, in 1883.

First, your eyes go to *1883*. Then your eyes go to *began building*. You have found the answer to the question—*in 1883*.

MATCHING   **A**   Read the questions below. Match each question to the type of information needed to answer it.

_____ 1. How far is Rapa Nui from Chile?   a. height

_____ 2. When did people probably first come to Rapa Nui?   b. year

_____ 3. Where did these people come from?   c. distance

_____ 4. How tall are the statues?   d. place

SCANNING   **B**   Now scan the following paragraph for the answers to the questions above. Underline the words in the paragraph that contain the answers.

Rapa Nui (Easter Island) is an island in the Pacific Ocean located 2,300 miles (3,700 kilometers) west of Chile. It's home to the mysterious *moai* statues— enormous figures carved from stone. It's not clear when the island was first settled. Experts guess that a few brave sailors somehow sailed west to Rapa Nui from the Polynesian islands around A.D. 800. There are 900 *moai* statues across the island. These are about 13 feet (4 meters) tall and weigh as much as 14 tons (12,700 kilograms). Most scholars think that the *moai* were created to honor ancestors, chiefs, or other important people.

IDENTIFYING RELEVANT INFORMATION   **C**   Scan the reading passage on pages 145–148 to find answers to the questions below.

1. When did Gaudí die?   _____

2. Who has worked on La Sagrada Família in recent years?   _____

3. When will La Sagrada Família be completed?   _____

Video

A DARING DESIGN

BEFORE VIEWING

A Read the information about Florence. Then answer the questions.

Florence—the capital of Italy's Tuscany region—is famous for its history, art, and culture. One place tourists like to visit is the Ponte Vecchio, the oldest bridge in Florence. Its current appearance dates back to 1345. The bridge is lined with shops that sell jewelry and souvenirs. There are also several museums in Florence where you can see famous works of art such as Michelangelo's *David* and Botticelli's *The Birth of Venus*. The historic center of Florence is commonly referred to as an "open-air museum," with its beautiful architecture, streets, and gardens.

1. What can tourists do on the Ponte Vecchio?

   _____

2. Why do you think the historic center of Florence has been called an "open-air museum"?

   _____

B The words in **bold** below are used in the video. Match the correct form of each word to its definition.

> In many theaters, the seat rows are arranged in a **semicircle**. This curved design enables every person in the audience to see the stage.
>
> Architect Frank Gehry is famous for designing buildings with **irregular** sides. For example, the Guggenheim Museum in Bilbao, Spain, has many curved sides of different sizes.
>
> Many houses are built with **bricks** that are held together by **cement**.

1. _____ (adj) not even or balanced in shape or arrangement

2. _____ (n) a small, rectangular block made of clay, used in building

3. _____ (n) half of a circle

4. _____ (n) a powdery substance that hardens when it is mixed with water

WHILE VIEWING

UNDERSTANDING
MAIN IDEAS

A ▶ What is special about Brunelleschi's dome? Watch the video and check (✓) the sentences that are true.

☐ 1. No one knows exactly how it was built.

☐ 2. Its base is a semicircle.

☐ 3. It was built without a central support system.

☐ 4. Its base has no true center.

☐ 5. It was constructed very quickly.

☐ 6. It is the largest brick dome in the world.

UNDERSTANDING
DETAILS

B ▶ Watch the video again. Fill in the missing information.

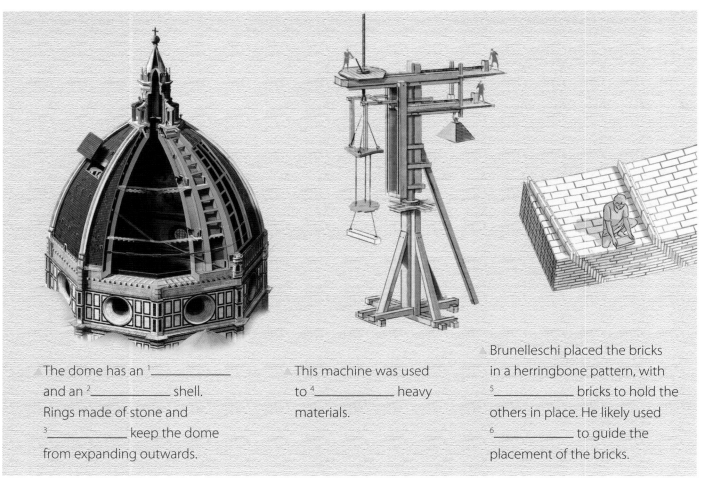

The dome has an ¹_____ and an ²_____ shell. Rings made of stone and ³_____ keep the dome from expanding outwards.

This machine was used to ⁴_____ heavy materials.

Brunelleschi placed the bricks in a herringbone pattern, with ⁵_____ bricks to hold the others in place. He likely used ⁶_____ to guide the placement of the bricks.

AFTER VIEWING

REACTING TO
THE VIDEO

A Brunelleschi had no formal architectural training. How do you think this might have helped him? Discuss with a partner.

CRITICAL THINKING:
SYNTHESIZING

B Write a few sentences comparing La Sagrada Família and Brunelleschi's dome. Consider the following:

• Where is each structure located?

• Which structure took / is taking longer to build?

• Which structure is older?

• What is the purpose of each structure?

Reading 2

PREPARING TO READ

A The words and phrases in **blue** below are used in the reading passage on pages 154–155. Read the sentences and then circle the best definition for each word or phrase.

1. The Pyramids of Giza **consist of** heavy blocks. Each block weighs about two and a half tons.
   a. are inspired by
   b. are formed from

2. It took 16 years to **construct** the dome of the Cathedral of Santa Maria del Fiore.
   a. build
   b. discover

3. Experts continue to **debate** the purpose of some ancient monuments. There are many opinions because there is not yet enough evidence.
   a. discuss
   b. agree on

4. A wedding is a religious ceremony for many people. The event often occurs in a **holy** place.
   a. very old
   b. sacred

5. The pillars inside La Sagrada Família **represent** trees. They are branched and slightly tilted, not straight, just like real trees.
   a. symbolize
   b. damage

6. Some building projects **require** hundreds of people to work together.
   a. hurt
   b. need

7. The ancient Mayan people worshipped various gods related to nature, including the gods of the sun and the moon. They went to the **temple** to honor their gods.
   a. place for entertainment
   b. place for religious activities

8. How did ancient people **transport** heavy stones? At the time, they didn't even have wheels.
   a. move
   b. carve

B Discuss these questions with a partner.

1. What are some methods of **transporting** heavy objects over long distances?
2. Have you visited any famous **temples**? Where were they and what were they like?
3. What skills are **required** to be an architect?

C Skim the first paragraph of the reading passage on pages 154–155, and look at the photos and captions. Consider the following:

How old do you think these structures are? What do you think was the purpose of each structure?

Discuss your ideas with a partner. Then check your ideas as you read the passage.

AMAZING STRUCTURES

A For thousands of years, people have been inspired to create giant monuments. Here are two great architectural achievements, located on opposite sides of the world.

CHICHÉN ITZÁ

B Chichén Itzá was a major city of the Maya Empire from A.D. 750 to 1200. Made of stepped pyramids, temples, and other stone structures, the ancient city is now one of Mexico's most visited tourist destinations. The largest building in Chichén Itzá is the Temple of Kukulkan—a pyramid with 365 steps. A kind of calendar, the temple shows the change of seasons. On the spring and autumn equinoxes[1] each year, a shadow falls on the pyramid in the shape of a snake. As the sun sets, this shadowy snake goes down the steps to eventually join a carved snake head on the pyramid's side.

C The Mayans constructed the pyramids with carved stone. Amazingly, they worked without wheels or metal tools. To build a pyramid, Mayan workers created a base and added smaller and smaller levels as the structure rose. Building the pyramids required many workers. Some pyramids took hundreds of years to complete.

D Chichén Itzá was both an advanced city center and a religious site. Spanish records show that the Mayans made human sacrifices[2] to a rain god here. Archaeologists have found bones, jewelry, and other objects that people wore when they were sacrificed. Experts also know that the Mayans were knowledgeable astronomers.[3] They used the tops of the pyramids to view Venus and other planets.

[1] An **equinox** is a time in the year when day and night are of equal length.
[2] A **sacrifice** is a religious ceremony in which people or animals are killed.
[3] An **astronomer** is a person who studies stars, planets, and other objects in space.

**Temple of Kukulkan,
Chichén Itzá, Mexico**

GÖBEKLI TEPE

Göbekli Tepe, in southeastern Turkey, is one of the oldest man-made structures on Earth. Experts believe it was built about 12,000 years ago. The structure **consists of** dozens of stone pillars arranged in rings. Many pillars are covered with carvings of animals. The tallest pillars are 18 feet (5.5 meters) in height and weigh 16 tons (more than 14,500 kilograms).

At the time that Göbekli Tepe was built, there was no writing system, and people did not use metal. Even wheels did not exist. Amazingly, though, the builders were able to cut, shape, and **transport** 16-ton stones. Archaeologists found Stone Age[4] tools such as knives at the site. They think hundreds of workers carved and put the pillars in place.

Archaeologists are still **debating** the purpose of Göbekli Tepe. Klaus Schmidt—the archaeologist who originally excavated[5] the site—believed that Göbekli Tepe was a **holy** meeting place. According to his theory, the T-shaped pillars **represent** human beings. The pillars face the center of the circle and perhaps represent a religious ceremony.

New evidence suggests that large feasts took place at the site. Archaeologists found thousands of small animal bones nearby, with stone containers large enough to hold more than 40 gallons (150 liters) of liquid. They also found smaller pillars similar to Göbekli Tepe's in areas over 125 miles (200 kilometers) away. It's as though Göbekli Tepe were a cathedral and the other structures were local churches.

[4]The **Stone Age** was a prehistoric period when tools were made of stone, not metal.
[5]When people **excavate** a site, they remove earth to find items buried underground.

Göbekli Tepe, Turkey

UNDERSTANDING THE READING

UNDERSTANDING THE MAIN IDEA

A Choose the best alternative title for the reading passage.

    a. Mysterious Modern Structures
    b. Architectural Wonders of the Ancient World
    c. Religious Architectural Styles

UNDERSTANDING DETAILS

B What do Chichén Itzá and Göbekli Tepe have in common? Check (✓) the sentences that are true.

    ☐ 1. Both structures are located in the Americas.
    ☐ 2. Both structures were built from stone.
    ☐ 3. Carvings of animals appear on both structures.
    ☐ 4. Both structures were built using metal tools.
    ☐ 5. Both structures were constructed amazingly quickly.
    ☐ 6. Both structures likely served a religious purpose.

IDENTIFYING EVIDENCE

C According to the writer, what was the purpose of each structure? What evidence does the writer give? Scan the reading passage again and note your answers.

Chichén Itzá

Purpose(s): _____

Evidence: _____

_____

Göbekli Tepe

Purpose(s): _____

Evidence: _____

_____

CRITICAL THINKING: EVALUATING AN ARGUMENT

D Work with a partner. Discuss the following questions about the reading passage.

    1. Look back at paragraphs D, G, and H. What language does the writer use to describe the purpose(s) of each structure? How does the writer introduce the evidence? Consider the levels of certainty expressed.
    2. Do you find the argument explaining the purpose of Chichén Itzá or of Göbekli Tepe more convincing? Why?

CRITICAL THINKING: REFLECTING

E Do you think it is a good thing or a bad thing that ancient sites like Chichén Itzá and Göbekli Tepe have been opened up to the world? What are the pros and cons? Discuss with a partner and note your ideas below.

Pros: _____

Cons: _____

Writing

EXPLORING WRITTEN ENGLISH

A Complete the sentences using the phrases in the box. One phrase is extra.

NOTICING

not as old as	more expensive than	less expensive than	older than

1. Göbekli Tepe was built about 12,000 years ago. Stonehenge was built about 5,000 years ago.

   Göbekli Tepe is _____ Stonehenge.

2. The Ponte Vecchio in Florence was built in 1345. The dome of the Cathedral of Santa Maria del Fiore was completed in 1436.

   The dome of the Cathedral of Santa Maria del Fiore is _____ the Ponte Vecchio.

3. The Guggenheim Museum Bilbao was built at a cost of about US$89 million. The National Museum of African American History and Culture was built at a cost of about US$540 million.

   The construction of the Guggenheim Museum Bilbao was _____ the construction of the National Museum of African American History and Culture.

LANGUAGE FOR WRITING Using Comparative Adjectives

One way to make comparisons is to use the comparative forms of adjectives. We use comparative adjectives when talking about **two** things (not three or more things). There are two ways to form a comparative adjective:

- adjective + -er + than (with most adjectives that have one syllable).

- more / less + adjective + than (with most adjectives that have two or more syllables).

  *St. Peter's Basilica in Vatican City is **larger than** the Seville Cathedral in Spain.*

  *The design of St. Patrick's Cathedral in New York City is **less complex than** the design of La Sagrada Família.*

  *Chichén Itzá is **more accessible than** Machu Picchu, which is located high in the Andes Mountains in Peru.*

Use (not) as + adjective + as to say things are (or are not) the same.

  *The Wharf Times Square in Wuxi, China, is **as tall as** Moscow's Mercury City Tower.*

  *The Empire State Building in New York City is **not as tall as** the Tokyo Skytree in Japan.*

B Complete the sentences using the correct comparative form of the adjectives in parentheses.

1. The Tokyo Skytree has a height of 2,080 feet (634 meters). The Canton Tower in Guangzhou, China, has a height of 1,982 feet (604 meters).

    The Tokyo Skytree is _____ (*tall*) the Canton Tower.

2. The Chrysler Building in New York City is 1,046 feet (319 meters) tall. Global City Square—a skyscraper in Guangzhou, China—is the same height.

    China's Global City Square is _____ (*tall*) the Chrysler Building.

3. St. Paul's Cathedral in London has a traditional design. The design of St. Mary's Cathedral in Tokyo is partly traditional and partly modern.

    The design of St. Paul's Cathedral is _____ (*traditional*) the design of St. Mary's Cathedral.

4. The Great Wall of China is 13,171 miles (21,196 kilometers) long. Hadrian's Wall in northern England is 73 miles (117 kilometers) long.

    Hadrian's Wall is _____ (*long*) the Great Wall of China.

5. The Golden Gate Bridge in San Francisco is about 220 feet (67 meters) above water. The Ponte Vecchio in Florence, Italy, is about 14 feet (4 meters) above water.

    The Golden Gate Bridge is _____ (*high*) the Ponte Vecchio.

C Using comparative adjectives, write three comparison sentences about places.

1. _____

    _____

2. _____

    _____

3. _____

    _____

WRITING SKILL Writing a Comparison Paragraph

When you write a comparison paragraph, first choose a topic—that is, the items you wish to compare. Next, think of two or three points about the items that you want to discuss. Then think of one or two details to include about each point.

When comparing two items, you can write about similarities or differences. Transition words and phrases in your paragraph help the reader understand your ideas.

Similarities: *Similarly, Both, Also, Like*

Differences: *However, On the other hand, Unlike, In contrast*

> **Both** *Göbekli Tepe and Stonehenge are ancient monuments.* **However**, *Göbekli Tepe is much older.*

> *The Temple of Kukulkan in Chichén Itzá shows the change of seasons.* **Similarly**, *some experts think that ancient people used Stonehenge as a kind of calendar.*

D Read a student's paragraph below comparing two libraries. In what ways are the libraries similar? In what ways are they different? Use the information in the paragraph to complete the Venn diagram.

The Grant Library and the Barrett Library are both important resources for student research at my university, but there are some differences between the two structures. First, the buildings have very different styles. The Grant Library, built in 1890, is older than the Barrett Library and was built in the classical style. For example, there are tall marble columns at the entrance, which make the library look like a Greek temple. The Barrett Library, on the other hand, has a more modern design. It was built in the early 20th century in the craftsman style and is made entirely of wood. The purposes of the two libraries are also different. The Barrett Library also functions as a museum, so it's open only seven hours a day. The Grant Library, however, is open 24 hours a day, so students can do research or study there for a longer time. The two buildings have different styles and purposes, but both are excellent examples of the variety of architectural styles at my university.

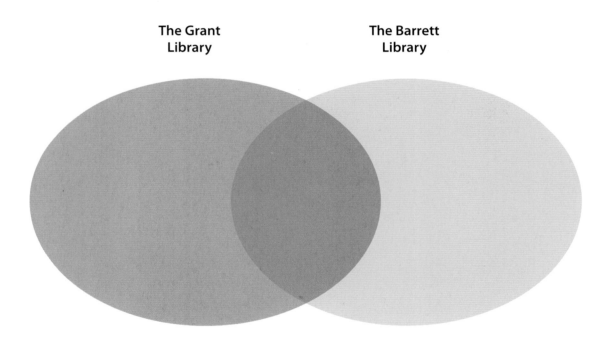

The Grant Library

The Barrett Library

E Look again at the paragraph in exercise D and answer the questions below.

1. What are the two points about the buildings that the writer is comparing?

_____

2. Find and underline two detail sentences for each of the points of comparison.

3. What transition words or phrases does the writer use to show comparison? Circle them.

WRITING TASK

GOAL You are going to write a paragraph on the following topic:

Compare two structures in terms of their age, size, purpose, and/or the length of time it took to build each one.

PLANNING **A** Follow these steps to plan your comparison paragraph.

Step 1 Label the two circles of the Venn diagram with the names of the two structures you are going to compare. Use structures from this unit or your own ideas.

Step 2 Think of two or three points of comparison (e.g., age, size, purpose, construction, design) and write them below the Venn diagram.

Step 3 Write the similarities in the space where the two circles intersect (meet). Write the differences in the outer parts of the circles. Add details and examples. Don't write complete sentences.

Step 4 Write a topic sentence that tells the reader whether you are going to write about similarities, differences, or both.

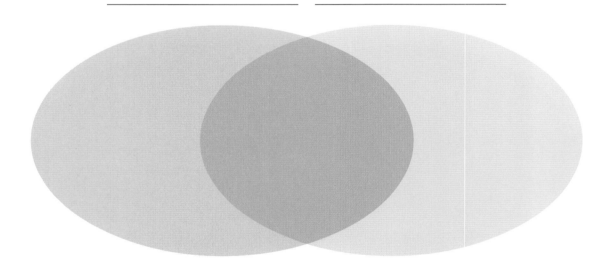

Point 1: _____ Point 2: _____ Point 3: _____

Topic Sentence: _____

_____

FIRST DRAFT **B** Use the information above to write a first draft of your paragraph.

REVISING PRACTICE

The drafts below are similar to the one you are going to write. They compare the Golden Gate Bridge in San Francisco and the Brooklyn Bridge in New York City.

What did the writer do in Draft 2 to improve the paragraph? Match the changes (a–d) to the highlighted parts. Some can be used more than once.

a. added a detail to a point of comparison
b. added a transition phrase to show difference
c. added a concluding sentence
d. corrected a comparative adjective mistake

▲ **Golden Gate Bridge**   ▲ **Brooklyn Bridge**

Draft 1

The Golden Gate Bridge and the Brooklyn Bridge are both examples of amazing engineering. They have a similar design. Both are steel suspension bridges—bridges with a deck that is hung from cables. However, at 1.7 miles (2.7 kilometers) long, the Golden Gate Bridge is more long than the Brooklyn Bridge, which is 5,989 feet (1.8 kilometers) long. In addition, the Golden Gate Bridge is newer than the Brooklyn Bridge. The Golden Gate Bridge was opened to the public in 1937. The Brooklyn Bridge was completed in 1883.

Draft 2

The Golden Gate Bridge and the Brooklyn Bridge are both examples of amazing engineering. They have a similar design. Both are steel suspension bridges— bridges with a deck that is hung from cables. Both have tall towers that hold the cables in place. However, at 1.7 miles (2.7 kilometers) long, the Golden Gate Bridge is longer than the Brooklyn Bridge, which is 5,989 feet (1.8 kilometers) long. In addition, the Golden Gate Bridge is newer than the Brooklyn Bridge. The Golden Gate Bridge was opened to the public in 1937. The Brooklyn Bridge, on the other hand, was completed in 1883 and is one of the oldest suspension bridges in the United States. In short, the two bridges have some similarities, but are different in terms of size and age.

C Now use the questions below to revise your paragraph.   REVISED DRAFT

☐ Does the topic sentence introduce the main idea?
☐ Are there at least two points of comparison?
☐ Is there enough detail for the points of comparison?
☐ Are there transition words or phrases to show similarities and differences?
☐ Is there a concluding sentence?

EDITING PRACTICE

Read the information below.

In sentences with comparative adjectives, remember to:
- use *more / less … than* with most adjectives that have two or more syllables.
- not use *more / less* with comparative adjectives ending in *-er than*.
- not use *than* with *(not) as … as*.

Correct one comparative adjective mistake in each sentence below.

1. The Seville Cathedral is more smaller than St. Peter's Basilica.
2. In my opinion, La Sagrada Família is attractiver than St. Mary's Cathedral.
3. The Temple of Angkor Wat in Cambodia is not as ancient than the Borobudur Temple in Indonesia.
4. Göbekli Tepe is more old than the Parthenon in Greece.
5. The Tokyo Skytree is not tall as the Burj Khalifa in Dubai, which has a height of almost 2,723 feet (830 meters).
6. The construction of the Barrett Library was less expensiver than the construction of the Morrison Library.
7. The Brooklyn Bridge is not as longer as the Golden Gate Bridge.

FINAL DRAFT **D** Follow these steps to write a final draft.

1. Check your revised draft for mistakes with comparative adjectives.
2. Now use the checklist on page 218 to write a final draft. Make any other necessary changes.

UNIT REVIEW

Answer the following questions.

1. Which of the buildings or structures in this unit would you most like to visit? Why?

_____

_____

2. What is one way to form a comparative adjective?

_____

_____

3. Do you remember the meanings of these words? Check (✓) the ones you know. Look back at the unit and review the ones you don't know.

Reading 1:

☐ architect ☐ committed to AWL ☐ illustrate AWL
☐ inspiration ☐ religious ☐ sculpture
☐ structure AWL ☐ style AWL ☐ symbol AWL
☐ theme AWL

Reading 2:

☐ consist of AWL ☐ construct AWL ☐ debate AWL
☐ holy ☐ represent ☐ require AWL
☐ temple ☐ transport AWL

FORM AND FUNCTION 9

A male bird of paradise uses its feather display to attract females.

THINK AND DISCUSS

1 Why do you think some animals have fur, skin, or scales?
2 What man-made objects or machines were inspired by nature?

A Look at the information on these pages and answer the questions.

1. What is an example of (a) a physical adaptation and (b) a behavioral adaptation?

2. What are some other examples of adaptations in the natural world?

B Match the correct form of the words in blue to their definitions.

_____ (v) to develop gradually, often into a better or more advanced state

_____ (n) an idea or a set of ideas that is intended to explain something

_____ (n) a feature or quality that makes a person, thing, or group different from others

ANIMAL ADAPTATION

The flight sequence of a collared kingfisher over the Kinabatangan River, Borneo

An adaptation is a change in an organism—a living plant or animal—that helps it survive in its environment. These changes are the result of mutation. Mutations are passed down through genes from one generation to the next. As more organisms inherit (receive) the mutation, the species evolves. Eventually, the adaptation becomes a normal characteristic of the species.

An adaptation can affect an organism physically. For example, some plants adapt to living in the desert by storing water in their stems. Adaptations can also affect behavior. Migration is a behavioral adaptation that allows animals to move to places where they can mate or find food. For example, gray whales give birth in warm water but travel to cold water for food.

Sometimes an adaptation develops for one purpose but is used for another. For example, one theory about feathers is that they were probably an adaptation to provide insulation (i.e., to prevent heat from escaping) but were later used for flying.

Reading 1

PREPARING TO READ

BUILDING VOCABULARY

A The words in **blue** below are used in the reading passage on pages 167–168. Complete each sentence with the correct form of the word. Use a dictionary to help you.

display	evidence	flexible	advantage	layer	clue	attract

1. _____ is anything that you see, experience, read, or are told that helps prove something.

2. A(n) _____ of material is a quantity that covers something or is between two other things.

3. If something is _____, it can bend easily without breaking.

4. A(n) _____ is a benefit or gain.

5. A(n) _____ is a piece of information that helps you find the answer to a problem, question, or mystery.

6. Something that is for _____ is designed to be seen by other individuals.

7. If something _____ people or animals, it has features that cause them to come to it or have a liking for it.

USING VOCABULARY

B Discuss these questions with a partner.

1. Can you name a famous scientist who developed a **theory**? What kind of theory did they develop?
2. What are some strategies that animals use to **attract** a mate?

BRAINSTORMING

C What are some of the main characteristics of birds? Make a list and share your ideas with a partner.

1. _____Birds lay eggs._____   3. _____

2. _____   4. _____

PREDICTING

D Skim the first paragraph of the reading passage on pages 167–168, and look at the subheads. How might feathers help with each function? Note your ideas and discuss them with a partner. Then check your ideas as you read the passage.

Insulation _____

Attraction _____

Flight _____

WHAT ARE FEATHERS FOR?

A coat of feathers provides warmth to a resting greater flamingo.

A Paleontologists[1] think feathers have existed for millions of years. Fossils of a 125-million-year-old dinosaur called a theropod show that it had a thin **layer** of hair on its back—**evidence** of very primitive[2] feathers. Discoveries such as this are helping scientists understand how and why feathers **evolved**.

INSULATION

B Some paleontologists speculate that feathers began as a kind of insulation. Paleontologists have found theropod fossils with their front limbs[3] spread over their nests. They think this shows that the dinosaurs were using feathers to keep their young warm. In addition, many young birds are covered in light, soft feathers, which keep the birds' bodies warm. Even when they become adult birds, they keep a layer of warm feathers close to their bodies.

[1]A **paleontologist** studies fossils—the remains of prehistoric animals found inside rocks.
[2]If something is **primitive**, it is in a very early stage of development.
[3]A **limb** is an arm or a leg, or a bird's wing.

ATTRACTION

Another **theory** is that feathers evolved for **display**—that is, to be seen. Feathers on birds show a huge range of colors and patterns. In many cases, the purpose of these beautiful feathers is to **attract** the opposite sex. A peacock spreads its brightly colored tail to attract a peahen. Generally, the more eyespots and the bigger the tail, the better the peacock's chances are of attracting a mate. Other birds use crests—feathers on their heads.

In 2009, scientists found evidence that supported this theory. They discovered very small sacs[4]—called melanosomes—inside theropod feathers. Melanosomes give feathers their color. The theropod melanosomes look the same as those in the feathers of modern birds.

FLIGHT

We know that feathers help birds to fly. Here's how they work: A bird's feathers are not the same shape on each side. They are thin and hard on one side, and long and **flexible** on the other. To lift themselves into the air, birds turn their wings at a particular angle. This movement allows air to go above and below the wings. The difference in air pressure allows them to fly.

Paleontologists are now carefully studying the closest theropod relatives of birds. They are looking for **clues** to when and how feathers were first used for flight. A 150-million-year-old dinosaur called *Anchiornis* may hold the answer. The size of a chicken, it had black-and-white arm and leg feathers. These feathers were similar to modern bird feathers, except that they were the same shape on both sides. Because of this, *Anchiornis* probably wasn't able to fly.

However, scientists also found a small, movable bone in *Anchiornis* fossils. This bone allowed it to fold its arms to its sides, keeping its arm feathers off the ground as it walked. Modern birds use a similar bone to pull their wings toward their bodies as they fly upwards. According to scientists, this common **characteristic** suggests that feathered dinosaurs such as *Anchiornis* evolved flight by moving their feathered arms up and down as they ran, or by jumping from tree to tree.

Research therefore shows that feathers probably evolved because they offered several **advantages**. The evidence suggests that their special design and bright colors helped dinosaurs—and later on, birds—stay warm, attract mates, and finally fly high into the sky.

◀ **Fossil evidence suggests that *Anchiornis* had black-and-white feathers and a red crest.**

[4]A **sac** is a small part of an animal's body that is shaped like a little bag.

UNDERSTANDING THE READING

A What is the main idea of the reading passage?

UNDERSTANDING
THE MAIN IDEA

   a. Feathers mainly evolved for warmth rather than flight.
   b. Feathers evolved because they perform a number of functions for birds.
   c. Feathers will continue to evolve and offer birds new advantages.

B Scan the reading passage for information to complete the chart below. Note your answers to the following questions.

IDENTIFYING
DETAILS

   1. How does the author support the ideas about the purpose of feathers? Note at least one modern-day example from the reading passage for each purpose.
   2. What fossil evidence have scientists found relating to each purpose?

Purpose	Modern Examples	Fossil Evidence
Insulation	Many _____ birds have light, _____ that keep their bodies warm.	
Attraction		
Flight	Modern bird feathers are _____ on one side and _____ on the other—so birds can lift themselves into the air. They have a _____ that helps them pull their wings toward their bodies as they fly upwards.	Feathered dinosaurs such as *Anchiornis* had a small, _____ that allowed them to fold their arms to their sides. This may eventually have helped them use their feathers to fly.

> **CRITICAL THINKING** When you **evaluate evidence**, you decide if it supports the writer's claims. Consider whether the evidence is *relevant* (does it relate to the main idea?), *logical* (does it make sense?), and *sufficient* (does it give enough support for the idea?).

C Look at the chart in exercise B again. Then discuss the questions below with a partner.

CRITICAL THINKING:
EVALUATING
EVIDENCE

   1. In your opinion, does the fossil evidence help support each theory about feathers? Do you see a clear link?
   2. Do you think the writer gives enough fossil evidence and modern-day examples for each theory?
   3. Which theory about feathers do you find most or least convincing? Why?

DEVELOPING READING SKILLS

READING SKILL Identifying Theories

Writers use certain words and expressions to differentiate theories from facts. A **fact** is an idea that has been proven to be true. A **theory** is an idea that is based on evidence and reasoning but has not yet been proven. Scientists develop theories in order to explain why something happens, or happened, in a particular way.

Writers use verbs such as *think, speculate, believe,* and *suggest* to indicate theories.

   *Paleontologists **think** feathers have existed for millions of years.*

   *Some paleontologists **speculate** that feathers began as a kind of insulation.*

Writers also use words such as *probably* and *perhaps* to indicate theories.

   *Because of this, Anchiornis **probably** wasn't able to fly.*

IDENTIFYING THEORIES

A Read the information about a fossil discovery in China. Then underline the theories and circle the words that introduce them.

Feathered dinosaurs such as *Microraptor gui* may have flown by gliding from tree to tree.

Many scientists think that a group of dinosaurs closely related to today's birds took the first steps toward flight when their limbs evolved to flap[1] as they ran. They theorize that this arm flapping eventually led to flying. But recently discovered fossils in China are showing a different picture.

Paleontologists discovered the fossils of a small, feathered dinosaur called *Microraptor gui* that lived between 110 and 120 million years ago. The Chinese scientists who studied the fossils don't think this animal ran or flapped well enough to take off from the ground. Instead, they believe this animal flew by gliding[2] from tree to tree. They speculate that the feathers formed a sort of parachute[3] that helped the animal stay in the air.

Not everyone agrees with this theory. Some researchers suggest that *M. gui*'s feathers weren't useful for flight at all. They think that the feathers possibly helped the animal to attract a mate, or made the tiny dinosaur look bigger.

[1] When a bird **flaps** its wings, the wings move up and down.
[2] When birds or airplanes **glide**, they float on air currents.
[3] A **parachute** is a device made of cloth that allows a person to jump safely from an airplane.

IDENTIFYING THEORIES

B Look back at the reading passage on pages 167–168. Underline two theories and circle the words that introduce them.

Video

A Draco lizard—or "Flying Dragon"—in mid-flight

FLYING REPTILES

BEFORE VIEWING

A Look at the photos above and on the next page. How do you think these animals move through the air? Discuss your ideas with a partner.

PREDICTING

B Read the information about wingless animals that can fly. Then answer the questions.

LEARNING ABOUT THE TOPIC

Some wingless animals can fly by gliding. One such animal is the flying squirrel. Flying squirrels have a layer of skin connecting their front paws to their back paws. When they jump off a tree, the skin acts like a parachute, keeping them in the air until they reach the next tree. They use their tails to steer as they glide. Another example is the flying fish. This animal has long fins shaped like a pair of wings. When they need to get away from bigger fish, they flap their fins very quickly to come out of the water. Then they use their fins to glide for a short distance over the surface of the water.

1. What body parts do flying squirrels and flying fish use to glide?

   _____

2. What factors do you think affect how far these animals can glide?

   _____

C The words in **bold** below are used in the video. Match the correct form of each word to its definition.

VOCABULARY IN CONTEXT

> The flying squirrel does not actually fly, but rather **launches** itself downward from a tall tree toward another tree or toward the ground.
> A number of animals have evolved gliding abilities in order to **escape** from predators.
> Flying squirrels are **prey** for a variety of predators like owls, hawks, and cats.

1. _____ (v) to succeed in getting away from something

2. _____ (v) to send something into the air

3. _____ (n) an animal that is hunted by other animals for food

WHILE VIEWING

A ▶ Watch the video. Explain in your own words what the two animals have in common.

_____

_____

B ▶ Watch the video again. Circle **T** for true or **F** for false.

1. The snake hangs off a tree in a "J" shape before taking off.   **T**   **F**

2. The snake can flatten itself to about twice its normal width.   **T**   **F**

3. The snake can turn in the air.   **T**   **F**

4. The paradise tree snake is prey for the Draco lizard.   **T**   **F**

5. The Draco can glide between trees up to 100 meters apart.   **T**   **F**

AFTER VIEWING

A Gliding has evolved mainly among rain forest animals, such as the paradise tree snake pictured below. Why do you think this is? Discuss with a partner.

B Read the following quote from the video:

"The lizard puffs itself up as a warning, but the snake doesn't seem put off by this display."

What does the narrator mean by "… the snake doesn't seem put off by this display"?

_____

A paradise tree snake launches itself from one tree to the next.

Reading 2

PREPARING TO READ

A The words in **blue** below are used in the reading passage on pages 174–175. Complete each sentence with the correct word. Use a dictionary to help you.

BUILDING VOCABULARY

adjust	industry	involved	vary
process	solid	surface	unique

1. Natural selection is the _____ by which species adapt to their environment.

2. Nature has given us ideas for products in many different areas of business and manufacturing, such as the automobile _____ .

3. An increasing number of chemists, engineers, and materials scientists are now getting _____ in biomimetics.

4. Nearly all male birds of paradise use movement to attract the opposite sex. However, the types of movements _____ between species.

5. Some animals see well at night because their eyes can _____ to the dark.

6. A toucan's beak, or bill, is very light because it contains a lot of air. It is not _____ inside.

7. The _____ of a bird's beak is smooth, but underneath, it is actually made of many small pieces of bone.

8. The desert beetle's shell is _____ in that it can collect water. Other beetle shells can't.

B Discuss these questions with a partner.

USING VOCABULARY

1. What are some characteristics that make humans a **unique** species?
2. Which objects in your classroom have rough **surfaces**? Which have very smooth surfaces?

C Look at the photos and the subheads of the reading passage on pages 174–175. What connection might there be between the things below? Note your ideas and discuss them with a partner. Then check your ideas as you read the passage.

PREDICTING

Toucan bills and car safety _____

_____

Shark scales and swimsuits _____

_____

DESIGN BY NATURE

🎧 2.08

A All living organisms are **uniquely** adapted to the environment in which they live. Scientists are studying the design and the biological **processes** of these organisms to get ideas for products and technologies. This field of study is called biomimetics. Here are two examples.

TOUCAN BILLS AND CAR SAFETY

B Toucan bills are so enormous that it's surprising the birds don't fall on their faces. One species of toucan, the toco toucan, has an orange-yellow bill that is six to nine inches (15–23 centimeters) long—about a third of the bird's entire length. Biologists aren't sure why toucans have such large, colorful bills. Charles Darwin[1] theorized that these bills attract mates. Other researchers think that the large bills are used for cutting fruit, for fighting, or for warning predators to stay away. A new study suggests that the enormous bills help control body temperature—the more blood flows into the bill, the more the toucan can cool down.

C One thing scientists are certain of is that the toucan's beak is designed to be both strong and light. The **surface** is made of keratin, the same material in human fingernails and hair. But the inside of the bill has a foam-like structure, and is made up of a network of light, thin pieces of bone. It contains a lot of air, and some areas of the beak are hollow, not **solid**. This design makes the bill hard but very light.

D Marc André Meyers is a materials scientist at the University of California, San Diego. He thinks the automotive and aviation **industries** can use the design of the toucan bill to make cars and planes safer. Studies show that the beak's structure can absorb high-energy impacts very well. "[Car body panels] that mimic[2] toucan bills may offer better protection to motorists **involved** in crashes," Meyers says.

Foam

Keratin

Hollow core

[1] **Charles Darwin** was a 19th-century English naturalist who developed the theory of evolution by natural selection.

[2] To **mimic** means to copy or imitate.

Despite its size, the toucan's bill is very light.

SHARK SCALES AND SWIMSUITS

E Shark skin may look smooth, but it's actually rough. Sharks are covered in scales made from the same material as their teeth. Viewed up close, the scales actually look like tiny teeth. These scales protect the shark and help to keep it clean. They are also flexible and can turn or bend in the water. This movement reduces the water's drag[3] on the shark and helps it to swim quickly.

F Amy Lang, an aerospace engineer at the University of Alabama, studied the scales on the shortfin mako. Shortfin makos are one of the fastest and strongest fish in the ocean, and are a relative of the great white shark. Lang and her team discovered that the shortfin mako's scales **vary** in size and flexibility over its body. For instance, the scales on the sides of the body are tapered—wide at one end and narrow at the other. Because they are tapered, these scales move very easily. They can turn up or flatten to **adjust** to the flow of water around the shark and to reduce drag.

G Lang believes that shark scales can inspire designs for machines that experience drag, such as airplanes. Coating airplanes with a material that mimics shark skin would probably help increase their speed. Designers are also getting ideas from shark scales for designing swimwear and coating ship bottoms.

[3]**Drag** is a force that opposes the motion of an object moving in water or air.

A close-up view of shark skin shows tooth-like scales.

UNDERSTANDING THE READING

UNDERSTANDING
THE MAIN IDEA

A Write a definition of *biomimetics* in your own words.

_____

_____

IDENTIFYING
DETAILS

B Scan the reading passage for information to complete the chart below. Note your answers to the following questions.

1. What are the biological purposes (or possible purposes) of each animal part?
2. What products or technologies are these animal parts inspiring?

	Purposes	Products/Technologies
 Toucan bills		
 Shark scales		

IDENTIFYING
THEORIES

C Look back at paragraph B of the reading passage. Underline three theories and circle the words that introduce them.

CRITICAL THINKING:
APPLYING

D Read the following. Check (✓) the options that are examples of biomimetics. Then discuss your answers with a partner.

☐ 1. putting bird feathers in a jacket to stay warm in cold weather
☐ 2. designing a glider based on the movements of a Draco lizard
☐ 3. inventing a material for making cars that has the same structure as a toucan bill
☐ 4. attaching shark skin to the bottom of a ship to make it go faster in the water

CRITICAL THINKING:
SYNTHESIZING

E Find three animals mentioned earlier in this unit. How is each one uniquely adapted to its environment? Discuss with a partner.

Writing

EXPLORING WRITTEN ENGLISH

A The sentences below are excerpts from the reading passages. Match the underlined words in the sentences to the words in the box (a–e) that have the same meaning. Then refer back to the reading passages to check your answers.

NOTICING

> **a** young   **b** look like   **c** theory   **d** evolved   **e** new

_____ 1. Discoveries such as this are helping scientists understand how and why feathers <u>developed</u>.

_____ 2. They think this shows that the dinosaurs were using feathers to keep their <u>babies</u> warm.

_____ 3. Another <u>idea</u> is that feathers evolved for display—that is, to be seen.

_____ 4. A <u>recent</u> study suggests that the enormous bills help control body temperature.

_____ 5. Viewed up close, the scales actually <u>resemble</u> tiny teeth.

LANGUAGE FOR WRITING Using Synonyms

When you write a summary of a passage, you should restate information as much as possible in your own words. This is also known as paraphrasing. One way to do this is to replace some of the original words or phrases with synonyms—words that have a similar meaning. For example, look at the two sentences below:

Original: *Some paleontologists speculate that feathers began as a kind of insulation.*

Paraphrase: *Some experts think that feathers initially developed as a way for animals to keep warm.*

> *paleontologists* → *experts*
>
> *speculate* → *think*
>
> *began* → *initially developed*
>
> *a kind of insulation* → *a way to keep warm*

One way to find synonyms is to use a **thesaurus**, a type of dictionary that has synonyms and antonyms (words with an opposite meaning). Not all synonyms are an exact match for a word, so it's important to understand the context in which you are using a word in order to choose the best synonym. For example, look at the following sentence:

> The Stenocara *beetle uses its shell to collect drinking water from the atmosphere.*

Synonyms in a thesaurus for *atmosphere* might include: *air, sky, feeling,* and *mood.* Only *air* is correct in this context.

B Read the sentences below. Choose the best synonym for each underlined word.

1. This design makes the toucan bill <u>hard</u> but very light.
   a. difficult
   b. firm

2. The bird's feathers are <u>stiff</u> on one side.
   a. inflexible
   b. formal

3. The *Stenocara* beetle can survive in a very <u>dry</u> environment.
   a. uninteresting
   b. arid

4. The Draco lizard can be found in the <u>dense</u> rain forests of Southeast Asia.
   a. unintelligent
   b. thick

C Choose four sentences from the reading passages in this unit and paraphrase them. Include a synonym of at least one word in each sentence.

1. _____

   _____

2. _____

   _____

3. _____

   _____

4. _____

   _____

WRITING SKILL Writing a Summary Paragraph

When you write a summary paragraph, you explain the key ideas of an original text in your own words. A summary paragraph has the following characteristics:
- It's shorter than the original text.
- It includes all the key ideas but fewer details.
- It does not contain new information.
- It presents the key ideas in the same order as the original.
- It has a topic sentence that expresses the main idea of the original.
- It should not contain your own opinions.

To write a summary:
- First, read the original text and highlight the key ideas as you read.
- Then write the key ideas in your own words.

D Read the paragraph below about biomimetics. Highlight the key ideas as you read.

Scientists are studying the adaptations of living organisms in order to use their designs in products and technologies for humans. This field of study is known as biomimetics. Velcro is one example of biomimetics. In 1948, a Swiss engineer named George de Mestral removed a bur stuck to his dog's fur. De Mestral studied it under a microscope and noticed how well the hooks on the bur stuck to things. He copied the design to make a two-piece fastening device. One piece has stiff hooks like the ones on the bur. The other piece has soft loops that allow the hooks to attach to it.

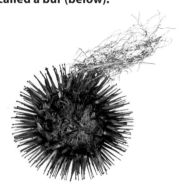

◀ **A close-up view of a piece of Velcro shows its hook-and-loop design, inspired by a type of seedpod called a bur (below).**

E Number the sentences (1–4) to put the key ideas in the same order as the original paragraph in exercise D.

_____ A Swiss engineer, George de Mestral, <u>noticed</u> how well a bur <u>stuck</u> to his dog's fur.

_____ An example of biomimetics is Velcro.

_____ He <u>made</u> a two-part fastener by mimicking the hooks on the bur and the softness of his dog's fur.

_____ Biomimetics involves studying the ways in which <u>organisms</u> adapt to their environments in order to develop useful products and technologies for <u>humans</u>.

F Now write the sentences from exercise E in the correct order to form a summary paragraph. Replace the underlined words with synonyms. Use a thesaurus to help you.

_____

_____

_____

_____

_____

_____

WRITING TASK

GOAL You are going to write a paragraph on the following topic:
Summarize a section of the reading passage on pages 174–175.

BRAINSTORMING **A** Without looking back at the reading passage on pages 174–175 ("Design by Nature"), try to remember the main ideas of each section. Note your ideas below. Check (✓) the section that you remember better.

☐ Toucan Bills and Car Safety: _____

_____

☐ Shark Scales and Swimsuits: _____

_____

PLANNING **B** Follow these steps to plan your summary paragraph.

Step 1 Choose a section of the reading passage to summarize. Write the title in the summary chart below.

Step 2 Read the section you chose again. Highlight the key ideas as you read.

Step 3 Paraphrase the key ideas of that section in the summary chart. Remember to keep the original ideas, but use your own words. Don't write complete sentences.

Step 4 Write a topic sentence that introduces the main idea of the original text.

SUMMARY

Title of Original Text: _____

Topic Sentence: _____

_____

Key Ideas: _____

_____

_____

_____

_____

_____

_____

_____

_____

FIRST DRAFT **C** Use the information in your summary chart to write a first draft of your paragraph.

REVISING PRACTICE

The drafts below are similar to the one you are going to write. They are summaries of the text entitled "Animal Adaptation" on page 165.

What did the writer do in Draft 2 to improve the paragraph? Match the changes (a–d) to the highlighted parts. Some can be used more than once.

a. used a synonym
b. made the topic sentence stronger
c. added a key idea from the original text
d. deleted new information

Draft 1

An adaptation is a change in a plant or an animal. These changes are the result of mutation. As more organisms inherit a mutation, it eventually becomes a normal characteristic of the species. In other words, the mutation becomes an adaptation. There are two kinds of adaptation: physical and behavioral. A desert plant that can store its own water is an example of a physical adaptation. Whale migration is an example of behavioral adaptation. Canadian geese flying south during the winter is another example of behavioral adaptation. Occasionally an adaptation occurs for a particular reason, but then evolves to have a different function.

Draft 2

An adaptation is a change in a plant or an animal that helps it survive in its environment. These changes are caused by genetic mutations. As more organisms inherit a mutation, it eventually becomes a common feature of the species. In other words, the mutation becomes an adaptation. There are two kinds of adaptation: physical and behavioral. A desert plant that can store its own water is an example of a physical adaptation. Whale migration is an example of behavioral adaptation. Occasionally an adaptation occurs for a particular reason, but then evolves to have a different function. Feathers are an example of this type of adaptation.

D Now use the questions below to revise your paragraph.

REVISED DRAFT

- ☐ Is there a topic sentence that introduces the main idea of the original text?
- ☐ Does your paragraph include all the key ideas that were in the original?
- ☐ Are the key ideas in the same order as the original?
- ☐ Is there enough paraphrasing of the language of the original (i.e., use of synonyms)?
- ☐ Are there any unnecessary details and opinions?
- ☐ Does your paragraph contain information that is not in the original?

EDITING PRACTICE

Read the information below.

In sentences using synonyms, remember to:
- use a synonym that works in the same context as the original word.
- choose a synonym that is the same part of speech as the original word.

Circle the correct word to complete each sentence below.

1. Feathers are one of nature's most **well-dressed / elegant** inventions.

2. The baby bird was covered in **light / easy**, soft feathers.

3. Scientists think dinosaurs used feathers to keep their **young / new** warm.

4. Paleontologists found theropod fossils with their front limbs **broadcast / spread** over their nests.

5. Drops of water roll down the bumps on the *Stenocara* beetle's **bomb / shell**.

6. Mutations that are **friendly / helpful** to a plant or an animal are passed down from one generation to the next.

7. Koalas have adapted to mainly eat the **leaves / departs** of eucalyptus trees, which are native to Australia.

FINAL DRAFT **E** Follow these steps to write a final draft.

1. Check your revised draft for mistakes with synonyms.

2. Now use the checklist on page 218 to write a final draft. Make any other necessary changes.

UNIT REVIEW

Answer the following questions.

1. Which of the animals mentioned in this unit would you like to know more about? Why?

_____

_____

2. What are three characteristics of a summary paragraph?

a. _____

b. _____

c. _____

3. Do you remember the meanings of these words? Check (✓) the ones you know. Look back at the unit and review the ones you don't know.

Reading 1:

☐ advantage ☐ attract ☐ characteristic
☐ clue ☐ display AWL ☐ evidence AWL
☐ evolve AWL ☐ flexible AWL ☐ layer AWL
☐ theory AWL

Reading 2:

☐ adjust AWL ☐ industry ☐ involved AWL
☐ process AWL ☐ solid ☐ surface
☐ unique AWL ☐ vary AWL

SMART ADVICE

10

Sheryl Sandberg of Facebook delivers a speech at Tsinghua University, China.

ACADEMIC SKILLS

READING Taking notes (Part 2)
WRITING Giving details that support advice
GRAMMAR Using the zero conditional to give advice

THINK AND DISCUSS

1 What is the best piece of advice you have ever received?

2 Who would you talk to if you needed career

EXPLORE THE THEME

A **Look at the information on these pages and answer the questions.**

1. Which of the jobs mentioned here would you be interested in? Why?
2. Why do you think these job opportunities are increasing?

B **Match the correct form of the words in blue to their definitions.**

_____ (adv) in a detailed way; completely and carefully

_____ (n) a difficult task or problem

_____ (n) special skill or knowledge in a particular subject

THE FUTURE OF JOBS

A study by Economic Modeling Specialists Intl. has revealed some of the fastest growing job areas in the United States. People who are thinking about making a career change or starting their own business should research these areas **thoroughly**.

Leading the way is the online shopping industry, where jobs are expected to increase by 32 percent between 2016 and 2021. Some jobs in this industry include software engineer, website designer, and personal shopper.[1] Translation and interpretation services are next. People in this industry have foreign language **expertise**. They usually translate books and other documents, or speeches at business and government meetings. Also on the list are jobs related to environmental, conservationist, and wildlife organizations. People who work for these organizations deal with **challenges** like reducing pollution and protecting endangered animals.

[1] A **personal shopper** is someone who helps people shop by giving advice and making suggestions.

The fastest growing jobs
Expected job growth between 2016 and 2021 in the U.S.

Online shopping	79,919 new jobs expected	**32% increase**	
Translation and interpretation services	10,547	**28%**	
Physical, occupational, and speech therapy	92,217	**25%**	
Environmental, conservationist, and wildlife organizations	11,833	**19%**	
Computer system design services	183,682	**19%**	
Nail salon services	26,987	**19%**	
Pet care services	17,907	**18%**	
Sports and recreation instruction	26,238	**15%**	

An interpreter at the World Economic Forum, 2014

Reading 1

PREPARING TO READ

BUILDING
VOCABULARY

A The words in **blue** below are used in the reading passage on pages 187–188. Complete each sentence with the correct word. Use a dictionary to help you.

empower	exchange	monitor	reality	promote	funding	initiative

1. A(n) _____ is the act of giving or taking one thing in return for something else.

2. _____ refers to the state of things as they actually are, as opposed to imagined or theoretical ideas.

3. If you _____ something, you check its development or progress over a period of time.

4. _____ is money that is provided for a special purpose, especially by an organization or a government.

5. To _____ a product means to encourage people to buy, use, or support it.

6. When you _____ people, you give them the ability to take more control of their lives and become stronger.

7. If you have _____, you tend to make decisions and take action without needing other people to tell you what to do.

USING
VOCABULARY

B Discuss these questions with a partner.

1. What are your favorite subjects in school? What is your area of **expertise**?
2. What is the biggest **challenge** you have faced in school or at work? How did you overcome it?
3. What are some things a manager can do to **empower** employees?

BRAINSTORMING

C What three areas of your life would be most affected if you didn't have Internet access? Share your ideas with a partner.

1. _____   2. _____   3. _____

PREDICTING

D Skim the first and last paragraphs of the reading passage on pages 187–188. Then look at the pictures and captions. What do you think Ken Banks did? Complete the sentence below. Then check your ideas as you read the passage.

I think Ken Banks created _____

that helps _____

_____

SOCIAL ENTREPRENEURSHIP AND INNOVATION

INTERNATIONAL CASE STUDIES AND PRACTICE

KEN BANKS

KoganPage

TURNING IDEAS INTO REALITY

🎧 2.09

▲ Ken Banks addresses
an audience in
Washington, D.C.

A   The Internet has a huge influence on the lives of those who use it. It empowers people by enabling the global exchange of knowledge and information. However, many rural communities around the world still live in areas with little to no Internet access. As a result, they are largely cut off. An entrepreneur[1] named Ken Banks found a solution to this problem by using his expertise in mobile technology.

A SIMPLE SOLUTION TO A BIG PROBLEM

B   While working in South Africa in 2003 and 2004, Banks saw that there were many organizations that were trying to help local communities. Since many villages didn't have Internet access, communication was a big challenge. Banks noticed, however, that many villagers had cell phones.

C   Banks had an idea. He created some computer software called FrontlineSMS, which allows users to send information from computers without using the Internet. Users install[2] the software on a computer. Then they connect the computer to a cell phone. To send information, users select the people they want to send it to. The cell phone sends the information to groups of people as a text message. Individuals can then reply on their own cell phones, creating a two-way messaging system between phone users and the computer.

[1]An **entrepreneur** is a person who starts a business.
[2]When you **install** a computer program, you set it up or connect it for use on your computer.

D FrontlineSMS is free and can work almost anywhere in the world. In Malawi, a rural healthcare program uses it to contact patients. As a result, health workers no longer have to visit patients' homes to update medical records or pass along important information. The software has also been used to monitor elections in Nigeria and to help disaster relief efforts in Haiti. Today, it is used in over 190 countries.

CREATING A SUCCESSFUL PRODUCT

E FrontlineSMS is a good example of taking an idea and making it a reality. So what should you do if you have an idea for making the world a better place? Banks offers the following advice:

F Don't immediately try to get money—most donors[3] want to see that you have a good idea first. "[D]onors don't tend to respond so well to people who just reach for money without actually showing they can do something," Banks explains. So start by researching your idea or product thoroughly. Do people really need it? To find out if you have a good idea, go into the community and talk to people.

G Once you have a workable idea, promote it. Use all the social media tools that you can: Start a Facebook group, use Twitter, or create a website. Start a blog and write about what you're doing. Connect online with other people who are working in the same field as you. The more you post, the easier it will be for search engines to find you.

H If you have a good idea, and you've gotten your message out, people will notice you. Now is the time to try to get funding. Your social networks are a good place to start raising money. Waiting until you have gotten this far shows potential donors that you have initiative, Banks says. It also shows that you are committed.

I We're currently living in the best time to create a product that can reach millions of people. More and more entrepreneurs are developing and promoting products that have the potential to solve the world's greatest challenges. All you need is an idea. As Banks puts it, "Innovation … is about someone standing in a rural village somewhere and suddenly realizing, 'If I did this … *that* could happen.'"

[3]A **donor** is a person or group that gives something (e.g., money) to help a person or organization.

▶ "FrontlineSMS gives [people] tools to create their own projects and make a difference," Banks says.

UNDERSTANDING THE READING

A Choose the best alternative title for the reading passage.

UNDERSTANDING
THE MAIN IDEA

   a. Innovative Solutions to Improve the World
   b. Tips for Managing a Business in a Developing Country
   c. A Day in the Life of an Entrepreneur

B Answer the questions below using information from the reading passage.

UNDERSTANDING
DETAILS

1. What gave Ken Banks the idea for FrontlineSMS?

   _____

2. Why is FrontlineSMS a good solution for developing countries?

   _____

3. What is one example of how FrontlineSMS has been used?

   _____

4. According to Banks, what should you do if you have an idea for making the world a better place? Summarize his three steps.

   a. _____

   b. _____

   c. _____

C How does FrontlineSMS work? Number the steps from 1 to 5 to show the correct sequence.

IDENTIFYING
SEQUENCE

   _____ Cell phone users can reply to the text message.

   _____ The cell phone sends information as a text message from the computer.

   _____ Then they connect a cell phone to the computer.

   _____ Users select the people they want to send information to.

   _____ Users install the FrontlineSMS software on a computer.

> **CRITICAL THINKING** **Applying an idea** to another real-world situation can help you evaluate the pros and cons of that idea. Ask yourself: In what situation(s) would that idea be useful? Who would benefit most from it?

D How might FrontlineSMS be used to solve the following problems? Which situation would it be more useful for? Discuss your ideas in small groups.

CRITICAL THINKING:
APPLYING AN IDEA
TO A NEW CONTEXT

   1. to protect an endangered animal
   2. to help children who don't have access to education

E The writer states, "We're currently living in the best time to create a product that can reach millions of people." Why do you think this is? Discuss with a partner.

CRITICAL THINKING:
INFERRING

DEVELOPING READING SKILLS

> **READING SKILL** Taking Notes (Part 2)
>
> In Unit 3 (page 48), you learned why taking notes on a reading passage is helpful. You also learned about different types of graphic organizers and practiced how to complete a flow chart.
>
> Another note-taking method is to identify the main idea and the supporting details of each paragraph, or section, as you read. If you read a long or difficult passage, you may forget some of the important ideas soon after you have finished reading. Summarizing the main ideas and details in a chart will help you review the content more easily later. See pages 8 and 28 for tips on identifying the main idea and details.
>
> When completing a summary chart, remember to note only the key points. Don't write complete sentences. Try to use your own words as much as possible.

TAKING NOTES **A** Complete the following chart with notes on "Turning Ideas into Reality" (pages 187–188).

Paragraph	Main Idea	Details
B	*how Banks got the idea for FrontlineSMS*	*- lived in S. Africa in 2003–04* *- trouble communicating w/out Internet, but had cell phones*
C		
D		
F		
G		
H		

APPLYING **B** Use the notes you took in exercise A to write a summary of "Turning Ideas into Reality." See Unit 9 (page 178) for tips on writing a summary paragraph.

Video

THE COMMUNITY BUILDER

Martín Andrade (kneeling) with local children at a project site in Chile

BEFORE VIEWING

A Read the information about Martín Andrade and his foundation. Then answer the questions.

LEARNING ABOUT THE TOPIC

The World Health Organization (WHO) recommends 9 square meters of green space per person. However, in certain urban areas of Chile, the reality falls short of this recommendation. While working as an architect in Santiago, Martín Andrade became aware that most of the public spaces in the city's poor areas were dirty and ugly. Many families didn't have access to beautiful green parks where they could spend time with their loved ones or enjoy nature. Andrade believed that if nothing was done to improve these public spaces, future generations born into this environment would be more vulnerable[1] to drug and alcohol abuse. He and a few other architects therefore started a foundation with the aim of improving the lives of low-income Chilean families. Because of his work, Andrade was named Chile's "Social Entrepreneur of the Year" in 2012.

[1]If you are **vulnerable** to something, you can be easily harmed or affected by it.

1. What problem did Andrade notice in Chile?

    _____

2. What is the goal of his foundation?

    _____

3. How do you think the foundation attempts to achieve this goal?

    _____

B Below are some quotes from the video. Match the correct form of each **bold** word or phrase to its definition.

> "… the scenery in many places is **breathtaking**."
>
> "Mi Parque … was **founded** by Martín Andrade and a few other architects."
>
> "Don't let the big problems facing society **get you down**."

1. _____ (v) to set up or establish (an institution or organization)

2. _____ (v) to make you feel sad or lose hope

3. _____ (adj) extremely beautiful or amazing

WHILE VIEWING

A ▶ Watch the video. Check (✓) the topics that are discussed.

☐ 1. how Andrade's career as an architect began

☐ 2. the lack of green space in some Chilean communities

☐ 3. how the foundation gathered construction materials for its first park

☐ 4. the foundation's plans to expand to other countries

B ▶ Watch the video again and answer the questions below.

1. What was one of the biggest challenges Andrade faced in getting his foundation started?

   _____

2. Which achievement is Andrade most proud of?

   _____

3. What two pieces of advice does Andrade give to people who want to start their own foundation?

   a. _____

   b. _____

AFTER VIEWING

A How might increasing people's access to green spaces improve their quality of life? Discuss your ideas with a partner.

B In the video, Andrade says:

"If you're focused on the resources that you currently have, you'll find that there are simple things that you can do now to make the world a better place."

What are some "simple things" that can make a difference? Find three examples from this book or use your own ideas. Discuss with a partner.

Reading 2

PREPARING TO READ

A The words in **blue** below are used in the reading passage on pages 194–195. Complete each sentence with the correct form of the word. Use a dictionary to help you.

BUILDING
VOCABULARY

passion	sensible	defining	consumer
quality	worth	reputation	demanding

1. A _____ person shows good judgment and makes careful decisions.

2. Given the rise in college fees, some students aren't sure if getting a college education is _____ the cost.

3. When choosing a college, students will usually think about whether the school has a good academic _____ .

4. Many _____ who own Apple products are very loyal. They are more likely to buy Apple products than similar items from other companies.

5. One way to figure out what type of career you will enjoy is to think about what activities you love doing and have a _____ for.

6. People who are _____ are not easily satisfied or pleased.

7. Graduating from college is a _____ moment for many people. It usually marks the time when people first enter the workforce.

8. Attention to detail is an important factor in making sure that products are of the highest _____ .

B Discuss these questions with a partner.

USING
VOCABULARY

1. Besides graduating from college, what are some other **defining** moments in our lives?
2. What are some brands that are known for having excellent product **quality**?
3. Who is the most **sensible** person you know? Describe that person.

C The reading passage on pages 194–195 is about business lessons that Guy Kawasaki has learned throughout his career. Scan the reading passage for the lessons he has learned, and note them below. Then check your answers as you read the passage.

PREDICTING

_____

_____

_____

LESSONS IN BUSINESS

Tech entrepreneur Guy Kawasaki speaks at a festival in Austin, Texas.

🎧 2.10

A   Guy Kawasaki is perhaps best known for his efforts in promoting Apple's early products like the Macintosh computer. He has since gone on to build a career as a successful entrepreneur, author, and speaker. Along the way, he has learned many important lessons from the people he's worked with.

B   After receiving his M.B.A. from UCLA in 1979, Kawasaki entered the jewelry business. The president of the company he worked for was a man named Martin Gruber. One of the biggest lessons Kawasaki learned from Gruber was how to sell a product. "It's not about selling a commodity[1] or the features of a product but to sell the benefits," Kawasaki says. This lesson proved to be valuable in his next job at Apple.

C   Working at Apple was the turning point in Kawasaki's life. At the time, the company was just starting to take off. Kawasaki gave himself the job title "chief evangelist." As an evangelist, he promoted Apple's products and shared his **passion** for them with other people.

D   Kawasaki learned how to handle office politics from Al Eisenstat, general counsel[2] at Apple. "[Eisenstat] showed me how corporate politics works—to not burn your bridges and to be nice to everyone," he explains. This **sensible** piece of advice helped Kawasaki during a power struggle between the company's leaders in the mid-80s.

[1] A **commodity** is a product (as opposed to a service) that is sold for money.
[2] A **general counsel** is a company's chief lawyer.

Another leader who influenced Kawasaki was Steve Jobs, co-founder of Apple. Kawasaki worked for Jobs—a famously tough boss—not once, but twice. He has described working for Jobs as one of the defining experiences of his life. Here are four things Kawasaki learned from the Apple boss:

People cannot describe their needs. Customers often don't know what they want until they see it. For example, the first Apple computer was very different from the personal computers available at the time. Customers didn't know they needed something different until Apple created it. A successful entrepreneur identifies problems that need solving before anyone else does.

Design counts. *Simple. Elegant. Fun.* All these words describe Apple's design philosophy. Apple products are well-known for their beautiful design, and enjoy great sales as a result. If your product looks good, consumers will be more likely to buy it, even if the price is high. An attractive design tells consumers that a product is of good quality and is worth the price.

You get the best results when you give people big goals. Don't simplify things for employees; give them big challenges instead. Jobs was well-known for his attention to detail. In fact, he had a reputation for being a very demanding boss. But, as Kawasaki explains, "I, and Apple employees before me and after me, did their best work because we had to do our best work to meet the big challenges."

Most experts are clueless. Experts—including consultants, analysts, and journalists—are often disconnected from customers. So don't trust the experts—their opinions aren't always accurate. As Kawasaki puts it, "Steve Jobs did not listen to experts … [E]xperts listened to him." Kawasaki advises entrepreneurs to do their own research and to reach out to consumers directly. The best way to do this, he says, is by using social media.

▼ **Apple co-founder Steve Jobs, 1988**

SELLING A PRODUCT

Here are four tips from Guy Kawasaki on using social media to sell a product:

1. Post frequently.

2. Post things that improve people's lives.

3. Include a video or a picture with every post.

4. Repeat your posts, because people live in different time zones and work on different schedules.

UNDERSTANDING THE READING

UNDERSTANDING
THE MAIN IDEA

A What is the main purpose of the reading passage?

a. to explain why Steve Jobs was a great boss
b. to describe what it is like to work for Apple
c. to share important business lessons from Guy Kawasaki

IDENTIFYING
OPINIONS

B Would Guy Kawasaki agree with the following statements? Circle **Y** (Yes), **N** (No), or **NG** (Not Given) if there isn't enough information in the reading passage.

1. When selling a product, it's more important to describe its features than its benefits.	Y	N	NG
2. Entrepreneurs should design products based on what consumers say they want.	Y	N	NG
3. Consumers are more likely to value design over price.	Y	N	NG
4. Entrepreneurs should keep environmental issues in mind when designing a product.	Y	N	NG
5. It's important to give employees challenging tasks.	Y	N	NG
6. It's important to rely on experts if you're starting a business.	Y	N	NG
7. When using social media to promote something, you should post the same information more than once.	Y	N	NG

CRITICAL THINKING:
INFERRING MEANING

C Find and underline the following **bold** words and phrases in the reading passage. Use context to identify their meanings. Then match each word or phrase to its definition.

turning point (paragraph C)   **power struggle** (paragraph D)
take off (paragraph C)   **philosophy** (paragraph G)
burn your bridges (paragraph D)   **clueless** (paragraph I)

1. _____ (n) a fight for control between two or more people

2. _____ (n) a time when an important change happens

3. _____ (n) a set of ideas about how to do something

4. _____ (adj) having no knowledge about a particular subject

5. _____ (v) to suddenly start being successful

6. _____ (v) to do something that makes it impossible to return to an earlier situation or relationship

CRITICAL THINKING:
SYNTHESIZING

D Compare the advice given by Ken Banks, Martín Andrade, and Guy Kawasaki. What similarities or differences do you see? Discuss with a partner.

Writing

EXPLORING WRITTEN ENGLISH

A Read the sentences (1–4). Then answer the question below.

NOTICING

1. <u>If you have a good idea for a new product</u>, you should promote it on social media.

2. Go into the community and talk to people <u>if you want to find out whether they like your idea</u>.

3. <u>If you have an idea for making the world a better place</u>, you should follow Ken Banks's advice.

4. Pay attention to product design <u>if you want consumers to buy your product</u>.

What do the underlined clauses show?

a. something that happens as a result of something else

b. a condition that can cause something to happen

LANGUAGE FOR WRITING Using the Zero Conditional to Give Advice

Conditional sentences include an *if* clause and a result clause. The *if* clause states a condition, and the result clause explains what happens when the condition occurs. In zero conditional sentences, we use the simple present tense in both clauses.

We can use the zero conditional with modal verbs to give advice. For example:

*If a company wants to promote a new product, it **should use** social media.*

*If you want to find out whether a school has a good academic reputation, you **can check** its ranking.*

We can also use the zero conditional with imperative verbs to give advice. For example:

*If you want to make a good impression at a job interview, **dress** professionally.*

*If you want to start your own web design company, **research** the industry thoroughly.*

Note that when the *if* clause appears at the beginning of a sentence, it is followed by a comma. When the *if* clause appears at the end of a sentence, there is no comma.

Dress professionally if you want to make a good impression at a job interview.

You should join a club or association if you want to make new friends in college.

B Match the following conditions and results.

Conditions	Results
____ 1. need money for college fees	a. shouldn't simplify things for employees
____ 2. want to apply for an internship	b. visit lots of campuses
____ 3. want to find the right college	c. get a part-time job
____ 4. want your business to succeed	d. talk to a career counselor

C Using the conditions and results in exercise B (page 197), write four sentences giving advice.

1. If _____

   _____

2. _____

   if _____

3. If _____

   _____

4. _____

   if _____

D In each pair of phrases, underline the condition. Then combine the condition and result phrases into zero conditional sentences.

1. talk to your teacher / you don't understand your homework assignment

   _____

   _____

2. you can't afford to pay for college / you can apply for a scholarship

   _____

   _____

3. you can't decide on a college major / take time to try out different classes

   _____

   _____

4. you should talk to your manager / you have a problem with another employee

   _____

   _____

WRITING SKILL Giving Details that Support Advice

As you learned in Unit 2, detail sentences give descriptions, reasons, facts, and examples about supporting ideas to help the reader understand them. When you write about advice, it's important to include details that explain:

- *why* the advice is important.
- *how* to follow the advice.

The following paragraph gives advice on how to succeed at a new job. What does each colored sentence do?

If you want to succeed at a new job, follow these tips. First, find a mentor who can show you how to do your job well. A mentor can teach you things that would take you a long time to learn on your own. To find a mentor, identify someone who has been working at the company for a long time and knows a lot about different jobs within the company. Second, you should . . .

The **red** sentence explains *why* it's important to find a mentor. The **blue** sentence describes *how* to find a mentor.

E The paragraph below summarizes Ken Banks's advice on page 188. Label the highlighted parts of the paragraph with these items (a or b).

a. a *why* detail sentence   b. a *how* detail sentence

According to Ken Banks, if you want to turn an idea into a product, you should follow these steps. First, make sure you research your idea or product thoroughly. Find out if people really need it. You don't want to spend time working on something that isn't really useful. To find out if you have a good idea, go into the community and talk to people. Once you have a workable idea, start promoting it. Use all the social media tools that you can: Start a Facebook group, use Twitter, create a website, or write a blog. The more you post, the easier it will be for search engines to find you. Finally, after you've gotten your message out, try to get funding. You can use your social networks to help raise money. Waiting until you have gotten this far shows potential donors that you have initiative and you are committed to the product.

F Look back at Guy Kawasaki's advice on page 195. Write *why* or *how* detail sentences for each of the following supporting ideas.

1. If you want to know what customers need, don't ask the customers themselves.

   Why: _____

2. Pay attention to product design if you want consumers to buy your product.

   Why: _____

3. Don't simplify things for employees; give them big challenges instead.

   Why: _____

4. Don't rely on expert opinions.

   Why: _____

   How: _____

WRITING TASK

GOAL You are going to write a paragraph on the following topic:

Imagine someone has asked you for advice about preparing to go to college. What advice would you give?

BRAINSTORMING **A** Below are some topics that people might need advice about when they are preparing to go to college. Check (✓) the one that you know the most about.

☐ how to choose a college
☐ how to make friends in college
☐ how to choose a major
☐ how to pay for college

With a partner, brainstorm at least three tips for the topic you chose.

_____

_____

_____

PLANNING **B** Follow these steps to complete an outline for your paragraph.

Step 1 Write your three best tips from exercise A in the outline below.

Step 2 Write *why* or *how* details that explain the advice in each supporting idea. Don't worry about grammar or spelling. Don't write complete sentences.

Step 3 Write a topic sentence that introduces your supporting ideas.

Step 4 Write a concluding sentence for your paragraph.

OUTLINE

Topic Sentence: _____

_____

Supporting Idea (Tip 1): _____

Detail(s): _____

Supporting Idea (Tip 2): _____

Detail(s): _____

Supporting Idea (Tip 3): _____

Detail(s): _____

Concluding Sentence: _____

_____

FIRST DRAFT **C** Use the information in your outline to write a first draft of your paragraph.

REVISING PRACTICE

The drafts below are similar to the one you are going to write, but they are on a different topic:

Imagine someone has asked you for advice about how to deal with a difficult colleague. What advice would you give?

What did the writer do in Draft 2 to improve the paragraph? Match the changes (a–d) to the highlighted parts. Some can be used more than once.

a. deleted unrelated information
b. corrected a conditional sentence
c. improved the concluding sentence
d. added a detail sentence

Draft 1

You have a problem with someone at work, you can try a few strategies to resolve the issue. Many people have trouble when they first start a new job. First, try telling your colleague that their behavior is bothering you. You can also try to avoid the person. Finally, you can try talking to your manager about your problem. Calmly describe the facts of the situation. Your manager may decide to fire your colleague or move them to a different department. This will create a more pleasant working environment.

Draft 2

If you have a problem with someone at work, you can try a few strategies to resolve the issue. First, try telling your colleague that their behavior is bothering you. This is a good idea because the colleague might not even realize that their behavior is bothersome. You can also try to avoid the person. Minimize direct contact as much as possible, for example, by emailing rather than speaking face-to-face. Finally, you can try talking to your manager about your problem. Calmly describe the facts of the situation. Your manager may decide to fire your colleague or move them to a different department. These tips should help you deal with a difficult colleague and create a more pleasant working environment.

D Now use the questions below to revise your paragraph.

REVISED DRAFT

☐ Does the topic sentence introduce the main idea of the paragraph?
☐ Does the paragraph include three supporting ideas that relate to the main idea?
☐ Does the paragraph include details for the advice in the supporting ideas?
☐ Does the paragraph use the zero conditional correctly?
☐ Is there any information that doesn't belong?
☐ Is there a concluding sentence?

EDITING PRACTICE

Read the information below.

In sentences using the zero conditional to give advice, remember to:
- use the simple present tense in the *if* clause.
- use a modal verb or an imperative verb in the result clause.
- use the base form of the verb after a modal.
- use the base form of the verb in the imperative.
- use a comma after the *if* clause when it appears at the beginning of a sentence.
- not use a comma before the *if* clause when it appears at the end of a sentence.

Correct one mistake with the zero conditional in each sentence below.

1. If you want to make new friends in college attend as many school-related events as you can.

2. If you wanted to find out if a particular college is right for you, visit the campus before classes start.

3. You can apply for a scholarship, if you don't have enough money for college.

4. If you plan to ask your boss for a raise, you should writes a list of your recent accomplishments at work.

5. You can get a bank loan, if you don't have enough money to start a business.

6. If you want your employees to feel empowered, making sure that they have the necessary resources and expertise to do their jobs.

FINAL DRAFT   **E**   **Follow these steps to write a final draft.**

1. Check your revised draft for mistakes with the zero conditional.

2. Now use the checklist on page 218 to write a final draft. Make any other necessary changes.

UNIT REVIEW
Answer the following questions.

1. Which piece of advice in this unit do you find most helpful? Why?

_____

_____

2. What are two ways you can use the zero conditional to give advice?

_____

_____

3. Do you remember the meanings of these words? Check (✓) the ones you know. Look back at the unit and review the ones you don't know.

Reading 1:

☐ challenge AWL   ☐ empower   ☐ exchange

☐ expertise AWL   ☐ funding AWL   ☐ initiative AWL

☐ monitor AWL   ☐ promote AWL   ☐ reality

☐ thoroughly

Reading 2:

☐ consumer AWL   ☐ defining AWL   ☐ demanding

☐ passion   ☐ quality   ☐ reputation

☐ sensible   ☐ worth

VOCABULARY EXTENSION   UNIT 1

WORD PARTNERS Expressions with *living*

Below are definitions for common expressions with the word *living*.

standard of living: the level of wealth someone has

cost of living: the average cost of the basic necessities of life

living the dream: experiencing the achievement of all your career or life goals

make a living: to earn enough money from a job to pay for housing, food, etc.

do (something) for a living: to have a job or career

A Complete each sentence using an expression from the box above.

1. It is hard to _____ as a waiter because wages are often quite low.

2. The well-educated generally enjoy a high _____.

3. The _____ in cities like San Francisco and New York is higher than in rural areas. One of the reasons is that housing is so expensive.

4. She has the job she has always wanted—she is _____!

5. He just finished college but is not sure yet what he wants to _____.

WORD FORMS Words as Nouns and Verbs

Some words can be both nouns and verbs. Some examples are *offer*, *pick*, and *taste*. If a word follows an adjective, it is more likely to be a noun.

NOUN
*She is the most hardworking **volunteer** at the hospital.*

VERB
*She **volunteers** at the local hospital every week.*

B Read the sentences below. Write **N** for *noun* or **V** for *verb* above each underlined word.

1. Many young adults get financial <u>support</u> from their parents when buying their first house.

2. Many homeless shelters need <u>volunteers</u> to help in the kitchen.

3. After three interviews, the company <u>offered</u> me the job.

4. People tend to be happier when they have easy <u>access</u> to good, affordable healthcare.

5. The supermarket <u>rewards</u> customers who shop regularly in the store by giving them a discount.

VOCABULARY EXTENSION   UNIT 2

Below are definitions for common collocations with the word *power*.

full power: the maximum amount of power that something can produce

solar power: electricity produced using energy from the sun

power failure: a loss of the electric power to a particular area

power line: a cable that carries electricity into a building

power plant: a building or group of buildings where electricity is produced

A Match the sentence parts in the columns to complete each sentence.

_____ 1. Some countries are building large nuclear   a. full power.

_____ 2. The storm brought down trees that cut several   b. solar power.

_____ 3. It takes a few minutes for the machine to reach   c. power plants.

_____ 4. The lights aren't working—there must be a   d. power failure.

_____ 5. A popular form of renewable energy is   e. power lines.

WORD LINK *-able* and *-ible*

Some adjectives end with the suffix *-able* or *-ible*, which means "able to." Adjectives formed from nouns and verbs often end in *-able* (e.g., *comfort—comfortable*). If the noun or verb ends in *-e*, drop the *-e* and add *-able* (e.g., *advise—advisable*).

Other adjectives not formed from nouns and verbs usually end in *-ible* (e.g., *incredible*).

B Circle the correct form of the word to complete each sentence.

1. Advances in technology have made many low-cost innovations **possable / possible**.

2. A patent—the exclusive legal right to make or sell an invention for a limited period of time—can be a very **valueable / valuable** business asset.

3. Most mobile apps are **compatable / compatible** with different smartphone models.

4. The baby-warmer invention is an **affordable / affordible** solution for developing countries.

5. Space travel became technologically **feasable / feasible** in the twentieth century.

VOCABULARY EXTENSION   UNIT 3

Some collocations are in adjective + noun form. Adding an adjective before the word *contribution* gives more information about the kind of contribution being described. Below are some common collocations with *contribution*.

positive contribution	small contribution
scientific contribution	large contribution
financial contribution	generous contribution

A Circle the correct word to complete each sentence.

1. Most crowdsourcing participants are not professional scientists. However, projects are carefully designed so that anyone can make a **generous / scientific** contribution.

2. By taking part in scientific online experiments, participants feel like they are making a **positive / financial** contribution to advancing human knowledge.

3. Crowdfunding projects raise money through **financial / positive** contributions from a large number of people.

4. Anyone who makes a contribution to a crowdfunding campaign, even if it is a **small / large** contribution, can make a difference.

5. People who make **scientific / large** contributions to crowdfunding campaigns receive certain rewards. For example, donors who gave over $2,299 to one campaign received a 3D printer.

WORD LINK *-al*

The suffix *-al* can mean "relating to." Add *-al* to some nouns to make them adjectives. For example, *global* means "relating to the whole world" (i.e., the globe).

B Complete each sentence using a word from the box below.

environmental	global	normal	tribal	virtual

1. Greenpeace and other _____ groups use the Internet to inform the public about pollution issues.

2. For many teenagers today, it is _____ to communicate with each other mainly through social media websites.

3. Some researchers think that _____ communities are not a good substitute for meeting people face-to-face.

4. English has become a(n) _____ language—there are English speakers in most countries around the world today.

5. Some _____ groups are concerned about the threat of logging to their traditional way of life.

VOCABULARY EXTENSION   UNIT 4

WORD FORMS   Changing Nouns into Adjectives

Some nouns can be made into adjectives by adding -ial, which means "connected or related to." For nouns ending in -e or -y, drop the -e or -y and add -ial.

NOUN	ADJECTIVE
commerce	commercial
industry	industrial

A   Complete each sentence using the adjective form of a word from the box below.

> commerce   face   finance   manager   office

1. The government's _____ definition of unemployment includes people who are "jobless, actively seeking work, and available to take a job."

2. According to one estimate, _____ fishing has wiped out 90 percent of large fish in the ocean.

3. A key _____ skill is the ability to motivate employees.

4. A(n) _____ advisor gives clients advice on how to manage their money.

5. _____ expressions are an important form of nonverbal communication.

WORD PARTNERS   verb + on

Many collocations are formed with prepositions like *in, on,* or *out.* Below are definitions for common collocations with the preposition *on.*

rely on: to depend on someone or something

get on: to have a good relationship with someone

build on (success): to continue to achieve more success

take on (work): to begin to deal with more work

move on: to progress or become more modern

B   Complete each sentence using the correct form of a collocation from the box above.

1. We _____ the ocean for many things including food and oxygen.

2. In the past, local fishermen used traditional gear like spears and hooks to catch fish. Modern fishing technology has _____ a great deal since then.

3. Many well-known chefs _____ their success by publishing cookbooks and presenting cooking shows on TV.

4. Waiters who _____ well with customers often receive a bigger tip.

5. Since becoming the office manager, she has had to _____ new responsibilities.

VOCABULARY EXTENSION   UNIT 5

WORD FORMS Changing Nouns and Adjectives into Verbs

The suffix -ize means "cause to become." Add -ize to some nouns and adjectives to make them into verbs. For nouns and adjectives ending in -y, drop the -y and add -ize.

ADJECTIVE	**VERB**
visual	visualize
NOUN	**VERB**
memory	memorize

A Complete each sentence using the verb form of a word from the box below.

> hospital   memory   modern   social   summary

1. I have a history test tomorrow. I need to _____ a lot of dates and names of places.

2. The community center is a good place for people to _____ with their neighbors.

3. The business will lose money if it doesn't _____ and adopt new technology.

4. A good reading comprehension strategy is to _____ the article in your own words.

5. A doctor may quickly _____ a patient if that patient needs immediate medical care.

WORD PARTNERS Expressions with *state*

Below are definitions for common expressions with the word *state*.

state of affairs: a situation or set of circumstances

state of emergency: a severe situation in which the government has increased powers to deal with a problem

state of repair: the physical condition of something (e.g., a building)

state of shock: the condition of being very upset because of something unexpected

state-of-the-art: the best available or the newest

B Complete the information using the expressions from the box above.

According to a recent report, the average age of a typical American public school building is 44 years. Some of these schools are in a bad ¹_____—broken roofs, doors, and windows. Other schools have poor lighting and heating systems. This ²_____ can lead to poor student performance.

Many people are in a ³_____ over the poor condition of American public schools. The cost of improving these schools is estimated to be about $145 billion. Unfortunately, many school districts already face funding shortfalls. Some authorities have declared a ⁴_____ in their school districts. More investment is needed to turn these public schools into modern, ⁵_____ centers of learning.

VOCABULARY EXTENSION   UNIT 6

WORD LINK *en-*

The prefix *en-* means "putting or causing to be in a certain condition." For example, if an animal is *endangered*, it is put in danger.

A Complete the paragraph using the correct form of the words from the box below.

> enact   encourage   endanger   enrich   ensure

In 1973, the U.S. ¹_____ a law to protect animals and plants threatened by extinction. The law ²_____ local authorities to look after a species before it becomes threatened. Scientists think this law has saved more than 200 critically ³_____ species. For example, the law helped ⁴_____ that there was adequate habitat for grizzly bears—today there are over five times as many grizzlies as in 1975. Conservationists think these amazing animals and plants ⁵_____ our environment and our lives in many ways.

WORD WEB Adjectives for Emotion

Using a variety of adjectives to accurately describe emotion can make your writing more interesting and effective. For example, instead of using *excited,* use *thrilled* to express more excitement or *pleased* to express less excitement.

B Complete the chart with the adjectives from the box below. Use a dictionary to help you.

> annoyed   distressed   furious   nervous   overjoyed   satisfied

LESS		EMOTION	MORE
		worried	
		angry	
		happy	

VOCABULARY EXTENSION   UNIT 7

WORD LINK ex-

The prefix *ex-* can mean "from" or "out of." For example, *extend* means "to stretch out from one place to another."

A Complete each sentence using the correct form of a word from the box below.

> exit   explain   explore   export   extend

1. After the airplane landed, the passengers _____ the plane through the front door.

2. The Amazon River _____ from the mountains of Peru to the coast of Brazil.

3. Many cavers have _____ the Krubera Cave—the world's deepest cave—in Georgia.

4. Scientists cannot fully _____ why some storms form into massive hurricanes and other storms don't.

5. Japan manufactures a large number of cars. In 2016, it _____ over $90 billion worth of cars to other countries around the world.

WORD FORMS Changing Adjectives into Adverbs

Many adverbs are formed by adding *-ly* to the end of adjectives. For adjectives ending in *-le*, replace the final *-e* with *-y*. For adjectives ending in *-y*, remove the final *-y* and add *-ily*.

ADJECTIVE	ADVERB
frequent	*frequently*
appropriate	*appropriately*
possible	*possibly*
easy	*easily*

B Circle the correct adjective or adverb in each sentence to complete the paragraph.

A [1]**particular / particularly** bad winter storm hit Argentina in July 2007. Snow fell in Buenos Aires for the first time in 89 years—an [2]**extreme / extremely** rare event. In [3]**remote / remotely** areas of the country, over 60 cm of snow fell. Temperatures were also [4]**significant / significantly** below normal. In the province of Rio Negro, temperatures dropped to –22 degrees Celsius. The storm left at least 46 people [5]**dead / deadly** in Argentina.

VOCABULARY EXTENSION UNIT 8

WORD PARTNERS adjective + *style*

Some collocations are in adjective + noun form. Adding an adjective before the word *style* gives more information about the kind of style being described. For example, if an item of clothing is in the *latest style*, that means it is up-to-date and popular.

A Circle the correct word to complete each sentence.

1. Many of architect Zaha Hadid's buildings have a **classical** / **modern** style. They feature unusual curves and non-traditional shapes.

2. Homeowners usually decorate their houses according to their own **personal** / **modern** style.

3. According to a recent survey, ranches—single-level homes—are the most **popular** / **regional** style of home for sale in the U.S. One reason people like them is because of their affordability.

4. The Southern house design is a **regional** / **personal** style developed in reaction to the hot, humid Southern climate of the United States.

5. The Parthenon, an ancient temple in Athens, Greece, is a good example of the **popular** / **classical** style of architecture.

WORD LINK *trans-*

The prefix *trans-* can mean "across" or "beyond." For example, to *transport* something means "to move it from one place to another." *Trans-* can also mean "to change completely." For example, *translate* means "to change from one language to another."

B Complete each sentence using the correct form of a word from the box below.

transact	transition	translate	transplant	transport

1. With the discovery of oil in the 1950s, Abu Dhabi _____ from a traditional economy to a global, oil-based economy.

2. The Abu Dhabi Crude Oil Pipeline can _____ up to 1.5 million barrels of oil per day.

3. When _____ from Arabic, *Abu Dhabi* means "Father of the Gazelle."

4. Abu Dhabi has a thriving healthcare sector. A new organ _____ center is scheduled to open in Abu Dhabi in 2018.

5. In a recent survey, Abu Dhabi ranked as one of the world's best cities to live, work, and _____ business in.

VOCABULARY EXTENSION   UNIT 9

Some collocations are in adjective + noun form. Adding an adjective before the word *advantage* gives more information about the kind of advantage being described. Below are some common collocations with *advantage*.

competitive advantage	full advantage
unfair advantage	main advantage
clear advantage	financial advantage
added advantage	mutual advantage

A Circle the correct word to complete each sentence.

1. With lower costs and higher profit margins, online booksellers have a **competitive** / **mutual** advantage over small bookstores.

2. A(n) **financial** / **added** advantage for online bookstores is that they also have a much larger range of books.

3. Some people like getting advice when they choose a book—a **clear** / **full** advantage for small bookstores that usually employ helpful staff.

4. Customers do not have to pay tax on purchases made at some online booksellers. Small bookstores are unhappy about this because it gives online booksellers a(n) **mutual** / **unfair** advantage.

5. Many customers take **main** / **full** advantage of days such as Cyber Monday when online booksellers offer big discounts.

The prefix *pro-* can mean "forward in place or time." For example, a *process* is a series of steps that lead to a particular result. Most of these kinds of *pro-* words include root words that do not typically mean anything on their own (e.g., the *-cess* in *process*).

B Match each word to its definition. Use a dictionary to help you.

_____ 1. promote   a. to assure someone that something will happen in the future

_____ 2. project   b. to defend against possible future harm

_____ 3. promise   c. to estimate or predict something based on current trends

_____ 4. proceed   d. to raise someone to a higher position or rank

_____ 5. protect   e. to start or continue an action or process

VOCABULARY EXTENSION   UNIT 10

WORD PARTNERS Expressions with *challenge*

Below are some common expressions with the word *challenge*.

*If a task **presents a challenge**, it appears to be difficult.*
*If you **meet a challenge**, you overcome or complete a difficult problem.*
*If a task is a **big challenge**, it is very difficult to do.*
*If you are looking for a **fresh challenge**, you are looking for something new and difficult to do.*

A Complete each sentence using the correct form of a word from the box below.

> big   fresh   meet   present

1. Climbing Mount Everest _____ a challenge for many climbers.

2. Edmund Hillary and Tenzing Norgay _____ that challenge when they became the first people to climb Everest in 1953.

3. Climbing a 40-foot vertical rock at the top of Everest was a _____ challenge for Hillary and Norgay.

4. After climbing Everest, Hillary wanted a _____ challenge, so he started an organization to build schools and hospitals for the Sherpa people of Nepal.

WORD PARTNERS Expressions with *quality*

Below are some common expressions with the word *quality*.

***Quality of life** is how good or bad a person's life is.*
***Air quality** is the degree to which the air in a particular place is pollution-free.*
***Star quality** is a special ability that makes someone seem better than other people.*
*If you spend **quality time** with someone, you give them all of your attention.*

B Write a sentence in response to each prompt. Use the **bold** expressions in your answers.

1. One way to improve your **quality of life**

   _____

2. One way to improve **air quality** in your city

   _____

3. Someone you think has **star quality**

   _____

4. Someone you like to spend **quality time** with

   _____

Independent Student Handbook

TIPS FOR READING FLUENTLY

Reading slowly, one word at a time, makes it difficult to get an overall sense of the meaning of a text. As a result, reading becomes more challenging and less interesting. In general, it is a good idea to first skim a text for the gist, and then read it again more closely so that you can focus on the most relevant details. Use these strategies to improve your reading speed:

- Read groups of words rather than individual words.
- Keep your eyes moving forward. Read through to the end of each sentence or paragraph instead of going back to reread words or phrases.
- Skip functional words (articles, prepositions, etc.) and focus on words and phrases carrying meaning—the content words.
- Use clues in the text—such as **bold** words and words in *italics*—to help you know which parts might be important and worth focusing on.
- Use section headings, as well as the first and last lines of paragraphs, to help you understand how the text is organized.
- Use context clues, affixes and parts of speech—instead of a dictionary—to guess the meaning of unfamiliar words and phrases.

TIPS FOR READING CRITICALLY

As you read, ask yourself questions about what the writer is saying, and how and why the writer is presenting the information at hand.

Important critical thinking skills for academic reading and writing:

- **Analyzing:** Examining a text in close detail in order to identify key points, similarities, and differences.

- **Applying:** Deciding how ideas or information might be relevant in a different context, e.g., applying possible solutions to problems.

- **Evaluating:** Using evidence to decide how relevant, important, or useful something is. This often involves looking at reasons for and against something.

- **Inferring:** "Reading between the lines"; in other words, identifying what a writer is saying indirectly, or *implicitly*, rather than directly, or *explicitly*.

- **Synthesizing:** Gathering appropriate information and ideas from more than one source and making a judgment, summary, or conclusion based on the evidence.

- **Reflecting:** Relating ideas and information in a text to your own personal experience and viewpoints.

TIPS FOR NOTE-TAKING

Taking notes will help you better understand the overall meaning and organization of a text. Note-taking also enables you to record the most important information for future uses— such as when you are preparing for an exam or completing a writing assignment. Use these techniques to make your note-taking more effective:

- As you read, underline or highlight important information such as dates, names, and places.

- Take notes in the margin. Note the main idea and supporting details next to each paragraph. Also note your own ideas or questions about the paragraph.

- On a separate piece of paper, write notes about the key points of the text in your own words. Include short headings, key words, page numbers, and quotations.

- Use a graphic organizer to summarize a text, particularly if it follows a pattern such as cause-effect, comparison-contrast, or chronological sequence. See page 48 for more information.

- Keep your notes brief by using these abbreviations and symbols. Don't write full sentences.

approx.	approximately	→	leads to / causes
e.g./ex.	example	↑	increases / increased
i.e.	that is / in other words	↓	decreases / decreased
etc.	and others / and the rest	& or +	and
Ch.	Chapter	b/c	because
p. (pp.)	page (pages)	w/	with
re:	regarding, concerning	w/o	without
incl.	including	=	is the same as
excl.	excluding	>	is more than
info	information	<	is less than

TIPS FOR LEARNING VOCABULARY

You often need to use a word or phrase several times before it enters your long-term memory. Here are some strategies for successfully learning vocabulary:

- Use flash cards to test your knowledge of new vocabulary. Write the word you want to learn on one side of an index card. Write the definition and/or an example sentence that uses the word on the other side.

- Use a vocabulary journal to note down a new word or phrase. Write a short definition of the word in English and the sentence where you found it. Write another sentence of your own that uses the word. Include any common collocations (see *Word Partners* in the Vocabulary Extensions).

- Make word webs or word maps. See below for an example.

- Use memory aids, or mnemonics, to remember a word or phrase. For example, if you want to learn the idiom *keep an eye on someone*, which means "to watch someone carefully," you might picture yourself putting your eyeball on someone's shoulder so that you can watch the person carefully. The stranger the picture is, the more likely you will remember it! See page 88 for more on mnemonics.

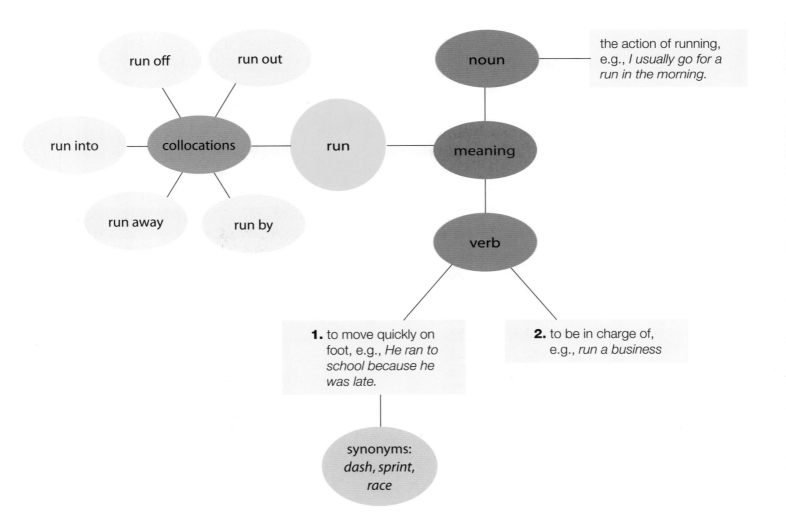

TIPS FOR ACADEMIC WRITING

There are many types of academic writing (descriptive, argumentative/persuasive, narrative, etc.), but most types share similar characteristics. Generally, in academic writing, you should:

- write in full sentences.
- use formal English. (Avoid slang or conversational expressions such as *kind of*.)
- be clear and coherent—keep to your main point; avoid technical words that the reader may not know.
- use signal words or phrases and conjunctions to connect your ideas. (See examples below.)
- have a clear point (main idea) for each paragraph.
- use a neutral point of view—avoid overuse of personal pronouns (*I*, *we*, *you*) and subjective language such as *nice* or *terrible*.
- use facts, examples, and expert opinions to support your argument.
- avoid using abbreviations or language used in texting. (Use *that is* rather than *i.e.*, and *in my opinion*, not *IMO*.)
- avoid using contractions. (Use *is not* rather than *isn't*.)
- avoid starting sentences with *or*, *and*, or *but*.

Signal Words and Phrases

Use signal words and phrases to connect ideas and to make your writing more academic.

Introducing supporting ideas	Giving details and examples
First (of all), …	One …
Secondly, …	An example of this is …
Another …	For example, …
Furthermore, …	For instance, …

Presenting similar ideas	Presenting contrasting ideas
Similarly, …	However, …
Both …	On the other hand, …
Like …	In contrast, …

Describing cause and effect	Describing a process
Therefore, …	First (of all), …
As a result, …	Then / Next / After that, …
Because of this, …	As soon as … / Once …
If …, then …	Finally, …

TIPS FOR EDITING

Capitalization

Remember to capitalize:

- the first letter of the word at the beginning of every sentence.
- proper nouns such as names of people, geographical names, company names, and names of organizations.
- days, months, and holidays.
- the word *I*.
- the first letter of a title such as the title of a movie or a book.
- the words in titles that have meaning (content words). Don't capitalize *a, an, the, and*, or prepositions such as *to, for, of, from, at, in,* and *on*, unless they are the first word of a title (e.g., *The Power of Creativity).*

Punctuation

- Use a period (.) at the end of any sentence that is not a question. Use a question mark (?) at the end of every question.
- Exclamation marks (!), which indicate strong feelings such as surprise or joy, are generally not used in academic writing.
- Use commas (,) to separate a list of three or more things. (*She speaks German, English, and Spanish.*)
- Use a comma after an introductory word or phrase. (*However, William didn't let that stop him.*)
- Use a comma before a combining word—*and, but, so, or*—that joins two sentences. (*Black widow spider bites are not usually deadly for adults, but they can be deadly for children.*)
- Use an apostrophe (') for showing possession. (*James's idea came from social networking websites.*)
- Use quotation marks (" ") to indicate the exact words used by someone else. (*"Our pleasures are really ancient," says psychologist Nancy Etcoff.*)

Other Proofreading Tips

- Print out your draft and read it out loud.
- Use a colored pen to make corrections on your draft so you can see them easily when you write your next draft.
- Have someone else read your draft and give you comments or ask you questions.
- Don't depend on a computer's spell-check. When the spell-check suggests a correction, make sure you agree with it before you accept the change.
- Check the spelling and accuracy of proper nouns, numbers, and dates.
- Keep a list of spelling and grammar mistakes that you commonly make so that you can be aware of them as you edit your draft.
- Check for frequently confused words:
  - *there, their,* and *they're*
  - *its* and *it's*
  - *your* and *you're*
  - *then* and *than*
  - *to, too,* and *two*
  - *whose* and *who's*
  - *where, wear, we're,* and *were*
  - *affect* and *effect*

EDITING CHECKLIST

Use the checklist to find errors in the second draft of your writing task for each unit.

	Unit				
	1	2	3	4	5
1. Is the first word of every sentence capitalized?					
2. Does every sentence end with the correct punctuation?					
3. Do your subjects and verbs agree?					
4. Are commas used in the right places?					
5. Do all possessive nouns have an apostrophe?					
6. Are all proper nouns capitalized?					
7. Is the spelling of places, people, and other proper nouns correct?					
8. Did you check for frequently confused words (see examples on page 217)?					

	Unit				
	6	7	8	9	10
1. Is the first word of every sentence capitalized?					
2. Does every sentence end with the correct punctuation?					
3. Do your subjects and verbs agree?					
4. Are commas used in the right places?					
5. Do all possessive nouns have an apostrophe?					
6. Are all proper nouns capitalized?					
7. Is the spelling of places, people, and other proper nouns correct?					
8. Did you check for frequently confused words (see examples on page 217)?					

GRAMMAR REFERENCE

UNIT 1
Language for Writing: Review of the Simple Present Tense

Affirmative and Negative Statements with *Be*					
Affirmative Statements			**Negative Statements**		
Subject	*Am/Are/Is*		Subject	*Am/Are/Is Not*	
I	**am**		I	**am not**	
You We They	**are**	happy. busy. online. at home.	You We They	**are not** **aren't**	happy. busy. online. at home.
He She It	**is**		He She It	**is not** **isn't**	

Affirmative and Negative Statements: Other Verbs				
Affirmative Statements		**Negative Statements**		
Subject	Verb	Subject	*Do/Does Not*	Verb (Base Form)
I You We They	**live** in Singapore.	I You We They	**do not** **don't**	**live** in Mexico.
He She It	**lives** in Singapore.	He She It	**does not** **doesn't**	

UNIT 2
Language for Writing: Review of the Simple Past Tense

Affirmative and Negative Statements with *Be*

Affirmative Statements			Negative Statements		
Subject	*Was/Were*		Subject	*Was/Were Not*	
I He She It	**was**	happy. busy. a doctor. a student. online. at home.	I He She It	**was not** **wasn't**	happy. busy. a doctor. a student. online. at home.
You We They	**were**		You We They	**were not** **weren't**	

Affirmative and Negative Statements: Other Verbs

Affirmative Statements		Negative Statements		
Subject	Verb (Past Form)	Subject	*Did Not*	Verb (Base Form)
I You We They He She It	**started** a project. **walked** home. **studied**. **went** to school.	I You We They He She It	**did not** **didn't**	**start** a project. **walk** home. **study**. **go** to school.

Past Forms of Commonly Used Irregular Verbs

become—became	fall—fell	read—read
begin—began	find—found	say—said
bring—brought	get—got	see—saw
build—built	give—gave	speak—spoke
buy—bought	have—had	take—took
choose—chose	hear—heard	tell—told
do—did	know—knew	think—thought
eat—ate	make—made	write—wrote

UNIT 3
Language for Writing: Using the Present Perfect Tense

Subject	*Have/Has (Not)*	Verb (Past Participle)	Time Marker (optional)
I You We They	**have** **have not / haven't**	**been** here **slept** **called** him	since last year. for 24 hours. recently.
He She It	**has** **has not / hasn't**		

Time Markers

Use *since* + a point in time, *for* + a length of time, *in the* + time period to describe something that began in the past and continues to the present.

> *I've lived in Denmark **since** 2010.*
> *He hasn't been here **for** three years.*
> *We've met a lot of people **in the past month**.*

Use *already* in affirmative statements to emphasize that something happened at an unspecified time in the past.

> *I've watched that movie **already**.*   *She's **already** gone home.*

Use *recently* or *lately* to emphasize that something happened or didn't happen at an unspecified time in the recent past.

> *Sarah has called several times **recently**.*   *The team hasn't shown much improvement **lately**.*

Use the present perfect tense when the time in the past is not important.

> *I **have been** to Fiji.*
> *He **has sung** that song many times.*
> *Her work **has protected** archaeological sites from looters.*

Past Participle Forms of Commonly Used Irregular Verbs

become—become	fall—fallen	read—read
begin—begun	find—found	say—said
bring—brought	get—gotten	see—seen
build—built	give—given	speak—spoken
buy—bought	have—had	take—taken
choose—chosen	hear—heard	tell—told
do—done	know—known	think—thought
eat—eaten	make—made	write—written

UNIT 5
Language for Writing: Using *By* + Gerund

Spelling Rules for Forming Gerunds

When forming gerunds, follow these rules for adding *-ing* to verbs:

1. Most verbs: Add *-ing*:

   sleep → sleeping   think → thinking   remember → remembering

2. Verbs that end with a consonant followed by *-e*: Drop the *-e* and add *-ing*:

   memorize → memorizing   store → storing   use → using

   By using *effective marketing techniques, companies can attract more customers.*

3. One-syllable verbs ending with a consonant + vowel + consonant: Double the final consonant and add *-ing*:

   get → getting   stop → stopping   put → putting

   (Exceptions: verbs that end in *-w*, *-x*, or *-y*; for example, say → saying)

   *You can get into college **by getting** good grades.*

4. Two-syllable verbs ending with a consonant + vowel + consonant, where the second syllable is stressed: Double the final consonant and add *-ing*:

   admit → admitting   begin → beginning   prefer → preferring

UNIT 8
Language for Writing: Using Comparative Adjectives

Spelling Rules for Forming Comparative Adjectives

When forming comparative adjectives, follow these rules:

1. With most one-syllable adjectives, add *-er*:

   hard → harder   fast → faster   slow → slower

2. With two-syllable adjectives ending in *-y*, change the *-y* to *-i* and add *-er*:

   easy → easier   busy → busier   happy → happier

3. With most adjectives of two or more syllables not ending in *-y*, use *more/less*:

   attractive → more attractive   famous → less famous

4. Some adjectives have irregular comparative forms:

   bad → worse   good → better

   *Mark's handwriting is **worse** than Mary's handwriting.*
   *The new design is **better** than the old design.*

UNIT 10
Language for Writing: Using the Zero Conditional to Give Advice

A zero conditional sentence includes an *if* clause and a result (or main) clause. In zero conditional sentences, we use the simple present tense in both clauses.

We usually use zero conditional sentences to describe general truths and facts.

If Clause (Condition)	Main Clause (Result)
If you heat ice,	it melts.
If a company goes out of business,	employees lose their jobs.
If someone gets promoted,	they receive a higher salary.

The zero conditional is often used with modal verbs to give advice. Include the modal verb in the result clause. The modal expresses ability, necessity, or permission. In the zero conditional sentence structure, you can use *should* or *can*, and their negative forms.

If Clause (Condition)	Main Clause (Result)
If you want to go to university,	you **should study** hard.
If you drink,	you **shouldn't drive**.
If you need advice about what to do,	you **can call** Bill.
If you have celiac disease,	you **can't eat** wheat.

We can also use the zero conditional with imperative verbs to give advice. Include the imperative verb in the result clause. These sentences are similar to saying: If the condition occurs, you must do this (in the result clause).

If Clause (Condition)	Main Clause (Result)
If you don't want to get lost,	**follow** the directions carefully.
If you want to be healthier,	**eat** less junk food and **exercise** more.
If you drink,	**don't drive**.

When the *if* clause appears at the end of a sentence, there is no comma between the clauses.

Main Clause (Result)	*If* Clause (Condition)
Employees lose their jobs	if a company goes out of business.
You should study hard	if you want to go to university.
Follow the directions carefully	if you don't want to get lost.

VOCABULARY INDEX

Word	Unit	CEFR Level	Word	Unit	CEFR Level
access*	1	B1	double(d)	4	B2
accurate*	3	B1	drug	5	B2
achievement*	5	B1	efficient	2	B1
adjust*	9	B2	electricity	2	A2
advance	6	B2	emotional	6	B2
advantage	9	B1	empower	10	-
advertise	3	B1	endanger(ed)	6	B2
afford	2	B1	environmental(ly)*	3	B2
appropriate*	7	B2	equal	1	B1
architect	8	B1	equipment*	2	B1
attract	9	B1	essential	4	B1
basic necessities	1	B2	estimate*	4	B2
benefit*	2	B1	eventually*	2	B2
block	7	B1	evidence*	9	B2
challenge*	10	B1	evolve*	9	C1
characteristic	9	B2	exchange	10	B1
climate	7	B1	experiment	6	B1
clue	9	B2	expertise*	10	B1
coast	7	B1	extend	7	B2
collaborate	3	C1	external*	5	B2
collide	7	-	factor*	1	B2
commercial	4	B2	familiar	5	B1
commit(ted) to*	8	B2	feature*	3	B2
community*	1	B2	financial*	1	B1
complex*	5	B2	flexible*	9	B2
concerned	6	B2	freedom	1	B2
condition	7	B1	frequent	7	B1
conduct*	6	B2	fuel	7	B1
consist of*	8	B1	funding*	10	C1
construct*	8	B2	global*	3	B2
consumer*	10	B2	gradual(ly)	5	B2
container	2	B2	grateful	1	B1
contribution*	3	B2	holy	8	C1
creative*	2	B1	identify*	2	B2
cure	6	B2	illustrate*	8	B2
data*	7	B2	impact*	4	B2
debate*	8	B2	indicate*	2	B2
declining*	4	B2	individual*	4	B1
defining*	10	B2	industry	9	B1
definite(ly)*	4	B2	informed	4	B1
demanding	10	B1	initiative*	10	C1
design*	2	B1	innovation*	2	C1
device*	2	B2	inspiration	8	B2
disease	6	B1	internal*	5	B2
display*	9	B1	invasive	6	-
diverse*	4	B2	investigate*	3	B2

Word	Unit	CEFR Level	Word	Unit	CEFR Level
involve(d)*	9	B1	side effect	6	C1
knowledge	6	B1	significant*	7	B2
laboratory	6	B1	socialize	1	B2
launch	3	B2	solid	9	B2
layer*	9	B2	species	4	B2
log in	3	B2	specific*	6	B2
long-term	1	B2	stable*	4	C1
memorize	5	B1	standard of living	1	B2
mental*	5	B2	state	5	B2
mission	6	B2	store	2	B1
monitor*	10	B2	stress*	5	B1
mood	1	B1	strike	7	B1
occur*	7	B2	structure*	8	B2
on purpose	7	B1	struggle	2	B2
on record	7	A2	style*	8	B1
participant*	3	C1	support	1	B2
particular(ly)	7	B1	surface	9	B2
passion	10	B2	survive*	4	B2
physical*	5	B2	symbol*	8	B2
possibility	6	B1	target*	6	B2
potential*	3	B2	technique*	5	B1
poverty	1	B2	temple	8	B1
power(ed)	2	B1	text*	5	A2
prevention	2	B1	theme*	8	B2
procedure*	6	B2	theory*	9	B2
process*	9	B2	thorough(ly)	10	B2
promote*	10	B1	threaten	7	B2
proof	5	B2	tool	3	B2
provide	1	B1	transfer*	5	B1
quality	10	B1	transport*	8	B1
quantity	4	B1	tribe	3	B2
reality	10	B2	unique(ly)*	9	B2
reduce	4	B1	valuable	2	B1
religious	8	B2	vary*	9	B2
rely on*	4	B2	violent	7	B2
remote	3	B2	virtual*	3	B2
represent	8	B2	visualize*	5	B2
reputation	10	B2	volunteer*	1	B2
require*	8	B1	voting	3	B1
resource*	6	B2	well-being	1	B1
restore*	4	B2	worth	10	B1
route*	5	B1			
sculpture	8	B1			
search	3	B1			
secure*	1	B2			
sensible	10	B1			
severe	4	B2			

*These words are on the Academic Word List (AWL). The AWL is a list of the 570 most frequent word families in academic texts. It does not include the most frequent 2,000 words of English.

ACKNOWLEDGMENTS

The Authors and Publisher would like to acknowledge the teachers around the world who participated in the development of the second edition of *Pathways*.

A special thanks to our Advisory Board for their valuable input during the development of this series.

ADVISORY BOARD

Mahmoud Al Hosni, Modern College of Business and Science, Oman; **Safaa Al-Salim**, Kuwait University; **Laila Al-Qadhi**, Kuwait University; **Julie Bird**, RMIT University Vietnam; **Elizabeth Bowles**, Virginia Tech Language and Culture Institute, Blacksburg, VA; **Rachel Bricker**, Arizona State University, Tempe, AZ; **James Broadbridge**, J.F. Oberlin University, Tokyo; **Marina Broeder**, Mission College, Santa Clara, CA; **Shawn Campbell**, Hangzhou High School; **Trevor Carty**, James Cook University, Singapore; **Jindarat De Vleeschauwer**, Chiang Mai University; **Wai-Si El Hassan**, Prince Mohammad Bin Fahd University, Saudi Arabia; **Jennifer Farnell**, University of Bridgeport, Bridgeport, CT; **Rasha Gazzaz**, King Abdulaziz University, Saudi Arabia; **Keith Graziadei**, Santa Monica College, Santa Monica, CA; **Janet Harclerode**, Santa Monica Community College, Santa Monica, CA; **Anna Hasper**, TeacherTrain, UAE; **Phoebe Kamel Yacob Hindi**, Abu Dhabi Vocational Education and Training Institute, UAE; **Kuei-ping Hsu**, National Tsing Hua University; **Greg Jewell**, Drexel University, Philadelphia, PA; **Adisra Katib**, Chulalongkorn University Language Institute, Bangkok; **Wayne Kennedy**, LaGuardia Community College, Long Island City, NY; **Beth Koo**, Central Piedmont Community College, Charlotte, NC; **Denise Kray**, Bridge School, Denver, CO; **Chantal Kruger**, ILA Vietnam; **William P. Kyzner**, Fuyang AP Center; **Becky Lawrence**, Massachusetts International Academy, Marlborough, MA; **Deborah McGraw**, Syracuse University, NY; **Mary Moore**, University of Puerto Rico; **Raymond Purdy**, ELS Language Centers, Princeton, NJ; **Anouchka Rachelson**, Miami Dade College, Miami, FL; **Fathimah Razman**, Universiti Utara Malaysia; **Phil Rice**, University of Delaware ELI, Newark, DE; **Scott Rousseau**, American University of Sharjah, UAE; **Verna Santos-Nafrada**, King Saud University, Saudi Arabia; **Eugene Sidwell**, American Intercon Institute, Phnom Penh; **Gemma Thorp**, Monash University English Language Centre, Australia; **Matt Thurston**, University of Central Lancashire, UK; **Christine Tierney**, Houston Community College, Houston, TX; **Jet Robredillo Tonogbanua**, FPT University, Hanoi.

GLOBAL REVIEWERS

ASIA

Antonia Cavcic, Asia University, Tokyo; **Soyhan Egitim**, Tokyo University of Science; **Caroline Handley**, Asia University, Tokyo; **Patrizia Hayashi**, Meikai University, Urayasu; **Greg Holloway**, University of Kitakyushu; **Anne C. Ihata**, Musashino University, Tokyo; **Kathryn Mabe**, Asia University, Tokyo; **Frederick Navarro Bacala**, Yokohama City University; **Tyson Rode**, Meikai University, Urayasu; **Scott Shelton-Strong**, Asia University, Tokyo; **Brooks Slaybaugh**, Yokohama City University; **Susanto Sugiharto**, Sutomo Senior High School, Medan; **Andrew Zitzmann**, University of Kitakyushu.

LATIN AMERICA AND THE CARIBBEAN

Raul Bilini, ProLingua, Dominican Republic; **Alejandro Garcia**, Colegio Marcelina, Mexico; **Humberto Guevara**, Tec de Monterrey, Campus Monterrey, Mexico; **Romina Olga Planas**, Centro Cultural Paraguayo Americano, Paraguay; **Carlos Rico-Troncoso**, Pontificia Universidad Javeriana, Colombia; **Ialê Schetty**, Enjoy English, Brazil; **Aline Simoes**, Way To Go Private English, Brazil; **Paulo Cezar Lira Torres**, APenglish, Brazil; **Rosa Enilda Vasquez**, Swisher Dominicana, Dominican Republic; **Terry Whitty**, LDN Language School, Brazil.

MIDDLE EAST AND NORTH AFRICA

Susan Daniels, Kuwait University, Kuwait; **Mahmoud Mohammadi Khomeini**, Sokhane Ashna Language School, Iran; **Müge Lenbet**, Koç University, Turkey; **Robert Anthony Lowman**, Prince Mohammad bin Fahd University, Saudi Arabia; **Simon Mackay**, Prince Mohammad bin Fahd University, Saudi Arabia.

USA AND CANADA

Frank Abbot, Houston Community College, Houston, TX; **Hossein Aksari**, Bilingual Education Institute and Houston Community College, Houston, TX; **Sudie Allen-Henn**, North Seattle College, Seattle, WA; **Sharon Allie**, Santa Monica Community College, Santa Monica, CA; **Jerry Archer**, Oregon State University, Corvallis, OR; **Nicole Ashton**, Central Piedmont Community College, Charlotte, NC; **Barbara Barrett**, University of Miami, Coral Gables, FL; **Maria Bazan-Myrick**, Houston Community College, Houston, TX; **Rebecca Beal**, Colleges of Marin, Kentfield, CA; **Marlene Beck**, Eastern Michigan University, Ypsilanti, MI; **Michelle Bell**, University of Southern California, Los Angeles, CA; **Linda Bolet**, Houston Community College, Houston, TX; **Jenna Bollinger**, Eastern Michigan University, Ypsilanti, MI; **Monica Boney**, Houston Community College, Houston, TX; **Nanette Bouvier**, Rutgers University – Newark, Newark, NJ; **Nancy Boyer**, Golden West College, Huntington Beach, CA; **Lia Brenneman**, University of Florida English Language Institute, Gainesville, FL; **Colleen Brice**, Grand Valley State University, Allendale, MI; **Kristen Brown**, Massachusetts International Academy, Marlborough, MA; **Philip Brown**, Houston Community College, Houston, TX; **Dongmei Cao**, San Jose City College, San Jose, CA; **Molly Cheney**, University of Washington, Seattle, WA; **Emily Clark**, The University of Kansas, Lawrence, KS; **Luke Coffelt**, International English Center, Boulder, CO; **William C. Cole-French**, MCPHS University,

Boston, MA; **Charles Colson**, English Language Institute at Sam Houston State University, Huntsville, TX; **Lucy Condon**, Bilingual Education Institute, Houston, TX; **Janice Crouch**, Internexus Indiana, Indianapolis, IN; **Charlene Dandrow**, Virginia Tech Language and Culture Institute, Blacksburg, VA; **Loretta Davis**, Coastline Community College, Westminster, CA; **Marta Dmytrenko-Ahrabian**, Wayne State University, Detroit, MI; **Bonnie Duhart**, Houston Community College, Houston, TX; **Karen Eichhorn**, International English Center, Boulder, CO; **Tracey Ellis**, Santa Monica Community College, Santa Monica, CA; **Jennifer Evans**, University of Washington, Seattle, WA; **Marla Ewart**, Bilingual Education Institute, Houston, TX; **Rhoda Fagerland**, St. Cloud State University, St. Cloud, MN; **Kelly Montijo Fink**, Kirkwood Community College, Cedar Rapids, IA; **Celeste Flowers**, University of Central Arkansas, Conway, AR; **Kurtis Foster**, Missouri State University, Springfield, MO; **Rachel Garcia**, Bilingual Education Institute, Houston, TX; **Thomas Germain**, University of Colorado Boulder, Boulder, CO; **Claire Gimble**, Virginia International University, Fairfax, VA; **Marilyn Glazer-Weisner**, Middlesex Community College, Lowell, MA; **Amber Goodall**, South Piedmont Community College, Charlotte, NC; **Katya Goussakova**, Seminole State College of Florida, Sanford, FL; **Jane Granado**, Texas State University, San Marcos, TX; **Therea Hampton**, Mercer County Community College, West Windsor Township, NJ; **Jane Hanson**, University of Nebraska – Lincoln, Lincoln, NE; **Lauren Heather**, University of Texas at San Antonio, San Antonio, TX; **Jannette Hermina**, Saginaw Valley State University, Saginaw, MI; **Gail Hernandez**, College of Staten Island, Staten Island, NY; **Beverly Hobbs**, Clark University, Worcester, MA; **Kristin Homuth**, Language Center International, Southfield, MI; **Tim Hooker**, Campbellsville University, Campbellsville, KY; **Raylene Houck**, Idaho State University, Pocatello, ID; **Karen L. Howling**, University of Bridgeport, Bridgeport, CT; **Sharon Jaffe**, Santa Monica Community College, Santa Monica, CA; **Andrea Kahn**, Santa Monica Community College, Santa Monica, CA; **Eden Bradshaw Kaiser**, Massachusetts International Academy, Marlborough, MA; **Mandy Kama**, Georgetown University, Washington, D.C.; **Andrea Kaminski**, University of Michigan – Dearborn, Dearborn, MI; **Eileen Kramer**, Boston University CELOP, Brookline, MA; **Rachel Lachance**, University of New Hampshire, Durham, NH; **Janet Langon**, Glendale Community College, Glendale, CA; **Frances Le Grand**, University of Houston, Houston, TX; **Esther Lee**, California State University, Fullerton, CA; **Helen S. Mays Lefal**, American Learning Institute, Dallas, TX; **Oranit Limmaneeprasert**, American River College, Sacramento, CA; **Dhammika Liyanage**, Bilingual Education Institute, Houston, TX; **Emily Lodmer**, Santa Monica Community College, Santa Monica, CA; **Ari Lopez**, American Learning Institute, Dallas, TX; **Nichole Lukas**, University of Dayton, Dayton, OH; **Undarmaa Maamuujav**, California State University, Los Angeles, CA; **Diane Mahin**, University of Miami, Coral Gables, FL; **Melanie Majeski**, Naugatuck Valley Community College, Waterbury, CT; **Judy Marasco**, Santa Monica Community College, Santa Monica, CA; **Murray McMahan**, University of Alberta, Edmonton, AB, Canada; **Deirdre McMurtry**, University of Nebraska Omaha, Omaha, NE; **Suzanne Meyer**, University of Pittsburgh, Pittsburgh, PA; **Cynthia Miller**, Richland College, Dallas, TX; **Sara Miller**, Houston Community College, Houston, TX; **Gwendolyn Miraglia**, Houston Community College, Houston, TX; **Katie Mitchell**, International English Center, Boulder, CO; **Ruth Williams Moore**, University of Colorado Boulder, Boulder, CO; **Kathy Najafi**, Houston Community College, Houston, TX; **Sandra Navarro**, Glendale Community College, Glendale, CA; **Stephanie Ngom**, Boston University, Boston, MA; **Barbara Niemczyk**, University of Bridgeport, Bridgeport, CT; **Melody Nightingale**, Santa Monica Community College, Santa Monica, CA; **Alissa Olgun**, California Language Academy, Los Angeles, CA; **Kimberly Oliver**, Austin Community College, Austin, TX; **Steven Olson**, International English Center, Boulder, CO; **Fernanda Ortiz**, University of Arizona, Tucson, AZ; **Joel Ozretich**, University of Washington, Seattle, WA; **Erin Pak**, Schoolcraft College, Livonia, MI; **Geri Pappas**, University of Michigan – Dearborn, Dearborn, MI; **Eleanor Paterson**, Erie Community College, Buffalo, NY; **Sumeeta Patnaik**, Marshall University, Huntington, WV; **Mary Peacock**, Richland College, Dallas, TX; **Kathryn Porter**, University of Houston, Houston, TX; **Eileen Prince**, Prince Language Associates, Newton Highlands, MA; **Marina Ramirez**, Houston Community College, Houston, TX; **Laura Ramm**, Michigan State University, East Lansing, MI; **Chi Rehg**, University of South Florida, Tampa, FL; **Cyndy Reimer**, Douglas College, New Westminster, BC, Canada; **Sydney Rice**, Imperial Valley College, Imperial, CA; **Lynnette Robson**, Mercer University, Macon, GA; **Helen E. Roland**, Miami Dade College, Miami, FL; **Maria Paula Carreira Rolim**, Southeast Missouri State University, Cape Girardeau, MO; **Jill Rolston-Yates**, Texas State University, San Marcos, TX; **David Ross**, Houston Community College, Houston, TX; **Rachel Scheiner**, Seattle Central College, Seattle, WA; **John Schmidt**, Texas Intensive English Program, Austin, TX; **Mariah Schueman**, University of Miami, Coral Gables, FL; **Erika Shadburne**, Austin Community College, Austin, TX; **Mahdi Shamsi**, Houston Community College, Houston, TX; **Osha Sky**, Highline College, Des Moines, WA; **William Slade**, University of Texas, Austin, TX; **Takako Smith**, University of Nebraska – Lincoln, Lincoln, NE; **Barbara Smith-Palinkas**, Hillsborough Community College, Tampa, FL; **Paula Snyder**, University of Missouri, Columbia, MO; **Mary Evelyn Sorrell**, Bilingual Education Institute, Houston, TX; **Kristen Stauffer**, International English Center, Boulder, CO; **Christina Stefanik**, The Language Company, Toledo, OH; **Cory Stewart**, University of Houston, Houston, TX; **Laurie Stusser-McNeill**, Highline College, Des Moines, WA; **Tom Sugawara**, University of Washington, Seattle, WA; **Sara Sulko**, University of Missouri, Columbia, MO; **Mark Sullivan**, University of Colorado Boulder, Boulder, CO; **Olivia Szabo**, Boston University, Boston, MA; **Amber Tallent**, University of Nebraska Omaha, Omaha, NE; **Amy Tate**, Rice University, Houston, TX; **Aya C. Tiacoh**, Bilingual Education Institute, Houston, TX; **Troy Tucker**, Florida SouthWestern State College, Fort Myers, FL; **Anne Tyoan**, Savannah College of Art and Design, Savannah, GA; **Michael Vallee**, International English Center, Boulder, CO; **Andrea Vasquez**, University of Southern Maine, Portland, ME; **Jose Vasquez**, University of Texas Rio Grande Valley, Edinburgh, TX; **Maureen Vendeville**, Savannah Technical College, Savannah, GA; **Melissa Vervinck**, Oakland University, Rochester, MI; **Adriana Villarreal**, Universidad Nacional Autonoma de Mexico, San Antonio, TX; **Summer Webb**, International English Center, Boulder, CO; **Mercedes Wilson-Everett**, Houston Community College, Houston, TX; **Lora Yasen**, Tokyo International University of America, Salem, OR; **Dennis Yommer**, Youngstown State University, Youngstown, OH; **Melojeane (Jolene) Zawilinski**, University of Michigan – Flint, Flint, MI.

CREDITS

Photos

Cover, iii WENN Ltd/Alamy Stock Photo, **iv** (from top to bottom) © Mac Kwan, Abbie Trayler-Smith/Panos Pictures, Jens Schlueter/Getty Images, David Doubilet/National Geographic Creative, Chip East/Reuters, **vi** (from top to bottom) David Doubilet/National Geographic Creative, Arnd Wiegmann/Reuters, Richard Conde/National Geographic Creative, Tim Laman/National Geographic Image Collection, VCG/Visual China Group/Getty Images, **1** © Mac Kwan, **5** Andrew Watson/Getty Images, **6** valentinrussanov/Getty Images, **9** David McLain/Aurora Photos, **12–13** Seiya Kawamoto/Getty Images, **14** Robert Clark/National Geographic Creative, **21** Abbie Trayler-Smith/Panos Pictures, **25** (b) Cengage Learning, Inc., (tr) Bobby Longoria/Getty Images, **26** Lucas Oleniuk/Toronto Star/Getty Images, **29** Emilio Flores/The New York Times/Redux, **32** (bl) Rebecca Hale/National Geographic, **32–33** (c) CB2/ZOB/WENN/Newscom, **33** (br) © Kris Krug, **37** Ruben Salgado Escudero/National Geographic Creative, **41** Jens Schlueter/Getty Images, **42–43** Lam Yik Fei/Getty Images, **45** © Erik Jepsen/Calit2/UCSD, **46** Sarah Parcak/National Geographic Creative, **49** Mike Hennig/National Geographic Creative, **52–53** © Dmitri Alexander, **55** © Ben Keene, **61** David Doubilet/National Geographic Creative, **62** (br) Hannele Lahti/National Geographic, **62–63** (c) Jason Edwards/National Geographic, **63** (tl) Richard Folwell/Science Photo Library/Getty Images, (c) Paul Chesley/National Geographic, (bl) David Doubilet/National Geographic Creative, **65** Brian J. Skerry/National Geographic Creative, **66** Roberto Caccuri/Contrasto/Redux, **69** Brian J. Skerry/National Geographic Creative, **72** (tr) Mark Thissen/National Geographic Creative, **72–73** (b) Mariel Furlong/Alejandro Tumas/National Geographic Image Collection, **81** Chip East/Reuters, **82–83** wragg/Getty Images, **85** Photo 12/Alamy Stock Photo, **86** Christopher Pledger/eyevine/Redux, **89** © Nelson Dellis, **90** Adam Simpson/National Geographic Creative, **92** PM Images/Getty Images, **101** David Doubilet/National Geographic Creative, **102** (bl) Brian J. Skerry/National Geographic Creative, (br) Pete Oxford/Minden Pictures/Getty Images, **102–103** (c) Mattias Klum/National Geographic Creative, **105** © Zoltan Takacs, **106** Mattias Klum/National Geographic, **109** Rebecca Hale/National Geographic Creative, **110** Joel Sartore/National Geographic, **112** Christian Science Monitor/Getty Images, **121** Arnd Wiegmann/Reuters, **122–123** (t) Mike Theiss/National Geographic Creative, **123** (b) Josh Edelson/Getty Images, **125** Mandel Ngan/Getty Images, **128** Gary Hincks/Science Source, **129** Stocktrek Images/National Geographic Creative, **132–133** Bruce Morser/National Geographic Image Collection, **139** Design Pics Inc/National Geographic Creative, **141** Richard Conde/National Geographic Creative, **142–143** Brent Stirton/Reportage Archive/Getty Images, **145** Gustavos Photos/Getty Images, **146–147** Fernando G. Baptista/National Geographic Magazine, **148** Ivan/Getty Images, **150** Stephen Alvarez/National Geographic, **151** Gavin Host/EyeEm/Getty Images, **152** Fernando G. Baptista/National Geographic Creative, **154–155** (c) Tetra Images/Getty Images, **155** (br) Design Pics Inc/National Geographic Creative, **161** (tc) Raymond Gehman/National Geographic, (tr) Richard Nowitz/National Geographic, **163** Tim Laman/National Geographic Image Collection, **164–165** © C.S. Ling Photography, **167** Tim Laman/National Geographic, **168** Xing Lida/National Geographic, **170** John Sibbick/National Geographic, **171** Chien Lee/Minden Pictures, **172** (cl) (bl) (br) Tim Laman/National Geographic, **174** (bc) Shawn Gould/National Geographic, **174–175** (c) Norbert Wu/Minden Pictures, **175** (br) Brian J. Skerry/National Geographic, (cr) Eye of Science/Science Source, **176** (t) Norbert Wu/Minden Pictures, (b) Eye of Science/Science Source, **179** (cl) (cr) Robert Clark/National Geographic Creative, **183** VCG/Visual China Group/Getty Images, **184–185** Thierry Falise/LightRocket/Getty Images, **187** Randall Scott/National Geographic Creative, **188** © Ken Banks, **191** Courtesy of Fundación Mi Parque, **194** DustinWireImage Finkelstein/Getty Images, **195** Douglas Kirkland/Corbis Premium Historical/Getty Images, **213** valentinrussanov/Getty Images

Texts/Sources

5–6 Based on information from the World Database of Happiness (worlddatabaseofhappiness.eur.nl); **12–13** Based on information from the TED Talks by Robert Waldinger, Nic Marks, Nancy Etcoff, Graham Hill, Michael Norton, and David Steindl-Rast (www.TED.com); **25–26** Adapted from "The Windmills of His Mind" by Marc Silver: National Geographic Blogs Oct 2009; **32–33** Adapted from "Big Ideas: Little Packages": NGM Nov 2010 and additional information from "Hayat Sindi": https://www.nationalgeographic.org/find-explorers/explorers/48FC9C7F/hayat-sindi/; **45–46** Based on information from "Watch: How to Become a Space Archaeologist" by Tom Clynes: http://news.nationalgeographic.com/2017/01/archaeologists-parcak-globalxplorer-looting-ted-prize/; Additional information from "How Crowdsourced Archaeology Could Help Solve the Mysteries of Peru" by Sarah Parcak: http://voices.nationalgeographic.org/2016/06/27/how-crowdsourced-archaeology-could-help-solve-the-mysteries-of-peru/, and "Conjuring Genghis Khan" by Luke Dittrich: http://adventure.nationalgeographic.com/2009/12/best-of-adventure/albert-lin/; **52–53** Adapted from "Welcome to the Tribe" by James Vlahos: National Geographic Adventure Feb 2007. Reprinted by permission; **65–66** Adapted from "Overfishing": http://www.nationalgeographic.com/environment/oceans/critical-issues-overfishing/; **72–73** Based on an original interview with Barton Seaver, and information from "Seafood Crisis" by Paul Greenberg: NGM Oct 2010; **85–86** Adapted from "Remember This" by Joshua Foer: NGM Nov 2007; **92–93** Adapted from "Memory Boosters: How to Help": NGM Nov 2007, and "Direct

Evidence of the Role of Sleep in Memory Formation Uncovered" by David Braun: http://voices.nationalgeographic.org/2009/09/15/sleep_and_memory/; **105–106** Based on information from "Zoltan Takacs": https://www.nationalgeographic.org/find-explorers/explorers/A93797E6/zoltan-takacs/; **112–113** Adapted from "Boom in Retiring Lab Chimpanzees Fills New Sanctuaries With Apes" by Virginia Morell: http://news.nationalgeographic.com/news/2014/09/140912-chimpanzee-haven-retired-research-animals/, and "Government Research Chimps Set to Retire" by Jani Actman and Rachael Bale: http://news.nationalgeographic.com/news/2015/11/20151119-chimpanzees-retired-medical-research-NIH/; **125–126** Adapted from "Joplin, Missouri, Tornado Strong but Not Surprising?" and "Monster Alabama Tornado Spawned by Rare 'Perfect Storm'" by Willie Drye: http://news.nationalgeographic.com/news/2011/05/110523-joplin-missouri-tornado-science-nation-weather/ and http://news.nationalgeographic.com/news/2011/04/110428-tuscaloosa-birmingham-alabama-news-tornadoes-science-nation/; Additional information from "Deadliest Tornado Outbreak in Decades Was Fueled by Smoke From Land Clearing" by Devin Powell: http://news.nationalgeographic.com/news/2015/02/150209-tornado-smoke-aerosol-storm-wind/; **132–133** Adapted from "Under Fire" by Neil Shea: NGM Jul 2008; **145–148** Adapted from "Gaudí's Masterpiece" by Jeremy Berlin: NGM Dec 2010; **154–155** Adapted from "The Birth of Religion" by Charles C. Mann: NGM Jun 2011, and "Chichén Itzá": http://www.nationalgeographic.com/travel/world-heritage/chichen-itza/; Additional information from "World's Oldest Temple to Be Restored" by Andrew Curry: http://news.nationalgeographic.com/2016/01/150120-gobekli-tepe-oldest-monument-turkey-archaeology/; **167–168** Adapted from "Evolution of Feathers" by Carl Zimmer: NGM Feb 2011; **174–175** Adapted from "Power Beak" by John Eliot: NGM Dec 2006, and "How Shark Scales Give the Predators Deadly Speed" by Christine Dell'Amore: http://news.nationalgeographic.com/news/2010/11/101123-shark-scales-speed-animals-environment/; **187–188** Based on information from "Ken Banks": https://www.nationalgeographic.org/find-explorers/explorers/CC6140D9/ken-banks/, and "How to Change the World" by Ford Cochran: http://voices.nationalgeographic.org/2010/10/22/how_to_change_the_world_poptec/; **194–195** Based on information from "Dreams of the World: Empowering and Inspiring Entrepreneurs With Former Apple Evangelist, Guy Kawasaki" by Kike Calvo: http://voices.nationalgeographic.org/2013/11/04/dreams-of-the-world-guy-kawasaki-former-apple-evangelist/

NGM = National Geographic Magazine

Maps and Infographics

2–3, **22–23**, **185** 5W Infographics; **62–63** (cl) Benjamin Halpern and others, National Center for Ecological Analysis and Synthesis, University of California, Santa Barbara; **126** National Geographic Maps

INDEX OF EXAM SKILLS AND TASKS

The activities in *Pathways Reading, Writing, and Critical Thinking* develop **key reading skills** needed for success on standardized exams such as TOEFL® and IELTS. In addition, many of the activities provide useful exam practice because they are similar to **common question types** in these tests.

Key Reading Skills	IELTS	TOEFL®	Page(s)
Recognizing vocabulary from context	✓	✓	7, 10, 14, 30, 50, 70, 89, 110, 130, 151, 171, 192, 196
Recognizing main ideas	✓	✓	7, 8, 14, 27, 54, 67, 74, 87, 114, 156, 169, 189, 190
Scanning for details	✓	✓	28, 84, 124, 150, 193
Making inferences	✓	✓	7, 14, 47, 54, 189, 196
Recognizing pronoun references		✓	114

Common Question Types	IELTS	TOEFL®	Page(s)
Multiple choice	✓	✓	7, 14, 27, 34, 47, 67, 74, 87, 107, 114, 156, 169, 189, 196
Completion (notes, diagram, chart)	✓		7, 27, 47, 48, 54, 67, 94, 114, 127, 128, 134, 149, 169, 176, 190
Short answer	✓		9, 14, 27, 29, 34, 49, 67, 68, 69, 74, 87, 89, 107, 129, 150, 151, 156, 171, 189, 191
Matching tasks (headers, features, information)	✓		8, 107, 127, 134, 149, 150
True / False / Not Given	✓		114, 134
Yes / No / Not Given	✓		74, 196
Prose summary		✓	54
Rhetorical purpose		✓	34, 127, 134, 149, 196

Level 2 of *Pathways Reading, Writing, and Critical Thinking* also develops **key writing skills** needed for exam success. The activities target paragraph-level writing. As a result, they do not directly mirror writing tasks in TOEFL® or IELTS (which require students to write essays or other long pieces). However, the skills provide an important foundation for the longer writing tasks practiced in higher levels of the series.

Key Writing Skills	Page(s)
Organizing ideas	18, 36, 37, 76, 77, 96, 97, 136, 137, 138, 179
Writing cohesively and coherently	36, 37, 95, 96, 100, 115, 116, 117, 120, 136, 137, 197, 198, 202
Expressing and justifying opinions	7, 18, 34, 149
Giving reasons and examples	7, 14, 18, 34, 44, 74, 134, 149, 169, 176, 198, 199, 200
Paraphrasing ideas and information	67, 176, 177, 178, 179, 180, 190
Making comparisons	152, 157, 158, 159, 160, 162
Expressing agreement and disagreement	116, 117, 118
Describing a graph or chart	68, 75, 76, 77, 78, 80

Pathways	CEFR	IELTS Band	TOEFL® Score
Level 4	C1	6.5–7.0	81–100
Level 3	B2	5.5–6.0	51–80
Level 2	**B1–B2**	**4.5–5.0**	**31–50**
Level 1	A2–B1	0–4.0	0–30
Foundations	A1–A2		